The Pr

TOPICS IN TRANSLATION

Series Editors:
Susan Bassnett (*University of Warwick*)
Edwin Gentzler (*University of Massachusetts, Amherst*)

Editor for Translation in the Commercial Environment:
Geoffrey Samuelsson-Brown (*Aardvark Translation Services Ltd*)

Other Books in the Series
Annotated Texts for Translation: French – English
    BEVERLY ADAB
Annotated Texts for Translation: English – French
    BEVERLY ADAB
Constructing Cultures: Essays on Literary Translation
    SUSAN BASSNETT and ANDRE LEFEVERE
Culture Bumps: An Empirical Approach to the Translation of Allusions
    RITVA LEPPIHALME
Linguistic Auditing
    NIGEL REEVES and COLIN WRIGHT
Paragraphs on Translation
    PETER NEWMARK
Practical Guide for Translators
    GEOFFREY SAMUELSSON-BROWN
The Coming Industry of Teletranslation
    MINAKO O'HAGAN
Translation, Power, Subversion
    ROMAN ALVAREZ and M. CARMEN-AFRICA VIDAL (eds)
Words, Words, Words. The Translator and the Language Learner
    GUNILLA ANDERMAN and MARGARET ROGERS

Other Books of Interest
About Translation
    PETER NEWMARK
Cultural Functions of Translation
    C. SCHÄFFNER and H. KELLY-HOLMES (eds)
Discourse and Ideologies
    C. SHÄFFNER and H. KELLY-HOLMES (eds)
More Paragraphs on Translation
    PETER NEWMARK

Please contact us for the latest book information:
Multilingual Matters, Frankfurt Lodge, Clevedon Hall,
Victoria Road, Clevedon, BS21 7HH, England
http:/www.multilingual-matters.com

TOPICS IN TRANSLATION 12
Series Editors: Susan Bassnett (*University of Warwick*)
Edwin Gentzler (*University of Massachusetts, Amherst*)

The Pragmatics of Translation

Edited by

Leo Hickey

MULTILINGUAL MATTERS LTD
Clevedon • Philadelphia • Toronto • Sydney • Johannesburg

Library of Congress Cataloging in Publication Data

The Pragmatics of Translation/Edited by Leo Hickey
Topics in Translation: 12
Includes bibliographical references and index
1. Translating and interpreting. 2. Pragmatics. I. Hickey, Leo. II. Series
P306.2.P7   1998
418'.02–dc21   98-21842

British Library Cataloguing in Publication Data

A CIP catalogue record for this book is available from the British Library.

ISBN 1-85359-405-9 (hbk)
ISBN 1-85359-404-0 (pbk)

Multilingual Matters Ltd

UK: Frankfurt Lodge, Clevedon Hall, Victoria Road, Clevedon BS21 7HH.
USA: 325 Chestnut Street, Philadelphia, PA 19106, USA.
Canada: OISE, 712 Gordon Baker Road, Toronto, Ontario, Canada M2H 3R7.
Australia: P.O. Box 586, Artamon, NSW, Australia.
South Africa: PO Box 1080, Northcliffe 2115, Johannesburg, South Africa.

Typeset by Archetype-IT Ltd (http://www.archetype-it.com).
Printed and bound in Great Britain by Cromwell Press Ltd.

Contents

Notes on Contributors

Peter Fawcett is a Lecturer in French at Bradford University. He has written on translation theory and practice and, as a practitioner, has translated a number of books.

Ernst-August Gutt has taught in universities in Germany and Ethiopia. He has published widely on translation including *Translation and Relevance: Cognition and Context* (1991).

Basil Hatim is a Professor of Arabic Translation and Linguistics at Heriot-Watt University. His major publications, including *Discourse and the Translator* (1990), have been written in collaboration with Ian Mason.

Sándor Hervey was, until his untimely death in 1997 shortly after completing his chapter for this volume, a Reader in Linguistics at the University of St Andrews. Among his publications are *Axiomatic Semantics* (1979) and *Semiotic Perspectives* (1982).

Leo Hickey is a Research Professor at the University of Salford. He has translated many books from Spanish and his publications on pragmatics include *Curso de pragmaestilística* (1987).

Ian Higgins is a Senior Lecturer in French at the University of St Andrews. Apart from his many literary translations from French, he is co-author, with Sándor Hervey, of *Thinking Translation*.

Juliane House is Professor of Applied Linguistics at the University of Hamburg. She is author of *A Model for Translation Quality Assessment* (1981) and *Translation Quality Assessment: A Model Revisited* (1997).

Frank Knowles is Professor of Language at Aston University. As well as his translations from, and studies of, the Slavonic languages, he has published widely on linguistic and pragmatic issues in Russian.

Kirsten Malmkjær is Assistant Director of Research in the University of Cambridge Research Centre for English and Applied Linguistics. She has published on translation and has edited *The Linguistics Encyclopedia* (1991).

Ian Mason is Professor of Interpreting and Translating at Heriot-Watt University. Among his publications is *The Translator as Communicator* (1997), written in collaboration with Basil Hatim.

Bill Richardson is a Lecturer in Spanish at Dublin City University. He has made a special study of deixis in literary translation, especially in the works of Federico García Lorca.

Christina Schäffner is a Lecturer in German and Co-Director of the Institute for the Study of Language and Society at Aston University. She has edited several volumes on language including her co-edition with Helen Kelly-Holmes of *Cultural Functions of Translation*.

Palma Zlateva is an Assistant Professor of English and American Studies at the St Kliment Ohridski University of Sofia. Her publications include her edition of *Translation as Social Action: Russian and Bulgarian Perspectives* (1993).

Introduction

LEO HICKEY

For as long as individuals have communicated with one another through the mediation of someone else, there has probably been a realisation that mediators do something more complex and more interesting than simply substitute their own words, one by one, for the originals. Since the early 1950s (Nida, 1952), however, there has been an upsurge in serious studies of translation, both in its theoretical, historical, didactic and professional dimensions and in its practice at the point when translators do something in response to their own reading of a text and which leads to the production of a second text. In particular, it is now understood that translators do not simply 'say' in one language what somebody or some piece of writing has 'said' in another. Whatever translation is in its entirety, it seems to involve semiotic, linguistic, textual, lexical, social, sociological, cultural and psychological aspects or elements, all of which are being studied nowadays as determining factors in whatever the translator does. It is also becoming clear that, as in any other form of rewriting (see Gentzler, 1993: ix and Lefevere, 1992), this implies manipulation and relates directly to ideology, power, value systems and perceptions of reality.

One of the many questions that recur, explicitly or implicitly, in these investigations is whether there is some objective entity, linguistic, semantic or psychological, expressed in or by an 'original', which can then be captured by a different text, the translation. In other words, is there something in, behind, underneath or belonging to a piece of writing in one language which can be extrapolated and safely packaged in another? After all, at first sight something seems to survive and pass more or less intact from one text to another in the process and the product of translation; we may therefore ask whether or how this actually happens and what that something may be. Certain aspects of language, such as words and grammar, appear to disappear or change completely in translation and yet the 'meaning', what might be termed the semantic import, usually survives the process quite well.

Beyond these first impressions, what is it, then, if anything, that is actually translated, transferred, between one text and another? Is it some part, ingredient or linguistic element of the text itself, or is it something less direct about the text, such as a particular reader's reaction or interpretation of it? And what happens to those elements which are not transferred? Are they irrelevant, surplus to requirements, treated as of no importance and simply ignored? Is translation some kind of science, pure or applied, prescriptive or descriptive, or is it a practical art or craft, which cannot be discussed until after the event, analogously to a conversation about the beauty of a sunset or a bird in flight? If the notion that something remains unscathed in the process of translation is too extreme, then perhaps there may be aspects of the original and the translation which, if not identical, are at least equivalent to one another. For some time now the notion of equivalence, or rather equivalences, has been debated with varying degrees of enthusiasm and conviction (see Bassnett, 1991: 23–9). It may also be that translation is merely an approximate, imprecise, procedure, and that any text has so many dimensions that equivalence on one may be incompatible with equivalence on some others. For example, linguistic equivalence (an extreme case of which would be word-for-word translation) may conflict with dynamic equivalence (stimulating an effect in the reader of the translation similar to that caused in the reader of the original), in the sense that if the linguistic surface of both texts is similar, the effect on their readers may necessarily be very different, and vice versa. And does translation deal with what the original author intended or simply what is expressed by the text?

Among the many approaches to research on translation which are yielding useful insights nowadays, Translation Studies has been in particular favour since the mid 1960s (see Bassnett, 1991: 6). Translation Studies concentrates on describing and analysing the procedure or processes, rather than commenting on the product itself and asking how well or badly any particular translation has been done. This non-prescriptive approach, among others, is interested in how translation is actually done, examining the methods that have been used throughout history and asking how texts fit into the receiving cultures.

Much work is also being carried out on the teaching of translation, with or without some kind of theoretical or academic underpinning. Universities and similar institutions educate graduates who go on to earn their living as translators. Some courses use translation merely as a methodological tool for language-teaching, without claiming to train translators, while others provide training in all aspects of the translator's work including practice in various registers, gathering and storing terminology, compiling data bases, documentation, IT etc. Closely related to teaching is assessment or evaluation, quality assurance or revision of translation, as part of the process itself or carried out on the product. It is done on various levels, from the practitioner's own impressionistic assessment of a first draft or a teacher's equally subjective, but perhaps more experience-based, comments on a student's piece of work to more academic attempts to develop systematic methods for the evaluation of professional work (House, 1976).

The profession of the translator, with its problems and practical considerations, is sporadically, though seldom systematically, treated in journals and newsletters. The practice of the profession under pressure, working to deadlines, satisfying different types of client, using dictionaries of all kinds, whether monolingual or multilingual, general or technical, hard-copy or computer-based, by in-house or freelance practitioners, making use of expert or other informants (often the clients themselves) is occasionally discussed, usually on an anecdotic level.

Despite much research and even calls for general theories and systems to explain or describe the translation process (Baker, 1993: 248), most work on the subject continues to address specific problems and individual elements or aspects of translation, including comparisons of brief texts with their originals. These studies range from the treatment of such detailed points as puns or culture-specific terms to advice on how to handle legal documents between systems which have neither terminology nor legal entities in common; they may rely on intuitive reactions to the 'readability' of a particular translation or on academic investigations of contrastive structural linguistics. The volume of work being done and the multiplicity of approaches used suggests that the study of translation is actively attempting to emerge from its infancy.

Much the same may be said of pragmatics. Since 1938, when Charles Morris defined semiotics as the use of signs governed by syntactic, semantic and pragmatic rules, but more particularly since 1959, when Rudolf Carnap explained that pragmatics refers to the relationships between signs and their users, the discipline has been developed with enthusiasm by philosophers and linguists alike. It entered an especially meaningful phase in 1962 when J. L. Austin's contribution to the subject was published under the title *How to Do Things with Words* (Austin, 1962), which showed that, when using language, people do not just talk or write to one another but rather they perform actions, they do things, usually in contexts that combine linguistic and nonlinguistic elements, part of the context in which they communicate consisting of the knowledge, beliefs and assumptions of all concerned.

Following Austin's work, pragmatics has focused on the conditions which permit speakers and writers to achieve what they want to achieve by bringing about certain modifications in the behaviour, knowledge, attitudes or beliefs of others. It studies what language-users mean, as distinct from what their language means, the rules and principles governing their use of language, over and above the rules of language itself, grammar or vocabulary, and what makes some uses of language more appropriate than others in certain situations.

However, apart from basic research on pragmatics which stresses, not so much what language is or how it is structured, as the links between its uses and users, developing general approaches to the subject which is seen as 'the study of language usage' (Levinson, 1983: 5), in practice certain specific areas of interest have become intimately associated with the discipline over the past 35 years. This is clear from general books on the subject (Levinson, 1983; Leech, 1983; Mey, 1993), specialist monographs (Sperber & Wilson, 1986; Brown & Levinson, 1987) and academic papers that appear in journals (such as *Pragmatics* or the *Journal of Pragmatics*). Here it is interesting to note that a distinction has emerged between what might be called the Anglo-American School and the mid-European School, in that the former works on a tightly defined agenda, dealing in effect with areas such as speech acts, politeness, cooperativeness and conversational implicature, relevance theory, the distribution of information in sentences and texts, presupposition, deixis, discourse markers, hedges or disclaimers and perhaps the structure of conversation. The mid-European School has a broader agenda, which investigates virtually all aspects of language seen as a social institution or, as Jacob Mey would say, 'the conditions of human language uses as these are determined by the context of society' (Mey, 1993: 42).

In general, pragmatic approaches attempt to explain translation — procedure, process and product — from the point of view of what is (potentially) done by the original author in or by the text, what is (potentially) done in the translation as a response to the original, how and why it is done in that way in that context. If we return to the question of whether there is something in an original text which is carried over in its translation, a pragmaticist might suggest that something does indeed survive the process, namely (at the very least) what is potentially done by or in the original text, since the translation has the same capability. We say 'at the very least' because, of course, if an original text, for example, informs, entertains, demands payment of a debt or apologises for some mistake, the translation will (be expected to) not only perform these actions but do so in a manner similar to the original: it will have to convey the same, and not different, information, the entertainment will have to be of the same kind in both texts (a shaggy dog story will not be translated by a one-line aphorism), the demand for payment must be for the same debt and the apology must be for the same mistake as in the original.

The last two examples well illustrate our insistence on the 'potential' for doing things. No text by itself does anything: the act performed always depends on certain conditions, sometimes called 'felicity' or 'happiness' conditions (see Austin 1962: passim). Here, for example, the demand for payment will be made only of the person to whom it is intentionally addressed (who may be the reader of the original, of the translation or of both), and not of everyone who happens to pick it up and scan it; the apology will be made only to whoever has been affected by the mistake (who may read the original, the translation or both). This factor places readers of the original and of the translation on the same footing, since the fact of being a reader of the one or of the other is irrelevant to being the goal of the act: sometimes the goal will be the reader of the original, sometimes it will be the reader of the translation, sometimes these will be the same person(s).

The 13 contributions to the subject contained in this volume begin from this firm basis, addressing questions such as what original texts and their translations are intended to achieve and how they attempt to achieve it, how writers set about cooperating with their readers, being polite and relevant, or how inter-cultural difference may be treated. On a more detailed level, such points as the handling of the distinction between old and new information, the transference of presupposition and deixis, connections between discourse elements and linguistic factors like hedges are discussed. The aim of the volume is to address an important level of translation, namely the pragmatic level, which is neither purely theoretical nor relevant merely to specific translation problems, but rather which is common to all translation.

In distinguishing syntactic from sentential units, Sándor Hervey defines sentence-building as endowing a meaningful linguistic unit with an illocutionary function. He explains that, although illocutionary functions can be understood across the most diverse cultural boundaries, their cultural relativity makes it difficult to transfer them in translation. He proposes a strategic approach which keeps very much in mind that, to convey these functions, English for example predominantly uses intonation, German prefers illocutionary particles while Hungarian resorts to sequential focus.

Kirsten Malmkjær examines Grice's theory of meaning and finds that, in applying his cooperative principle to literary texts and translations, difficulties arise from his postulate that understanding a speaker's utterance requires an audience's prior understanding of the actual words used.

There is thus no place for a mediator of messages and Grice's mechanism does not in itself provide a satisfactory theory of translation because of its crucial distinction between literal and non-literal meaning, which may not coincide across languages. She discusses a possible solution to this difficulty.

˒ The distinction developed in relevance theory between the descriptive use of language (intended to be taken as true) and the interpretive (representing what someone else said or thought) allows Ernst-August Gutt to place translation in this latter category, since it restates and 'resembles' an original text. On this basis, 'translation' is similar in role to other text categories such as 'novel' or 'essay'. However, like other quotations (which, in effect, is what it is), a translation is often encountered 'out of context', with attendant consequences for the skills of the translator.

Unlike Brown and Levinson's 'face-saving' approach, Juliane House treats both universal and varying aspects of politeness. In discussing politeness equivalence, she distinguishes overt from covert translation. The former, coactivating the original frame and discourse world, tends to be appropriate when the original is source-culture linked, has independent status in the source language community and operates like a quotation. In the covert mode, the translator seeks an equivalent speech event without co-activating the original discourse world, no easy task when working between languages such as German and English, which use politeness very differently.

Starting from Brown and Levinson's notion of politeness, Basil Hatim studies text politeness within socio-textual practice, which subsumes expressions of attitude, upholding genre conventions and maintaining rhetorical purposes through actual texts. He suggests that a translator's unjustified intervention may produce undue 'domestication' of a text, rather than respecting its 'foreignness'. Using varied examples, he detects a tendency in Western translators to impose order (connectors etc.) on seemingly chaotic texts and shows that it may be risky to tamper with the politeness of, rather than merely in, source texts.

The mechanisms available to signal the distinction between theme or information already known to readers and rheme or new information vary from language to language. Frank Knowles shows how inflection, rather than word order, largely fulfils this function in Russian. A translator then has to decide how to convey the theme–rheme structure of an original text using whatever means the target language can offer. A 'good fit' requires replication of the original theme–rheme structure, communicative value, message and thrust, while respecting the target language's grammar and style. Yet, just as willingness to risk deviance may mark a good writer, so also it may mark a good translator.

Presuppositions, as background assumptions built into utterances and allowing them to make sense, require that a reader or translator be able to link such utterances to their context. Using mostly French and German examples, Peter Fawcett points to collocation, or the probability that words will co-occur, and connotation, or secondary meaning, as posing special difficulties for translation, forcing the translator to decide whether, or to what extent, the target audience may need hints as to what is presupposed rather than explicitly conveyed in the original.

Deixis links utterances to their contexts via spatial, temporal and personal dimensions (e.g here/there, now/yesterday, I/they, respectively). A translator must therefore re-create the original message using a deictic perspective appropriate to the target language and avoiding undue influence of the original patterns. Bill Richardson argues, using Spanish and English texts, that seeking equivalent pragmatic effect when the context and participants of the original situation are no longer present involves constructing a new text with its own world-view and its own relations with other sets of worlds.

On a more detailed level, Palma Zlateva chooses pragmatic substitution and reference to show how non-coincidence across languages on such a specific point may make translational equivalence difficult to achieve. Analysing the non-structural use of deictic pro-forms (English *this/that*, Russian *eto*, Bulgarian *takova*) to avoid explicitness or lengthy explanation, as in 'She slapped him in the face . . . a good hard *one*', she finds no sharp boundary between pragmatic reference/substitution, which is a universal feature of language communication, and structural substitution, which she ascribes to the analytic nature of English and (to some extent) Bulgarian, in contrast with Russian.

Ian Mason asks what a translator should do when faced with suppressed discourse connectives as an interactive feature in a counter-argumentative source text. Since the markers of argumentative opposition ('Of course . . . ', 'True . . . ') are unexpressed, should the reader be left to infer what the relationship is between the different parts of the text by means of a Gricean-type implicature or should this be spelled out in the translation? Using English translations from French, he discusses the informative markedness and the politeness which motivates such ellipsis and concludes that explication should not be undertaken automatically.

Hedges, as devices which increase or decrease fuzziness, are much used in political texts in order to lessen a politician's commitment to the truth of a proposition or to mitigate possible negative effects on an audience. Adopting Pinkal's four-point classification, Christina Schäffner concentrates on 'specifying hedges' ('real', 'true', 'proper' . . .), which attenuate indeterminateness. Asking whether a reader will be able to identify their pragmatic function e.g. the implication that an opponent is being criticised, she examines German and English translations in which they have been deleted, added or changed.

In comparing a passage from Racine's _Andromaque_ (1667) with three English versions, Ian Higgins demonstrates how certain linguistic features, notably word order, caesura, rhyme and mute _e_ heard as a schwa, contribute to the illocutionary force of the written/spoken text. Since the original verse has major illocutionary potential, part of the translator's task is to ensure that this is realised also in the translation and ways must be found to stimulate its effects in readers of English, a language which thematises and emphasises mainly through intonation, unlike French, where grammatical devices tend to fulfil these functions.

Broadly speaking, perlocutionary effects are the thoughts, feelings and actions that result from reading a text. Leo Hickey suggests that, in some (e.g. legal) texts, clear signalling that a particular text is, in fact, a translation may produce similar effects with little need to explain the realities mentioned in the original, in others (literary), little such signalling and little explanation may be necessary, while in yet others (humorous), recontextualisation, or placing the text in a totally new context, may be required in order to stimulate in a reader effects equivalent to those stimulated by the original.

It is hoped that these 13 studies will together constitute a rounded vision of how pragmatics relates to translation and, in particular, of how pragmatic equivalence may be achieved in the process and product of the translator's art.

References

Austin, J. L. (1962) _How To Do Things With Words_. Oxford: Clarendon Press. Page references are to the 1986 OUP edition.

Baker, M. (1993) Corpus linguistics and translation studies: Implications and applications. In M. Baker, G. Francis and E. Tognini-Bonelli (eds) _Text and Technology: In Honour of John Sinclair_. Philadelphia/Amsterdam: John Benjamins.

Bassnett, S. (1980, revised 1991) _Translation Studies_. London: Routledge.

Brown, P and Levinson, S.C. (1987) _Politeness: Some Universals in Language Usage_. Cambridge: Cambridge University Press.

Carnap, R. (1959) _Introduction to Semantics_. Cambridge, MA: Harvard University Press.

Gentzler, E. (1993) _Contemporary Translation Theories_. London: Routledge.

House, J. (1976) _A Model for Translation Quality Assessment_. Tübingen: Gunter Narr.

Leech, G.N. (1983) *Principles of Pragmatics*. London: Longman.

Lefevere, A. (1992) *Translation, Rewriting, and the Manipulation of Literary Fame*. London: Routledge.

Levinson, S.C. (1983) *Pragmatics*. Cambridge: Cambridge University Press.

Mey, J.L. (1993) *Pragmatics: An Introduction*. Oxford: Blackwell.

Morris, C. (1938) Foundations of the theory of signs. In O. Neurath, R. Carnap and C. Morris (eds) *International Encyclopedia of Unified Science* (pp. 177–238). Chicago: University of Chicago Press.

Nida, E.A. (1952) *God's Word in Man's Language*. New York: Harper & Brothers.

Sperber, D. and Wilson, D. (1986) *Relevance: Communication and Cognition*. Oxford: Blackwell.

Chapter 1

Speech Acts and Illocutionary Function in Translation Methodology

SÁNDOR G. J. HERVEY

When ethologists studying the communicative behaviour of dolphins attempt to render in English the messages that these, in all probability highly intelligent, animals exchange with one another in the course of their daily lives, they face a nigh-on insurmountable problem: translating messages from 'dolphinese' presupposes that the content and the purport of the utterances of dolphins is neither entirely beneath, nor utterly beyond, a human conception of communicative acts. There is, in fact, no guarantee that grasping the nature of the pragmatics of dolphin communicative performance is not totally outside the scope of human imagination.

For all that cross-linguistic translation (translation proper) is notoriously problematic and fraught with difficulties, translators from English to German, Hungarian to French, Russian to Swahili, Chinese to Gujerati, and so on, at least do not face problems of such a magnitude as do 'translators from dolphinese'. Though translation proper is a cross-cultural puzzle, and scepticism about full translatability without distortion is, rightly, widespread among those who theorise about translation, there is no chance that the performance of communicative acts in another human society, no matter how strange and uncanny it may look at first sight when viewed from across a cultural boundary, could be beyond human imagining.

When human beings communicate, they perform acts that fall into the range of what other human beings, even those from vastly different cultural backgrounds, are in principle capable of empathising with. This presumption (and I stress that it *is* a presumption) defines the limits of a cautious 'universalism' or, more precisely, an intellectual position between universalism and relativism. What members of one culture do can be *imagined* by members of another culture, even if they *do* otherwise. It is to this extent that human communication is 'universal'.

Since the early work of Austin (1962), and subsequently of Searle (1969, 1979), the idea that utterances are forms of 'doing' has become to all intents and purposes an interdisciplinary commonplace. The view, spearheaded by the notion of *performative* utterances (Austin, 1962), according to which all utterances are means of performing intended actions has taken solid hold in recent 'pragmatic' approaches to semiotics (Parret, 1983), linguistics (Levinson, 1983; Brown & Levinson, 1978) — it has also made its influence felt in anthropology (Gumperz, 1982) and, of course, in theory of translation (Hatim & Mason, 1990). The performative intention behind, and embedded in, every utterance (in fact, every communicative act) is usually reified under the label of 'illocutionary force' (Searle, 1969); that is, the illocutionary force of an utterance — its most salient pragmatic purpose — is the performative intention which the utterance serves.

Since a discussion of illocutionary force entails an analytic appraisal of supposed intentions judged by external functional criteria, I prefer to designate this performative aspect of utterances by the term *illocutionary function*. A cautious form of universalism would grant that the illocutionary function of every human act of communication is, in principle, *knowable* (though, incidentally, the same cautious intellectual position would express a degree of scepticism about the knowability of the illocutionary functions of communication acts performed by non-human animals). Furthermore, in the light of the earlier presumption about human empathy, a qualified universalism would have to stretch to the belief that *illocutionary functions can be comprehended across the most diverse cultural boundaries*. This belief does not, however, extend to supposing that the cross-cultural appraisal of illocutionary functions is *easy*. On the contrary, cultural relativity makes this a highly sensitive and problematic issue.

Because the 'speech act theory' initiated by Austin and Searle is firmly embedded in a tradition of Western philosophy, the concept of 'illocutionary force', attempts at taxonomies of illocution (Searle, 1979), as well as examples of illocutionary acts, tend to be discussed in terms of an implicitly universalist framework: the culture-specificity and cross-cultural diversity of what I would prefer to call illocutionary functions is an issue that can hardly even arise in such a framework. In short, the familiar illocutionary functions of English appear 'naturally' in the role of universal illocutionary categories valid for the pragmatics of all human societies.

With the spread of the influence of 'speech act theory' beyond philosophy — into linguistics and into anthropology — came also a loosening of the bonds between illocutionary acts and pan-humanistic theorising (Ballmer & Brennenstuhl, 1980; Wierzbicka, 1985a, b, 1991). In particular, the work of Wierzbicka is directed at a substantial relativising of the notion of speech acts and, along with it, of notions of illocutionary function. For instance, her contrastive studies of how speech acts are performed in English and Polish, respectively, have a specifically de-universalising aim; as she herself puts it, in reference to the behaviour of speakers: 'It is not *people in general* who behave in the way described, it is the *speakers of English'*. In terms of my own position, equally balanced between linguistics and anthropology, the earlier mentioned compromise between universalism and relativism appears to offer the most plausible alternative: the illocutionary functions manifested in one language/culture are autonomous cultural/linguistic categories (relativism), but are imaginable by members of other cultures (qualified universalism) and, to some extent, are cross-culturally translatable, though not, of course, without translation loss.

Illocutionary functions are, in the simplest terms, the things that people *do* in making utterances. There is always something teleological about these functions, and about the utterances serving these functions: to formulate an illocutionary function is to express an assessment of the aim or purpose of an utterance. Thus, to assert that 'Have you read this book?' has the illocutionary function of a *question* is to attribute to such an utterance, in general, the aim or purpose of eliciting information from an interlocutor. True enough, on occasion one may conclude that the 'real' or 'ulterior' aim of uttering such a question is to patronise and belittle (perhaps even to embarrass); but 'patronise', 'belittle' and 'embarrass', too, contribute to the formulation of a teleological illocutionary function.

Two implications of these observations are worth spelling out. First, the example of utterances of 'Have you read this book?' points up a necessary distinction between grammatical form and pragmatic use: *all* utterances of 'Have you read this book?' are 'interrogative' in grammatical form, but not all its utterances share the plain illocutionary function of eliciting information. Second, the various illocutionary functions that 'Have you read this book?' can be imagined to fulfil in different contexts all have designations in the language/culture to which these illocutionary functions pertain. From linguistic evidence alone, one would have to conclude that members of a culture share a consensual awareness of the illocutionary functions operative in their language/culture. Investigating illocutionary functions in, say, English can safely take the form of a parallel investigation of English terms for 'doing things' with English utterances (Ballmer & Brennenstuhl, 1980). However, when it comes to designating the illocutionary functions of a given language/culture by labels drawn from another language, the situation is rather different: often such labels can at best be highly approximate glosses for illocutionary functions which have indigenous designations but are difficult to translate and require explanation by paraphrase. Though the cultural remove between Western Europe and Hungary can hardly be seen as vast (certainly not in comparison with the cultural distance between, say, Britain and China, or the United States and indigenous Amazonian tribes), the illocutionary function designated in Magyar by the term 'felköszönteni' (roughly, to greet and express good wishes to someone on a special occasion) provides a good example of the culture-specificity and cross-cultural non-transferability of illocutionary functions. What Hungarians do with utterances in performing the act designated as 'felköszönteni', though it may partially overlap with 'toasting someone's health', is simply not the kind of thing people do in British culture.

Implicit in what has been said so far is that illocutionary function is a property of 'utterances'; this, however, instantly raises the question: utterances of what? In so far as *greeting* refers to a particular type of illocutionary function (differently conceived and differently performed in different cultures), and because greetings vary in extent from the monosyllabic 'Hi!' in English to the multi-turn exchanges in Wolof (Irvine, 1974: 170–175), it follows that illocutionary function may pertain to a variety of different 'sizes' of linguistic unit. Some of these units clearly consist of a succession of sentences while others appear to fall below what would be consensually recognised by linguists as a 'complete sentence'.

The issue of definitions of 'sentence' across the vast variety of linguistic theories from traditional grammar to the plethora of current approaches is too complex to take up here; yet a commitment to some definition is unavoidable. I propose, therefore, to adopt a notion of sentencehood whereby 'sentence' corresponds to the minimum linguistic unit endowed with illocutionary function. That is to say, I take the view that utterances operating in context as complete, self-contained speech acts correspond to linguistic units that are either sentences or successions of sentences. This implies that such utterances as 'Hi!', 'Listen!', 'Where?', 'Please', 'Damn!', 'Really', and so on, in so far as they have properties of illocutionary function, correspond to sentences. A sentence, in other words, is defined here as *a minimum self-contained linguistic unit endowed with illocutionary function*.

With the signal exception of Tagmemics (Pike, 1982: 74), most major structural approaches to grammatical theory see the sentence as a 'synthetic' object which is the output of an unbroken *syntactic* hierarchy: that is to say as resulting from a continuous sequence of operations whereby words (whatever alias they might appear under) are combined into complex 'phrase-structures' until the process culminates in the formation of sentences.

It is evident that the present definition of sentencehood is incompatible with the views of most major structural approaches (barring Tagmemics). In the first instance, if 'Hi!' is recognised as a sentence, it follows that sentences cannot be defined as synthetic objects made up of combinations of words: unlike a proposition (e.g. 'Elizabeth II is the Queen of England'), a sentence need not be complex at all, and may contain only one word (e.g. 'Listen!'), or perhaps, no real words at all (e.g. 'Tut-tut').

In the second instance, if sentences are not defined by syntactic complexity, there can also not be a single continuous hierarchy by which, starting with words and applying a series of 'syntactic' processes, we arrive at sentences. We must therefore conclude that the processes by which syntactic complexes (phrase structures) are constructed constitute a separate linguistic hierarchy that cuts across a different set of processes by which meaningful linguistic units are raised to the status of sentences. This line of reasoning leads to the further conclusion that phrase-structural principles belong to one compartment of grammar, to *syntax*, and sentence-building principles to another, perhaps paralinguistic, *sentential level* (Gardner & Hervey, 1983; Hervey, 1990). The crux of sentential level processes — that is, sentence-building processes — is precisely the creation of units that answer our definition of 'sentence' by being endowed with illocutionary function (self-containedness is a by-product of this). *To build a sentence is to take some suitable (meaningful) linguistic unit and to endow it with an illocutionary function.*

The distinction between the syntactic and the sentential levels, besides being an inescapable corollary of the definition of sentence adopted here, offers additional advantages in avoiding paradoxes. For instance, if all sentences are syntactic in composition, it follows that all their constituents are words. This in turn implies that the 'please' of 'Please come home!', the 'hello' of 'Hello, this is Hervey speaking', not to mention the 'tut-tut' of 'Tut-tut, you really shouldn't have done that' must all be *bona fide* words. Yet it is blatantly obvious that these are *not* words in the same sense in which 'come', 'home', 'this', 'is', etc. are words: the two sets do not resemble each other either in function, or in denotation, which merely compounds the difficulties of arriving at any homogeneous, consistent sense of grammatical function or of lexical meaning. The recognition of a sentential level (as distinct from syntax) allows items such as 'please, hello, tut-tut' to be separated off from words, in a category of their own: for all their superficial resemblance to words, these are not syntactic, but sentential units.

Another paradox that is avoided by distinguishing between syntactic and sentential units can best be illustrated through an example from German. In superficial appearance an item such as 'schon' seems to preserve its identity over contexts like 'Er ist schon gekommen' and 'Er wird schon kommen'. Yet both the meaning and the function of 'schon' is evidently different in these two contexts: in the first it adverbially modifies the predicate 'ist gekommen' and has a meaning that can be glossed as 'already'; in the second it nuances the pragmatic import of the assertion 'er wird kommen' and has a meaning that may at best be glossed as 'surely' or 'don't worry'. This suggests, paradoxically, that 'schon' is a single grammatical invariant (word), but that 'schon' conceals two distinct grammatical invariants under the same formal guise. The example is further highlighted by the ambiguity of instances such as 'Ich komm schon' (alternately glossed as 'I'm already on my way' and 'Don't fuss, I will be coming'). For an approach that attributes all sentence-forming processes to syntax, these paradoxes and ambiguities create real difficulties: above all, because there is no alternative to recognising 'schon' *as a word*. The same difficulties do not arise if syntax is differentiated from the sentential level of grammar: in this case, the 'schon' of 'Er ist schon gekommen' is a word with a syntactic function, while the 'schon' of 'Er wird schon kommen' is a sentential marker with an illocutionary function; while the ambiguity of 'Ich komm schon' resides precisely in the fact that, unless the situational context resolves the issue, one cannot be sure whether the *word* 'schon' or the *sentential marker* 'schon' is intended in this instance.

The theoretical stance behind these examples (and my interpretation of them) is that, in every language, there is a set of sentential units whose function and meaning is illocutionary. For all that these units sometimes look like words (as do 'yes', 'please' and 'hello' in English and 'schon' in German), they are in fact quite different in nature (in function and in meaning) from words. Furthermore, these word-like non-words — which I refer to as *illocutionary particles* (see, for instance, Hervey & Higgins, 1992) — share their properties of sentence-forming function and illocutionary meaning with two other, formally rather different, types of sentential marker: *intonation* and *sequential focus* (Hervey & Higgins, 1992).

Units with a sentence-forming function and an illocutionary meaning, in theory, form the following triad of categories:

(1) illocutionary particles (e.g. the 'please' of 'Please come home'),
(2) intonation (e.g. the rising intonation of 'Come home?'),
(3) sequential focus (e.g. the 'marked' word-order of 'Home he came').

The first and the third of these categories are matched in a direct way in alphabetically written languages; the function of the second, intonation, is poorly substituted for by *punctuation*. In short, the extremely rich and expressive illocutionary system of intonation in spoken languages is parallelled in writing by a rather restricted and comparatively vastly less expressive system of punctuation. In what follows, we shall concentrate for the most part on spoken languages — even though our attention will, after this long preamble, gradually turn increasingly to translation issues, and translation tends to take for its object written texts. However, most of what I shall argue holds, *mutatis mutandis*, for written languages as well.

The task of conferring and conveying illocutionary function (whether in speech or writing) is, in every given language, unequally distributed between the three categories of sentential marker. It is, of course, conceivable for a particular language to make roughly equal use of illocutionary particles, intonation and sequential focus. It is just as likely, however, that in a given language one or other of these categories may blatantly predominate in terms of frequency and expressive potential. For instance, one may expect that in tonal languages (e.g. Standard Chinese), where the use of pitch modulation is extensively used for phonologically distinctive (as opposed to grammatical) purposes, intonation — also physically manifested in pitch modulation — is relatively less predominant than the use of illocutionary particles. Similarly, one may expect that languages in which word-order is the prominent carrier of distinctions in syntactic form (e.g. English 'people avoid snakes' versus 'snakes avoid people') there is less scope for the use of word-order as a sentential feature of sequential focus, than in languages where syntactic function is conveyed by morphological affixation (e.g. Latin 'puer amat puellam'/ 'puellam amat puer'/ 'puer puellam amat').

Though the issue hinges on tendencies (reinforced by frequency and stereotypicality), it can be reasonably asserted that some languages are particularly noted for the predominant sentential use they make of illocutionary particles, across a cross-section of textual genres. Thus, while clearly not all genres (oral and written) are equal in this respect, *the prominent use of illocutionary particles is nonetheless stereotypically characteristic of German*. (As a cross-generic generalisation, it is fair to observe that illocutionary function is clearly more often marked by illocutionary particles in German than, say, in English.) In token of this observation, we shall categorise German as a *particle-oriented* language.

In general, and certainly in comparison with German, or, say, with Latin, English makes a predominant sentential use of intonation for conveying illocutionary function. This is not to deny that certain genres of English text — for instance, casual oral conversation in particular — may be quite heavily interlarded with illocutionary particles ('you know', 'eh?', 'right?', 'wow!', etc.). Nonetheless, at least stereotypically the prominent use of intonation for conveying illocutionary meanings is characteristic of English; in token of which, English can be categorised as an *intonation-oriented* language.

Compared to both English and German, Hungarian has a strong tendency for conveying subtleties of illocutionary function by the use of sequential focus. Again, this is not to say that the sentential level of the Hungarian language (Magyar) is not rich in illocutionary particles and in the means for intonational nuancing of sentences. However, since syntactic functions in Hungarian are, for the most part, marked by morphological affixation rather than by word-order, this leaves word-order free to be widely deployed as a means of conveying illocutionary nuances through sequential focus. In a manner that parallels Latin, Hungarian 'a fiú szereti a lányt' [the boy loves the girl] contains a subject ('a fiú' = the boy) morphologically marked for subject function by the *nominative* case, and a direct object ('a lányt' = the girl + accusative) morphologically marked for object function by the *accusative* case. Consequently, word-order is not required for syntactic purposes: the underlying proposition 'the boy loves the girl' is unambiguously expressed by any of 'a fiú szereti a lányt', 'a lányt szereti a fiú', 'szereti a fiú a lányt', 'szereti a lányt a fiú', 'a fiú a lányt szereti', 'a lányt a fiú szereti'. These different permutations do not serve different syntactic functions, but allow for subtle illocutionary nuancing of sentences with different sequential focus. Such an illocutionary use of word-order permutations is stereotypically characteristic of Hungarian, in token of which the Magyar language can usefully be categorised as a *sequential-focus-oriented* language.

Recognising German as a particle-oriented language, English as an intonation-oriented language and Hungarian as a sequential-focus-oriented one has clear-cut implications for translation strategy. In the first instance, at the stage of comprehending the meanings of source texts (STs) — where translators are faced, among other things, with the need to grasp the illocutionary forces of ST sentences — the attention of translators from German should be drawn particularly to the textual role of illocutionary particles, the attention of translators from English should be especially drawn to the textual role of intonation and the attention of translators from Hungarian especially drawn to the textual role of sequential focus. This, of course, is not a recommendation for ignoring intonation and sequential focus in German STs, for ignoring illocutionary particles and sequential focus in English STs or for ignoring illocutionary particles and intonation in Hungarian STs. It is, however, a sound translation-strategic reminder that, in German, important, subtle and possibly problematic nuances of illocutionary meaning are likely to be concentrated in the use of illocutionary particles; that, in English, important and possibly not easily translated nuances of illocutionary meaning are likely to be concentrated in the use of intonation; and that, in Hungarian, such nuances of illocutionary meaning are likely to be encountered in the area of the use of sequential focus. In crude terms, these strategic points could be formulated as follows:

(1) when translating from German, be sure to pay special attention to illocutionary particles in the ST;
(2) when translating from English, be sure to pay special attention to the illocutionary function of intonation in the ST;
(3) when translating from Hungarian, be sure to pay special attention to the illocutionary function of sequential focus in the ST.

In the second instance, when it comes to the search for possible translational renderings of sentences with identified illocutionary functions a crucial strategic consideration arises from the observation that illocutionary meanings conveyed by particles in a ST do not necessarily find expression through the use of particles in a target text (TT); illocutionary meanings conveyed by intonation in a ST are not necessarily expressible through intonation in a TT; and illocutionary meanings conveyed by sequential focus in a ST are not necessarily capable of expression through the use of sequential focus in a TT. In short, the translational rendering of illocutionary functions in ST sentences can be regularly expected to involve *compensation in kind* (defined as 'compensating for [the loss of] a particular type of textual effect in the ST by using a textual effect of a different type in the TT' in Hervey & Higgins, 1992: 248).

When translating from German into English or Hungarian, therefore, general strategic considerations suggest that illocutionary functions negotiated through illocutionary particles in the ST may need to be handled by means other than the use of particles in the TT. Similarly, when translating from English into German or Hungarian, intonationally conveyed illocutionary functions of sentences may need to be reconstructed in the TT by using pragmatic devices other than intonation. Equally, when translating from Hungarian into German or English, it is to be expected that nuances of sequential focus in the ST may need to be conveyed by means other than sequential focus in the TT.

Furthermore, and still as a matter of general translation strategy, it makes good sense, when translating illocutionary meanings into German (by whatever means they are conveyed in the ST), to give priority to a search for appropriate particles that may be used in the TT. Along the same lines, when translating illocutionary meanings into English, it makes good sense to start by searching for appropriate intonational features that may be appropriate in the TT. In the same way, it is good strategy, when translating into Hungarian, to give first consideration to possible uses of sequential focus that might convey the appropriate illocutionary meanings in the TT.

These strategic pointers can be seen as indicating a degree of 'freedom' in the translation of illocutionary functions: freedom, that is, from a rigid adherence to one-to-one correspondences of particle for particle, intonation for intonation, and sequential focus for sequential focus between ST and TT. This is a well-motivated degree of freedom, given the observation of stereotypical differences between particle-oriented, intonation-oriented and sequential-focus-oriented languages. Yet again in crude terms, the following strategic points could be formulated:

(1) when translating illocutionary functions into German, be sure to consider possible illocutionary particles that might be appropriate;
(2) when translating illocutionary particles into English, be sure to consider possible intonational features that might be appropriate;
(3) when translating illocutionary particles into Hungarian, be sure to consider possible uses of sequential focus that might be appropriate.

These strategic recommendations are, as I have indicated before, based on sound theoretical principles relating to what I have established as the unity-in-diversity of illocutionary function in a given language (namely, they are predicated on the commonality of the function of particles, intonation and sequential focus), and to the trichotomy of particle-oriented, intonation-oriented and sequential-focus-oriented languages. In this sense, then, the strategies in question are deductively arrived at, rather than being inductively derived from examples and data. However, their practicality and usefulness cannot be fully appreciated until they have been tried in concrete cases. At the very least, then, it would be helpful to offer, in what follows, some typical instances that provide concrete exemplification.

Example (1a) German to English
ST: [from a Hyundai advertisement]
[. . .] Hyundai stellt Autos her, die zwar alles haben, was man von einem modernen Automobil erwartet [. . .]
TT: [. . .] Hyundai make cars that have *everything* you would expect of a modern automobile [. . .]

[Comment: In the ST the illocutionary particle 'zwar' has the function of heightening the sense of 'emphatic assertion' in the sentence: in explanatory terms this might be given the English gloss 'absolutely'. Indeed, a possible TT might have been '[. . .] Hyundai have absolutely everything [. . .]' —

but for the fact that this TT seems to be more over-stated than the ST and is excessively bombastic for British tastes. A safer option, with an adequately emphatic, less over-stated, illocutionary function, is to indicate (by the use of italics) that the TT sentence is to be read with a stressed falling pitch on the word 'everything'.]

Example (1b) German to Hungarian
ST: [from a Contax camera advertisement]
     [Eine gute Aktie wiegt weniger.] Sie macht aber auch nicht so schöne Bilder.
TT: Olyan jó képeket sem csinál viszont.
     [Such good pictures neither makes though]

[Comment: In the ST the illocutionary particles 'aber' and 'auch' have an adversative force, creating an illocutionary function that, in English, might be given the rough explanatory gloss 'but then [it takes] *not such good pictures*'. A possible Hungarian rendering of the ST might have been 'De nem is csinál olyan jó képeket' [interlineally: but not either makes such good pictures]. The disadvantage of this rendering is that it transfers the adversative force on which the persuasive impact of the advertisement hinges from *not such good pictures* to *does not take*. Sequential focus, shifting the constituent 'olyan jó képeket' [such good pictures–accusative] from the end of the sentence to the beginning, restores an illocutionary function in which the adversative force is fixed on *not such good pictures*.]

Example (2a) English to German
ST: [from an anthropological discussion of characters in an English village]
     Don't Doris and Fred remember the great times *they* had together as kids?
TT: Doris und Fred haben doch wohl nicht etwa schon vergessen, was für tolle Zeiten sie selber mal hatten als Kinder?

[Comment: In the ST, the illocutionary function of the emphatic questioning intonation involves conveying a mildly annoyed critical response to the inconsistent attitudes of Doris and Fred. [This illocutionary function is later increased to a much less mild *'why the hell?'* in a subsequent sentence of the text: 'So why the hell do they now forget . . . ?'] It is precisely this note of mild impatience, annoyance, and implied reproach that the particle 'doch wohl' attempts to recreate in the TT; an effect which is further enhanced by the sarcasm of the particle 'etwa', used here with mock tentative irony (Hervey *et al.*, 1995: 196). Though alternative TTs are doubtless available — for instance, the much more anodyne 'Haben Doris und Fred denn schon vergessen, was für tolle Zeiten . . . ?', which conveys no detectable note of impatience, only of mild reproach and regret — it is hard to imagine how, other than by the use of illocutionary particles, an appropriately nuanced TT might be constructed at all.]

Example (2b) English to Hungarian
ST: [from an anthropological discussion of characters in an English village]
[. . .] she warns him that she's not having *her* 15-year-old maligned
[. . .]
TT: figyelmezteti: az ö tizenöt éves lányát nem türi, hogy csepüljék
[warns the her 15 yeared daughter not put up that malign-they]

[Comment: Evidently, the illocutionary force of the intonational features indicated by italics is adversative: a rough explanatory paraphrase might be *'others: yes; her: no'*. While the use of italics, placing the illocutionary onus on intonation in the TT, would be possible, the focus of the adversative would be definitely blurred and dissipated between *'won't* have it' and *'her* no' in a rendering such as 'figyelmezteti: nem türi, hogy csepüljék az ö tizenöt éves lányát' [warns not put up that malign-they the her 15 yeared daughter-accusative]. In the preferred TT, sequential focus, shifting the constituent 'az ö tizenöt éves lányát [her 15-year-old daughter] from the end of the sentence to immediately after the main verb, concentrates the adversative force on '*her* no'.]

Example (3a) Hungarian to German
ST: [from a series of published Reformed Church sermons]
Nem ilyen szakadékony parton állsz te is?
[not such crumbling shore-on stand-thou also?]
TT: Stehst du nicht etwa auch auf einem so unfesten Ufer?

[Comment: The illocutionary nuance of the ST sentence invites an explanatory paraphrase along the lines of 'examine your conscience [in the light of the foregoing examples]! Be honest with yourself and admit that [you, too, face a similar crisis]!'; the persuasive import of the ST depends on this illocutionary function. Manipulation of sequential focus is not available for the German TT, and while something of the suggestion of turning in upon yourself might be conveyed by intonation in a possible version such as 'Stehst *du* nicht auch auf einem so unfesten Ufer?', this does not nearly do enough to convey the implicit nuance of the ST sentence. Similarly, while 'Du stehst auch auf einem so unfesten Ufer, nicht wahr?' issues a similar kind of invitation to honest admission, it does so in far too crude and explicit terms. Another possible version, using the rhetorical question form and adding the particle 'doch wohl' is, according to my German informants, far too direct, heavy-handed, over-loaded and lacking in any degree of tentativeness. The over-loading could be mitigated by abandoning the question form and keeping 'doch wohl' to produce 'Du stehst auch doch wohl . . . '; however, this remains too assertive and lacking in tentativeness. Restoring the question form seems to be the answer to avoiding excessive assertiveness, while an element of tentativeness can best be introduced by means of 'etwa'. It is, in other words, precisely the illocutionary particle 'etwa', used here in its genuinely tentative sense (Hervey *et al.*, 1995: 196), that most adequately approximates to the implicit nuance of the ST.]

Example (3b) Hungarian to English
ST: [from a paper on Hungarian woman writers]
      Egy ideig szoros barátság füzte Ritoók Emmát Ernst Blochhoz, a neves Német filozófushoz is.
      [a time-for close friendship tied Ritoók Emma Ernst Bloch-to, the famous German philosopher-to also]
TT: She also enjoyed a close friendship for a while with Ernst Bloch, the celebrated German philosopher.

[Comment: The illocutionary purport of the ST sentence is to provide an additional detail supporting, without overstatement, the importance of the particular woman writer discussed. The constituents moved to the front and to the very end of the sentence — 'egy ideig szoros barátság' [for a time close friendship] and 'is' [also] — both receive prominence of focus in this balance between claimed yet qualified praise. Simple copying of the ST's sequential focus, producing a TT in the form of 'For a while close friendship linked Ritoók Emma to Ernst Bloch, the celebrated German philosopher, too' would destroy this delicate illocutionary balance, besides creating a stilted effect by the outlying position of 'too'. In this version, excessive importance is attached to the qualifying 'for a while', and not enough to signalling that the sentence is intended to provide additional, parenthetical detail. Using 'also', which will attract intonational stress even without the device of italics, foregrounds the parenthetical nature of the information, moving 'for a while' to after 'close friendship' makes this a clear mitigating qualification, and terminating in 'the celebrated German philosopher' gives this claim the quality of a punchline.]

The purpose of these examples has been, as I indicated at the outset, to anchor my relatively abstract strategic hints and recommendations in the more concrete form of illustrations. (I am, incidentally, particularly indebted to my colleague Michael Loughridge, and to Annette Zimmermann, for their advice on points of German, though the responsibility for all the examples and comments rests ultimately with me.) These strategic pointers must further be seen in the light of what is to be understood by a 'translation strategy': this can under no circumstances be construed as a recipe, or a set of instructions to be followed blindly and unreflectingly. The whole issue of a strategic approach to translation — of dealing with translation problems as they arise, where they arise and on whatever level of language or text they arise — is to give careful thought to options and alternatives. A strategic approach to translating is intended to be a reflective and intelligent method. It is in this light that the whole of the foregoing discussion, including discussion of the illustrative examples, is to be considered.

When it comes to the illocutionary/sentential level of texts, a further consideration adds yet another strategic pointer worth mentioning here: good translation practice not only requires sound comprehension of, in this case, illocutionary functions in a ST, as well as a degree of flexibility in compensation, as opposed to one-to-one rendering of ST features — it also requires, under normal circumstances, that TTs be constructed and edited as *plausible* texts in the target language. A TT in English that consistently omitted the use of intonation as a means of conveying illocutionary nuances might be a 'precise' rendering of a ST; yet the cumulative effect of the absence of illocutionary devices stereotypical of English would be to render the TT less than plausible as a 'normal' target language text. Similarly, a TT in German that was manifestly devoid of illocutionary particles would, through its lack of devices stereotypical of German, induce a cumulative effect of implausibility as a 'normal' German text. In the same vein, a TT in Hungarian from which the illocutionary use of sequential focus was conspicuously absent would be cumulatively perceived as implausible as a 'normal' Hungarian text. In sum, the 'normalisation' of TTs (perhaps at the editing stage of the translation process) strongly suggests a strategy of ensuring that these texts are not unnaturally devoid of properties considered stereotypical of the target language: in particular, illocutionary particles in the case of particle-oriented languages, intonation in the case of intonation-oriented languages, and sequential focus in the case of sequential-focus-oriented languages. As we said earlier, these strategic points may be summarised as follows.

(1) when translating into German, use illocutionary particles;
(2) when translating into English, use the illocutionary function of intonation; and
(3) when translating into Hungarian, use the illocutionary function of sequential focus.

Such strategies have, of course, to be implemented with care: overloading a text with stereotypical devices has its own dangers of turning 'normalisation' into 'caricaturisation'. However, provided excesses are avoided, these further strategic recommendations add a useful component to translation practice with regard to handling the illocutionary level of texts.

It is undoubtedly the case that sensitive handling of the illocutionary functions of sentences (as speech acts) is an essential aspect of skill in translating and in interpreting. It is also evident that this skill can be improved through the application of translation strategies based on sound theoretical, descriptive, and contrastive linguistic principles. The aim of this chapter has been to develop and to illustrate such a set of translation strategies.

References
Austin, J.L. (1962) *How to Do Things with Words.* Oxford: Clarendon Press.

Ballmer, T.L and Brennenstuhl, W. (1980) *Speech Act Classification: A Study of the Lexical Analysis of English Speech Activity Verbs.* Berlin, New York: Springer.

Brown, P. and Levinson, S. (1978) Universals in language use: Politeness phenomena. In E. Goody (ed.) *Questions and Politeness: Strategies in Social Interaction* (pp. 56–311). Cambridge: Cambridge University Press.

Gardner, S. and Hervey, S. (1983) Structural sentence-types. *La linguistique* 19, 3–20.

Gumperz, J. (1982) *Discourse Strategies.* Cambridge: Cambridge University Press.

Hatim, B. and Mason, I. (1990) *Discourse and the Translator.* London: Longman.

Hervey, S. (1990) Sentences and linguistic data. *La Linguistique* 26, 17–27.

Hervey, S. and Higgins, I. (1992) *Thinking Translation.* London: Routledge.

Hervey, S., Higgins, I. and Loughridge, M. (1995) *Thinking German Translation.* London: Routledge.

Irvine, J. (1974) Strategies of status manipulation in the Wolof greeting. In R. Bauman and J. Scherzer (eds) *Explorations in the Ethnography of Speaking* (pp. 167–91). Cambridge: Cambridge University Press.

Levinson, S. (1983) *Pragmatics.* Cambridge: Cambridge University Press.

Parret, H. (1983) *Structural Semiotics and Integrated Pragmatics. An Evaluative Comparison of Conceptual Frameworks.* Amsterdam: John Benjamins.

Searle, J.R. (1969) *Speech Acts.* Cambridge: Cambridge University Press.

Searle, J.R. (1979) *Expression and Meaning.* Cambridge: Cambridge University Press.

Wierzbicka, A. (1985a) A semantic metalanguage for a cross cultural comparison of speech acts and speech genres. *Language in Society* 14, 491–513.

Wierzbicka, A. (1985b) Different cultures, different languages, different speech acts: Polish versus English. *Journal of Pragmatics* 9, 145–78.

Wierzbicka, A. (1991) *Cross Cultural Pragmatics: The Semantics of Social Interaction.* Berlin: Mouton de Gruyter.

Chapter 2

Cooperation and Literary Translation

KIRSTEN MALMKJÆR

Introduction

The notion of cooperation is relevant to the reading of literature in many ways. It underlies, for example, Coleridge's notion of the 'willing suspension of disbelief for the moment, which constitutes poetic faith' (1817: Ch. 14); to approach a text, whether fictional or not, as a literary work, constitutes a type of cooperation with the text and with the norms and expectations of the culture within which it exists and is accepted as a literary text. In fact, cooperation, perhaps of a rather more basic type, is an inherent feature of all kinds of linguistic communication, as Wittgenstein's (1958) argument against a private language forcefully shows and as most philosophers of language since have readily admitted. The most famous account of what linguistic cooperation amounts to which has emerged from the philosophy of language is Grice's (1975) account of some of the effects of communicative activity which fall beyond meaning proper, as he sees it (Grice, 1957). It is probably also the most systematic account, in so far as it appears to strike a reasonable balance between a potentially unstoppable proliferation of principles (cf. Leech, 1983) and a denial of the need for, or possibility of classification beyond one, overarching, principle (cf. Sperber & Wilson, 1986).

The Gricean account is developed primarily with spoken conversation in mind, that is, it addresses directly situations of the type to which Lyons (1977: 637) refers as 'the canonical situation of utterance' involving:

> one–one, or one–many, signalling in the phonic medium along the vocal–auditory channel, with all the participants present in the same actual situation able to perceive one another and to perceive the associated non-vocal paralinguistic features of their utterances, and each assuming the role of sender and receiver in turn.

As Lyons (1977: 638) goes on to point out:

Many utterances which would be readily interpretable in a canonical situation-of-utterance are subject to various kinds of ambiguity or indeterminacy if they are produced in a non-canonical situation: if they are written rather than spoken and dissociated from the prosodic and paralinguistic features which would punctuate and modulate them . . . ; if the participants in the language-event, or the moment of transmission and the moment of reception, are widely separated in space and time; if the participants cannot see one another, or cannot see what the other can see; and so on.

Literary texts, and in particular translated literary texts, tend to satisfy some or all of the criteria for problem-creation which Lyons mentions. So it cannot by any means be straightforwardly assumed that the Gricean account is directly applicable to the study of literary translation. I shall address this issue later. The next three sections are devoted to setting out the theory and its application to written (literary) texts in general.

Grice's Theory of Meaning

Grice's theory of cooperation in conversation (1975) forms a pragmatic complement to the semantic theory presented by Grice & Strawson (1956/1972) and Grice (1957). The semantic theory originates in an attempt to save the distinction between analytic and synthetic truths, which has traditionally been explained as a distinction between utterances that are true or false because of how the world is, and utterances that are true or false because of the meanings of the terms used in them. For example, 'My house is white' is true or false depending on the colour of my house, that is, on a state of affairs in the world; it is synthetically true or false. But 'My white house is red all over' must be false because of the relationship between the meanings of the terms 'white' and 'red'; it is analytically false.

Quine (1951) questions this distinction. He suggests that *all* truths and falsehoods are subject to revision in the light of experience, even those which appear analytic. Our experience is holistic and provides us with a unified physical theory to which our language relates. Given sufficiently radical revision of the theory, even apparently analytic truths can be given up. If this view seems extreme, consider what a change in physical theory did to the statement 'parallel, straight lines perpendicular to a third line will never meet' (Hookway, 1988: 41).

Nevertheless, it seems counter-intuitive to conflate the two kinds of statement in the Quinean way, and Grice and Strawson (1956) attempt to save the distinction between analytic and synthetic truths by relocating it in speakers' minds (cf. Putnam, 1962). They suggest that we can distinguish in terms of listener attitudes between the two statements (Grice & Strawson, 1956: 131):

(1) My neighbour's three-year-old child understands Russell's Theory of Types.
(2) My neighbour's three-year-old child is an adult.

The traditional position is that the first is a synthetic statement which could, logically speaking, be true, provided the child in question was most unusual. The second is an analytic statement which must be false because of the meanings of 'child' and 'adult' respectively. Grice and Strawson, however, wish to distinguish between the two in terms of listener reactions. Listeners would be likely to greet the first statement with doubt, but might be willing to alter their mental state to one of belief if the child were to demonstrate that it did, in fact, understand Russell's Theory of Types. In contrast, listeners would greet the second statement with uncompromising incomprehension: no matter what feats the child were to show itself capable of, they would never be prepared to concede that the child was an adult. So a distinction in types of meaning can be recast in terms of a distinction in types of mental state, and this reliance on the mental state of speakers is carried through to the theory of meaning presented in Grice (1957).

Here Grice (1957: 44) sets out to establish:

> the difference between . . . 'deliberately and openly letting someone know' and 'telling' and between 'getting someone to think' and 'telling'.

He ends up with three conditions for a proper case of telling, or meaning, to have taken place (adapted from Strawson's (1964: 28) formulation):

S means something by an utterance x if, and only if, S intends:

(1) to produce by uttering x a response r in an audience A and
(2) that A shall recognise S's intention (1) and
(3) that this recognition on the part of A of S's intention (1) shall function as A's reason, or part of the reason, for A's response r.

By response here is meant a belief. Notice that although the audience's beliefs figure large in the formulation, it is the speaker's intentions which are critical for a proper case of meaning something by an utterance to have taken place. Notice, further, that the basis on which A is able to pass from the speaker's words to his or her intentions is A's knowledge or assumption that, for the speaker, x means or has as one of its meanings x (Grice, 1968/1971: 63). That is, hearers recognise speakers' intentions because they understand their utterances.

Grice (1957: 47) goes on to stress that we must leave aside from the meaning of the action any secondary intentions the doer of the action might have; that is, any possible perlocutionary effect (Austin, 1962: Ch. VIII) cannot be said to have been part of the meaning of what was said. For example, if I utter 'The bus is full', intending to make the driver believe that the bus is full, and intending that this belief should have the effect that the driver should believe that it is time to drive off, then we must not be led into a position where the utterance 'The bus is full' *means* 'It is time to drive off'. This restriction is, in Grice's view, absolutely critical for any systematic theory of meaning. If it were not imposed, then, because of the potentially infinite number of further effects which any utterance may have, any utterance could mean anything. However, it is clear that the restriction also renders the theory incapable of accounting for a very great deal of what goes on in everyday linguistic interactions, and in 'Logic and conversation' (1975), Grice seeks to bridge the gap between that small part of language which semantics proper, as he sees it, can account for, and some of the rest. In this pragmatic addendum to the theory, also, the listener's role is made more prominent than in the formulation of the basic, semantic, theory.

Logic and Conversation

Grice (1975) begins by trying to preserve logic as a useful starting point for the study of natural language. The suitability of logic as such a starting point has often been doubted on the grounds that there seems to be no one-to-one correspondence between the sentence-forming operators of logic and their natural language counterparts; and if these do not correspond, then it is hard to see how logic can help us with the study of natural language. To provide a systematic account of meaning in natural language, it is necessary to account for the relationships between sentences and between the terms which occur in them. We must be able to produce generalisations about relationships between predicates such as 'is a flower' and 'is a tulip', for example, and to explain how such relationships affect relationships between sentences in which the predicates occur; and this is done using logical formulae in which the sentence-forming operators are used.

Grice's strategy is to reiterate the restriction on meaning and assign all other effects to the category *implicature*. Consider the sentence 'If Charles is English, he is brave'. In logic, the sentence-forming operator corresponding to 'if', usually represented by either '$\supset$' or '$\rightarrow$', is defined in such a way that the only circumstance in which a sentence of the form '$P \rightarrow Q$' is false is the circumstance in which 'P' is true while 'Q' is false. This is because it is one of the primary concerns of logic, the study of valid arguments, to prevent the derivation of false conclusions from true premises. This means, however, that the sentence about Charles would be classed as true in logic even if 'he is brave' is true while 'Charles is English' is false, and this seems to fly in the face of our conventional assumption that, in an if-sentence, the fact reported in the second clause (in this case, 'he is brave') is a consequence of the fact reported in the first clause ('Charles is English'). In other words, whereas in natural language the utterance, 'If Charles is English, he is brave' implies that his bravery is a consequence of his Englishness, in logic there is no such implication. But, according to Grice, this _conventional implicature_ is not, strictly speaking, part of the meaning of the words.

Other types of implicature are far less closely related to the conventional meanings of the words used. Grice (1975: 43) provides the following example:

> Suppose that A and B are talking about a mutual friend, C, who is now working in a bank. A asks B how C is getting on in his job, and B replies, _Oh quite well I think; he likes his colleagues, and he hasn't been to prison yet._

As Grice points out, the potential implicature here is vastly variable with circumstances. Is there any way of trying to systematise this variability?

Grice begins by considering 'a certain subclass of nonconventional implicatures' (1975: 45), namely **Conversational Implicatures**. These are 'essentially connected with certain general features of discourse', which arise from the fact that if our talk exchanges are to be rational, they must consist of utterances which are in some way connected to each other. What guarantees this connection is called the **Cooperative Principle**: 'Make your conversational contribution such as is required, at the stage at which it occurs, by the accepted purpose or direction of the talk exchange in which you are engaged' (1975: 45).

Under this principle fall four categories of maxim. The connection with human rationality is highlighted in the selection of categories deduced by Kant (1781; 1787) as part of what he considered an analysis of just that phenomenon. The categories and principles are the following (Grice, 1975: 45–6):

(I) **Maxims of quantity** (concerning the amount of information to be conveyed):
    (1) Make your contribution as informative as is required (for the current purposes of the exchange).
    (2) Do not make your contribution more informative than is required.

(II) **Maxims of quality**: Try to make your contribution one that is true. More specifically:

(1) Do not say what you believe to be false.
(2) Do not say that for which you lack adequate evidence.

(III) **Maxim of relation**: Be relevant.

(IV) **Maxims of manner** (concerning not so much *what* is said as *how* it is said): Be perspicuous. More specifically:
(1) Avoid obscurity of expression.
(2) Avoid ambiguity.
(3) Be brief (avoid unnecessary prolixity).
(4) Be orderly.
And there may be others.

There are various ways in which a participant in a talk exchange may fail to fulfil a maxim:

(1) by violation (which is likely to mislead);
(2) by opting out (saying, for example, *I don't want to talk about it*);
(3) there may be a conflict of maxims (you cannot be as informative as is required if you do not have enough evidence);
(4) by blatantly flouting a maxim.

It is in cases of the fourth type, when, as Grice (1975: 49) puts it, a maxim is being exploited, that conversational implicature is most characteristically generated. However, it is also possible to generate implicatures from cases in which no maxim is being violated and from cases in which a maxim is apparently violated because of a clash with another maxim.

In working out an implicature, the hearer relies on the following types of data (Grice, 1975: 50):

(1) the conventional meaning of the words used, and the referents of referring expressions;
(2) the cooperative principle and its maxims;
(3) the co-text and context;
(4) background knowledge;
(5) the supposition that all participants suppose that all relevant items falling under (1)–(4) are available to them all.

Finally, it is worth bearing in mind five features of conversational implicature, namely (Grice, 1975: 57–8):

(1) It can be cancelled, either by an explicit declaration that the speaker is opting out or, implicitly, by the co-text and context.
(2) It is non-detachable, insofar as saying the same thing in another way usually carries the same implicature.

(3) It is not part of the meaning of the expression, but is, rather, dependent on the prior knowledge of that meaning.

(4) It is not carried by what is said but by the saying of it; that is, by the entire speech act (Austin, 1962) rather than by the propositional content.

(5) It may be indeterminate: in many cases, the list of possible implicatures of an utterance is open.

In the next section I shall examine the applicability of this system to the study of written texts, in particular literary texts, before turning to its applicability to the study of *translated* literary texts.

Cooperation and Literary Texts

Before moving on to consider how Grice's theory of cooperation might account for literary translation, it is necessary to set aside some objections which might be raised to the project of applying the theory to the study of written texts that are not translated — in particular literary texts. I think it is possible to argue that these objections are spurious.

Most generally, as mentioned in the first section, in linguistic interaction involving only written language, cues to interpretation such as tone of voice, stress, intensity and cadence are lost. However, there are various orthographic measures, such as punctuation and variations in font, available to a writer wishing to convey different degrees of emphasis and other semantic nuances (besides such obvious devices as various reporting verbs — 'exclaimed', 'shouted' etc — and adverbs — 'emphatically', 'happily' etc) which skilled readers make use of in interpreting the text.

More serious difficulties may arise because of the physical and/or temporal distance between the interactants in communicative events involving writing only. They typically do not have access to the same immediate environment, which often supplies one of the types of evidence which Grice (1975: 50; see p. 30) claims that hearers need to rely on in working out implicature, namely the referents for referring expressions. However, most referents for referring expressions in literary texts are provided somewhere in the co-text and will take their place in the reader's representation of the fictional world. Those that are not provided can either typically be inferred, as one might infer them in spoken interaction, or they refer to items such as the sun, which readers import from the actual world into the fiction.

What may be worse is the inability of participants to check with each other whether they have reached mutual understanding, on the basis, partly, of shared background knowledge. In the case of literary texts, the text is generally the *only* point of contact between writer and reader and the amount of background knowledge which they share is obviously variable. This is a difficulty, but it is not one which distinguishes written from spoken interaction generically. Misunderstandings may be more likely to arise where a literary text is concerned, but they do undoubtedly also arise in the canonical speech situation. Grice's theory is not supposed to guarantee against misunderstanding; it is simply meant to account for what has to happen for an instance of linguistic communication to be successful: the audience understands the producer in the way that the producer intended, and it can very well be argued that this is as true a picture of successful communication by means of literary written texts as it is of successful communication in canonical speech situations.

Finally, difficulties might be thought likely to arise in applying the theory of conversational cooperation to the study of literary texts from the fact that the cooperative principle is formulated for instances in which interactants are interested in 'a maximally effective exchange of information' (Grice, 1975: 47). We cannot assume that a writer's primary purpose in writing a literary text is the effective exchange of information nor, even, that the writer necessarily intends the reader to grasp his or her intentions. Many writers expressly refuse to be drawn into critical debate concerning interpretations of their work. Nor can we assume that the readers' main purpose in reading a text as literature is to grasp the intentions of the writer or to be effectively informed. However, we *can* assume, I think, that the writer at least would like the reader to grasp the basic, literal meaning of his or her written utterance and that the reader shares this desire; as long as this is all that is meant by the effective exchange of information, I see no problem here. We should remember, also, that the list of potential implicatures is open, and that being able to establish exactly what implicatures can legitimately be drawn from texts is not what matters, especially not implicatures at the level of abstraction from the text which a full, critical interpretation of a literary work amounts to. Finally, we must draw, in this connection, a distinction between the reader as the writer's audience and the reader as a type of 'overhearer' of conversations and thought sequences involving characters in the text. Just above, I have dealt with the reader as the writer's audience only. Insofar as the reader as overhearer is concerned, there are grounds for arguing that a reader of literary texts is actually in a better position to draw implicatures than an 'overhearer' of others' conversations, such as a discourse analyst, for example. Schober and Clark (1989) demonstrate the serious limitations on comprehension imposed by overhearers' inability to collaborate with participants in a speech encounter — to ask for additional information, and so on. But in the case of reading a literary text, the reader is often provided by the co-text with the information required to comprehend conversational interactants' utterances and the implicatures which the interactants may be supposed to be drawing from them.

I think, then, that there are no insurmountable obstacles in the way of the application of the Gricean mechanism to the study of written literary texts. We must now see whether any may arise from the *translation* of such texts.

Cooperation and Literary Translation

The severest difficulties in applying the theory of conversational cooperation to the study of literary translation arise, in my opinion, from its situation within a theory of meaning according to which understanding the meaning of a speaker's utterance amounts to a recognition on the part of the hearer of the speaker's intentions in producing the utterance on the basis of the audience's prior (assumed) understanding of the speaker's words (see p. 27). As previously mentioned, in the case of the overwhelming majority of literary texts, the text presents the *only* point of contact between writer and reader; and in the case of translated texts, it is feasible to argue that the fact of translation severs this connection. More generally, however, and on the model of this argument concerning translation, it is feasible to argue that the very text (whether spoken or written) severs the connection between the utterer's intentions and the audience's recognition of them.

A theory of meaning according to which the recognition of speakers' intentions are tantamount to understanding what the speakers meant, *and* in which this recognition depends on the prior understanding of their utterances *cannot* also use the intentions as evidence for the meanings of the utterances. In Grice's theory, this understanding is taken for granted (see p. 27). It is easy to assume such understanding in the case of interactants who share a language. However, as Davidson (1973: 125) points out:

> The problem of interpretation is domestic as well as foreign . . . Speakers of the same language can go on the assumption that for them the same expressions are to be interpreted in the same way, but this does not indicate what justifies the assumption.

It seems, therefore, that we must, paradoxically, account for the phenomenon of translation even if we are to provide an account of how the participants in linguistic interactions involving just one language arrive at common understanding and the Gricean account does not do this. It is doubtful, therefore, whether it can account for mutual understanding where two languages are involved *and* there is intervention by a translator. The Gricean theory of meaning cannot answer Quine's (1960) challenge that translation is indeterminate. Elsewhere (Malmkjær, 1993) I report an answer to this challenge, provided by Davidson (1973). Davidson (1986) praises Grice for having done more than any other theorist to cast light on how we understand non-standard cases of meaning and it might be argued that, once situated within a theory which answers the indeterminacy thesis, the Gricean, pragmatic, wheels can be allowed to turn undisturbed. That is, once the problem of basic meaning is sorted out *à la* Davidson, the Gricean theory of cooperation can take care of the non-literal. However, examining translations casts doubt on its ability to account satisfactorily for at least some instances of translation. In the following section, I shall provide one such example among others which, however, suggest that many observed instances *can* be explained by the theory of cooperation.

Examples

I shall begin this section by trying to demonstrate the limitations of the Gricean account of cooperation as a theory of literary translation.

Consider the following text extract, taken from Barbara Haveland's translation (1995) of Peter Høeg's *Forestilling om det tyvende århundrede* (1988) [*The History of Danish Dreams* (1996: 331–2)]:

> All of this Mads senses, at this moment, with the kind of clarity that follows a bad hangover or a long illness — not because he is clairvoyant but because he was born to the sensitivity and confusion of this century. And I know what I am talking about, because I am him — from now on *you can call me Mads*. [My emphasis]

I doubt whether any competent reader of English would claim to have any difficulty in understanding any part of this extract, and it is a reasonably faithful translation, on the literal level, of the following (apart from the punctuation; see below) (Høeg, 1988: 334; my emphasis):

> og alt dette føler Mads dette øjeblik med en klarhed some efter svære tømmermænd eller lang tids sygdom, og det er ikke fordi han er clairvoyant men fordi han er født til dette århundredes følsomhed og forvirring, og jeg ved hvad jeg taler om, for det er mig der er ham, fra nu af *kan I kalde mig Mads.*

Compare the Danish phrase 'kan I kalde mig Mads' and the 'equivalent' in the translation, 'you can call me Mads'. Except for the inversion of subject and object in Danish, which the fronting in the clause of the prepositional adverbial phrase meaning 'from now on' demands in Danish, the two clauses correspond word for word ('I' = 'you'; 'kan' = 'can' 'kalde' = 'call'; 'mig' = 'me'). In addition to its literal meaning, however, the Danish clause standardly implicates what the English 'I am the Queen of Sheeba' implies. From it, therefore, in this particular context, the Danish reader can generate all manner of implicatures relating to the status of the story they have just been told with respect to reality (the clause occurs very near the end of the book, just before Mads explains why he has recorded the history of his family through the 20th century).

English readers probably cannot generate these implicatures from this clause, even though Haveland has undoubtedly *said* the same as Høeg. And saying the same, using a different form of expression should, on Grice's account, carry the same implicature, given the non-detachability criterion (see p. 30). Now, it might undoubtedly be argued that the reason why saying the same thing does not carry the same implicature in these two cases is to do with the lack of shared background knowledge about what the Danish expression standardly implicates. But, on Grice's account, it seems that we would then have to say that the implicature has not been translated and, therefore, that this text part has not been translated — at least not completely. The literal meaning has been translated, but the implicature has not. It could have been translated, not by means of translating the literal meaning but only by substituting this for 'the Queen of Sheeba' which would, in this context have been wholly inappropriate. *Ergo* this text part is, strictly speaking, untranslatable.

But trouble lies here. A reader of the English text, having no knowledge of what he or she is missing, will read calmly along and accept the text-extract as a translation; and what else, indeed, are we to call it? Toury (1980) demonstrates that source text (ST)-oriented theories of translation, according to which a translation is not a translation unless it conveys everything that the original conveyed, find themselves in difficulty when trying to account for the existence of things which are called translations but which, in the terms of the theories, would have to be defined as non-translations. And there is a danger that this difficulty might be encountered by a Gricean theory *per se*, even without examples such as that just quoted. According to the theory, for a proper case of telling to have taken place, the writer must intend the reader to form a belief in virtue of his or her recognition of the writer's intention that s/he form this belief. In translation, this picture is skewed by the intervention of the translator. The reader of a translation typically finds it meaningful; s/he feels that s/he is being told something. But s/he cannot be being told this because s/he recognises any intentions of the writer: s/he is recognising the telling-in-tentions of the translator. But the translator is not the author and there is no place in the theory for a mediator of messages. Perhaps such a place could be created. However, I think that such a project would run into difficulties because of the reliance it would have to make on intentions. The translator would be likely to be cast in the role, first, of a recogniser of the writer's intentions to produce responses in a readership, and next as a purveyor of these, via a new medium, to a different readership than any the writer is likely to have had in mind. Such a theory would share important characteristics with the theory of dynamic translation (Nida, 1964) and would, in my view, run into serious difficulties concerning the notion of equivalent effect — effect here being renamed response.

Besides, the exact conveyance of writers' original intentions, even at the level of literal meaning, is not necessarily what translations are intended by their creators to do, as, for example, Venuti's (1995) accounts of his own efforts as a translator clearly show. But this cannot be said to mean that Venuti's translations are not translations, unless we wish to return to the stalemate which Toury (1980) points to. When this difficulty is seen in conjunction with the argument which I have just put forward to the effect that the Gricean mechanism cannot account for all micro-instances of translation, I think it is clear that it is not a satisfactory theory of translation. It lacks full descriptive and explanatory power.

The trouble lies in the distinction drawn in the theory between literal and non-literal meaning. What we need, in my view, is a re-casting of that distinction as one between *first meaning* (Davidson 1986) and whatever else might be implicated. First meaning is whatever comes first in the order of interpretation. Now, it seems to me that it need not matter whether what comes first is, in fact, the same for readers of the ST and readers of the target text (TT), as long as everyone might in principle end up in the same place. And, adopting this point of view, I think that we can deem even the example I have just quoted to be a satisfactory translation *even from a ST-oriented point of view* which I do not endorse, but which it might make sense to adopt with respect to Haveland's translations of Høeg, because Haveland is, on the whole, scrupulously faithful to the original. She works closely with the author (Guido Waldman, personal communication) and is, presumably, guided by him in the way in which Tiina Nunnally refused to be. Nunnally is the initial translator of the text which, in an amended form to which Nunnally refused to lend her name, is marketed in Britain as translated by the non-existent F. David under the title, *Miss Smilla's Feeling for Snow.* Nunnally's translation, available in the United States, is called *Smilla's Sense of Snow,* and the difference is suggestive of Haveland's and Høeg's desire for accuracy, in this case, arguably, right down to rhythm and patterns of alliteration: Høeg's original is called *Frøken Smillas fornemmelse for sne.*

As mentioned earlier, at first sight, it looks as if English readers should not be able to generate the same implicatures from 'you can call me Mads' as Danish readers do. And I believe it is true that they will not generate this *as first meaning* of the clause. However, they might be able to generate it eventually, taking into consideration the entire context of the work. I think that the clause in its context invites implicatures concerning the relationship between this fiction and reality via implicatures which it gives rise to concerning the relationship between the narrator and the author. These implicatures arise partly because Høeg writes this book in a manner which has reminded many critics of magical realism (though I prefer to see it as realist fantasy) (see below), and partly because of the simple and sudden conflation of the narrator, who has so far not figured as a character in the novel but only as a writer and researcher of the social and personal history which it records, with one of the characters. Høeg employs a similar strategy in *De måske egnede* (1993: 247), translated by Haveland as *Borderliners* (1994; 1995: 224), when he lets the first-person narrator of the severe, institutional mistreatment to which he was subjected as a child reveal that he was adopted in 1973 by Karen and Erik Høeg, at the age of 15 (the author was born in 1957).

However, the Gricean mechanism's failure to stand as a full-blown theory of literary translation does not mean that there is not a great deal in a literary translation which can be described and explained in its terms or that translators would not be well advised to keep in mind the notion of implicature when translating.

For example, punctuation and other orthographic measures can be adjusted by editors/translators to suit a given readership, distanced either temporally or culturally or both from the writer; and such adjustment can be understood as a compensatory strategy explainable in terms of the principle of cooperation: the editor/translator can be said to be trying to ensure that the reader of the translated text has access to similar cues to interpretation as those available to the original audience. On the other hand, punctuation in a literary translation may also be widely at variance with that of the ST because of a desire on the part of translators or editors to produce a translation which is 'invisible' (Venuti, 1995). For example, whereas Høeg uses punctuation sparingly, particularly in certain parts of the source text for *Borderliners* (see above) and of the ST for *The History of Danish Dreams* (see the extract about Mads), to create a run-on, stream-of-consciousness effect, Haveland's translation normalises the punctuation, probably in order to encourage a calm, controlled, conventional reading-style. Consider, for example, the following paragraph from *De måske egnede*, p. 65; I have provided my own translation (a), which retains the

punctuation of the original, for comparison with the published translation
(b) by Barbara Haveland (*Borderliners*, p. 55):

Example (a)
At the Crust House the arrangement had been that if anyone had
personal problems they could turn to their class teacher, it was Willy
Ohrskov, who was popular and respected, he had a red MG, and drove
like a devil, when I had been there for half a year he died in a crash, and
besides it had always been considered wet to talk about yourself with a
teacher.

Example (b)
At Crusty House if you had any personal problems you were supposed
to consult your class teacher. That was Willy Ohrskov, who was popular
and respected. He had a red MG and drove like a madman. When I had
been there for six months he was killed in a car crash. And besides,
talking about yourself to a teacher had always been considered a bit wet.

I have argued elsewhere that this type of adjustment may significantly
interfere with the semantics of the text (Malmkjær, 1997), which, in turn,
may deprive readers of the translation of cues to implicature generation
which were available to the readers of the original. Obviously such cases
can also be explained by the theory, as cases of interference in the process
of communication between the original writer and the reader of the
translation.

Referents that are not provided by the co-text can be explained by
editors, as happens, for example, in the case of *The History of Danish Dreams*,
which includes at the end a list and brief notes about historical characters
referred to in the text, most of them Danish, which the British or American
audience is deemed unlikely to know anything about. This list provides
dates of birth and death, and helps generate the implicatures concerning
the relationship between fiction and reality mentioned earlier in connection
with the metaphor of Mads, right from the beginning of the book. On page
8 (which is the second page of the main text), for example, we find Casper
Bartholin (1585–1629) and Ole Rømer (1644–1710) present at the same
gathering of luminaries.

The theory can also account for various kinds of intratextual additions.
For example, F. David (1993: 1996 edn, p. 16; translation Høeg, 1992: 24)
adds the phrase in italics in the following passage (my emphasis):

Here they haven't put in a tennis court. But not for lack of space. It's probably because Loyn has a couple of them in his back garden in Hellerup, and two more *at his summer home* on Klitvej in Skagen.

The addition aids the generation of the implicature that Loyn is rich. However, the generation of this implicature is slightly different in the two texts. In the ST, addressed at Danes, it is generated from background knowledge that Skagen is a popular place for summer homes *and* that most summer homes there are owned by the rich; whereas the TT reader is only given the information that the two tennis courts which Loyn owns in Skagen are situated on his holiday property there. But having a summer home is less common in the UK than in Denmark and is, mainly, the prerogative of the rich. What is interesting, however, is that the co-text in fact contains plenty of evidence that Loyn is rich, including, of course, the mere fact of owning not just one, but a total of four tennis courts (wherever they may be). Perhaps, therefore, the addition is largely made in order to ensure against the possible generation of *inappropriate* implicatures by the absence of understanding, on the part of the TT reader, of the implication of having some of these in Skagen.

In sum, I believe that the notion of conversational cooperation is as applicable to literary translation as it is to language use in general. It cannot, on its own, serve as a theory of literary translation, because it cannot account for the phenomenon of translation as such and because it cannot account for all instances of translation. Nevertheless, many translational phenomena can be described fairly systematically using concepts and descriptive terms borrowed from it.

References

Austin, J.L. (1962) *How To Do Things With Words*. Oxford: Clarendon Press.

Coleridge, S.T. (1817) *Biographia Literaria*.

Davidson, D. (1973) Radical interpretation. *Dialectica* 27: 313–28. Reprinted in D. Davidson (1984), *Inquiries into Truth and Interpretation*. Oxford: Clarendon Press.

Davidson, D. (1986) A nice derangement of epitaphs. In E. LePore (ed.) *Truth and Interpretation: Perspectives on the Philosophy of Donald Davidson*. Oxford: Blackwell.

Grice, H. (1957) Meaning. *Philosophical Review* 66, 377–88. Reprinted in P. Strawson (ed.) (1967) *Philosophical Logic*. Oxford: Oxford University Press, 39–48.

Grice, H. (1968) Utterer's meaning, sentence-meaning, and word-meaning. *Foundations of Language*, 4, 1–18, Reprinted in J.R. Searle (ed.) (1971) *The Philosophy of Language* (pp. 54–70). Oxford: Oxford University Press.

Grice, H. (1975) Logic and conversation. In P. Cole and J.L. Morgan (eds) *Syntax and Semantics 3: Speech* Acts (pp. 41–58). New York Academic Press.

Grice, H.P. and Strawson, P.F. (1956) In defence of a dogma. *Philosophical* Review, 141–341. Reprinted in H. Feigl, W. Sellars and K. Lehrer (eds) (1972) *New Readings in Philosophical Analysis* (pp. 126–36). New York: Appleton-Century-Crofts.

Hookway, C. (1988) *Quine: Language, Experience and Reality* (Ch. 2). Oxford: Oxford Polity Press.

Høeg, P. (1988) *Forestilling om det tyvende århundrede*. Copenhagen: Munksgaard/Rosinante. Translation by B. Haveland (1995, 1996) *The History of Danish Dreams*. London: The Harvill Press.

Høeg, P. (1992) *Frøken Smillas fornemmelse for sne*. Copenhagen: Munksgaard/Rosinante. Translation by F. David (1993) *Miss Smilla's Feeling for Snow*. London: The Harvill Press.

Høeg, P. (1993) *De måske egnede*. Copenhagen: Munksgaard/Rosinante. Translation by B. Haveland (1994; 1995) London: The Harvill Press.

Kant, I. (1781 and 1787) *Immanuel Kant's Critique of Pure Reason*. Translation by N. Kemp Smith (1933). Second impression with corrections. London & Basingstoke: Macmillan.

Leech, G.N. (1983) *Principles of Pragmatics*. London: Longman.

Lyons, J. (1977) *Semantics* (two volumes). Cambridge: Cambridge University Press.

Putnam, H. (1962) The analytic and the synthetic. In H. Feigl and G. Maxwell (eds) *Minnesota Studies in the Philosophy of Science III*. Minnesota: University of Minnesota Press.

Malmkjær, K. (1993) Underpinning translation theory. *Target* 5 (2), 133–48.

Malmkjær, K. (1997) Punctuation in Hans Christian Andersen's stories and in their translations into English. In F. Poyatos (ed.) *Nonverbal Communication and Translation: New Perspectives and Challenges in Literature, Interpretation and the media*. Amsterdam and Philadelphia: John Benjamins.

Nida, E. (1964) *Toward a Science of Translating*. Leiden: E.J. Brill.

Quine, W.V.O (1951) Two dogmas of empiricism. *Philosophical Review* (Jan.). Reprinted in (1961 *From a Logical Point of View: 9 Logico-Philosophical Essays*, 2nd edn, revised (pp. 20–46). New York: Harper and Row.

Quine, W.V.O (1960) *Word and Object*. Cambridge, MA: Massachusetts Institute of Technology.

Schober, M. F. and Clark, H. H. (1989) Understanding by addressees and overhearers. *Cognitive Psychology* 21: 211–32.

Sperber, D. and Wilson, D. (1986) *Relevance: Communication and Cognition*. Oxford: Blackwell.

Strawson, P.F. (1964) Intention and convention in speech acts. *The Philosophical Review* LXXIII (4), 439–60. Reprinted in J.R. Searle (ed.) (1971) *The Philosophy of Language* (pp. 23–38). Oxford: Oxford University Press.

Toury, G. (1980) Translated literature: System, norm, performance: Toward a TT-orientated approach to literary translation. In G. Toury (1980) *In Search of a Theory of Translation* (pp. 35–50). Tel Aviv: The Porter Institute for Poetics and Semiotics, Tel Aviv University.

Venuti, L. (1995) *The Translator's Invisibility: A History of Translation*. London: Routledge.

Wittgenstein, L. (1958) *Philosophical Investigations*, 2nd edn. Translation by G.E.M. Anscombe. Oxford: Blackwell.

Chapter 3

Pragmatic Aspects of Translation: Some Relevance-Theory Observations

ERNST-AUGUST GUTT

Introduction

This chapter focuses on two important aspects of translation: the notion of 'translation' itself, and the significance of changes in context often involved in translation work. Both topics are looked at from the perspective of the relevance theory of communication as developed by Sperber and Wilson (1986 and 1995), which I believe provides concepts that can help to better understand the nature of translation and some of the problems it typically involves.

Basics of Relevance Theory

Since this study is founded on the relevance-theory framework, a few essential concepts of relevance theory are briefly introduced here.

The inferential nature of communication

According to relevance theory, communication not only requires encoding, transfer and decoding processes, but crucially involves inference in addition. Consider the following exchange:

Example 1
(a) Joe: 'Will Sarah be long?'
(b) Pam: 'She is with Frank now'.

Pam does not answer Joe's question directly; rather, she informs Pam that Sarah is with Frank. Now as case A, let us assume that Frank is known to be very quick with people; usually he deals with a matter in a few minutes. In this case, Joe would gather from Pam's answer that Sarah will not be long.

Alternatively, let us imagine a case B where Frank is known to be with someone whose office you could never leave in under half an hour. In this situation Joe would understand that Sarah would indeed be long.

How can the same utterance convey opposite meanings? The obvious reason is that its meaning depends, not only on its semantic content, but crucially on the context in which it is interpreted or, more technically, on the contextual information with which it is inferentially combined:

Case A

Premise 1	Utterance	Sarah is with Frank now.
Premise 2	Context A	Frank does not take long with people.
Conclusion	Implication	Frank will not take long with Sarah.

Case B

Premise 1	Utterance	Sarah is with Frank now.
Premise 2	Context B	Frank keeps people a long time.
Conclusion	Implication	Frank will keep Sarah a long time.

One rather obvious point of this illustration is that the success of communication can depend very much on whether the audience uses the right, that is, the speaker-intended, context. The use of wrong contextual information can lead to a complete failure of the communication attempt. This in turn raises the question: if the use of the right context is so crucial, how can it be achieved? In preparation for addressing that question, something needs to be said about the notion of context as understood in relevance theory.

Context

In relevance theory, the notion of 'context of an utterance' is 'a psychological construct, a subset of the hearer's assumptions about the world'; more specifically, it is 'the set of premises used in interpreting [that] utterance' (Sperber & Wilson, 1986: 15). Under this definition, 'context' is a very wide notion that can include virtually any phenomenon entertainable by the human mind:

> A context in this sense is not limited to information about the immediate physical environment or the immediately preceding utter-

ances: expectations about the future, scientific hypotheses or religious beliefs, anecdotal memories, general cultural assumptions, beliefs about the mental state of the speaker, may all play a role in interpretation. (Sperber & Wilson, 1986: 15f)

Note that this notion of context also includes the text surrounding an utterance, what has sometimes been called the 'co-text'.

A second important characteristic of context in relevance theory is that it is assumed to be organised, and that this organisation affects the accessibility of a particular piece of contextual information on a particular occasion. For example, having just talked about childhood memories, information about some of your toys may be very easily accessible. On another occasion, though, it might take considerable effort to remember the colour of your first big toy truck. Thus there is a correlation between the accessibility of information in our minds and the effort required to recall it. With this clarification about context we now return to the question of how it is possible for hearers to find and use the contextual information which the speaker intended them to use and which is necessary for understanding her correctly.[1]

Optimal Relevance

According to Sperber and Wilson (1986, 1995), the central factor that makes communication succeed is the pursuit of *optimal relevance* on the part of both the communicator and the addressee. An utterance is optimally relevant (a) when it enables the audience to find without unnecessary effort the meaning intended by the communicator[2] and (b) when that intended meaning is worth the audience's effort, that is, when it provides adequate benefits to the audience. These benefits are psychological in nature; they consist in modifications of a person's knowledge and are referred to technically as 'positive contextual effects'.[3] The function of optimal relevance in communication is captured in the principle of relevance, which is believed to be an innate constraint in our human psychological make-up.[4] According to this principle, whenever a person sets out to communicate something, she automatically communicates the presumption that what she is going to say is believed to be optimally relevant to the audience.

It is this claim to optimal relevance which guides the recipient in identifying the speaker-intended context for a given utterance in the following way. It makes him expect that the contextual information needed for the correct interpretation is readily accessible. Hence he begins the interpretation process from information most readily available to him at that time. Furthermore, he will assume that, when combined with the right context, the utterance will yield an interpretation that is worth the effort invested in processing it.

On these assumptions, the recipient will proceed with the interpretation process until he arrives at an interpretation that fulfils both conditions: it is derivable without unnecessary effort and yields adequate contextual effects. In other words, the claim to optimal relevance leads the hearer to accept the first interpretation consistent with the principle of relevance as the right, that is, the speaker-intended, interpretation. Thus, the search for optimal relevance guides the hearer not only to the speaker-intended context but also to the speaker-intended interpretation. It should be added here that people are not usually aware of these interpretation processes in their minds; they take place subconsciously.

Interpretive and descriptive use of language

One of the important claims of relevance theory is that there are two psychologically distinct modes of using language: the descriptive use and the interpretive use. Since these two terms are not necessarily self-explanatory they are now briefly introduced.

A language utterance is said to be *used descriptively* when it is intended to be taken as true of a state of affairs in some possible world.

An utterance is said to be *used interpretively* when it is intended to represent what someone said or thought.[5]

Example 2
(a)   Melody: 'Fred and Judy have got a divorce.'
(b)   Melody: 'Harry said, "Fred and Judy have got a divorce."'

Both examples contain the utterance 'Fred and Judy have got a divorce'. In the first example Melody uses that utterance to claim that the state of affairs it describes is true. In other words, she maintains that it is true that Fred and Judy have got a divorce. She is using that utterance descriptively. She would be wrong if Fred and Judy were not divorced.

In example (2b), however, Melody does not (necessarily) claim that Fred and Judy have got a divorce; all she does is report what someone else said. Therefore, here the utterance is used *interpretively*. Melody's utterance in (2b) would not be wrong if Fred and Judy had not got a divorce, but it would be wrong if Harry had not, in fact, made that statement.

Interpretive resemblance and faithfulness

The crucial factor in interpretive use is that there be a relationship of *interpretive resemblance* between the original utterance and that used to represent it. Such interpretive resemblance between utterances consists in the sharing of explicatures and implicatures. This implies that resemblance is a matter of degree. Thus, two utterances interpretively resemble each other more closely, the more explicatures or implicatures they share.[6] A direct quotation, as in example (2b), shows the highest degree of resemblance to the original: it shares all explicatures and implicatures of the original, though only under one important condition, to which we shall return below: that is, that the direct quotation is interpreted in the same context as the original.

By contrast, excerpts, paraphrases, summaries etc. can vary a great deal as to the degree and kind of resemblance they show. Thus if asked about the content of a particular lecture, the respondent or reporter would have a range of options open for her reply:

Example 3
(a) she could give a report with much detail of the lecture, which would show a high degree of interpretive resemblance;
(b) she could give a detailed report of one part of the lecture, summarising the rest;
(c) she could give a brief summary of the main points and so forth.

This raises the important question of what will determine which kind of report the speaker will give? Being engaged in interpretive use, the speaker will aim at interpretive resemblance to the original; being constrained by the principle of relevance, she will aim at resemblance in those aspects which she believes will satisfy the expectation of optimal relevance.[7] Thus, in interpretive use, the utterance of the speaker comes with a claim to *faithfulness*:

> The speaker guarantees that her utterance is a faithful enough representation of the original: that is, resembles it closely enough in relevant respects. (Wilson & Sperber, 1988: 137)

So if the reporter knows that the recipient is quite interested in the lecture as a whole, she will use option (3a), giving much detail. If she is aware that there is only one part which the recipient would find relevant, she is likely to choose option (3b), concentrating on that part of the lecture and so forth. Hence we find that relevance theory comes with a ready-made, context-sensitive concept of faithfulness, applying to the interpretive use of language in general.

The Pragmatic Role of the Notion of 'Translation'

Translation as an interpretive use of language

From the relevance-theory point of view, translation falls naturally under the interpretive use of language: the translation is intended to restate in one language what someone else said or wrote in another language. In principle it is, therefore, comparable to quoting or speech-reporting in intra-linguistic use. One of its primary distinctions setting it off from intra-lingual quoting or reporting is that original text and translation belong to different languages.[8]

It follows that, as an instance of interpretive use, translation will also be constrained by the notion of faithfulness introduced above. In other words, the translator will design her translation in such a way that it 'resembles [the original] closely enough in relevant respects' (Wilson & Sperber, 1988: 137).

Up to here things might seem straightforward enough were it not for the term and concept called 'translation'. In order to understand the rather ambivalent function of this term, let us consider the role of labels for types of texts or acts of communication in general.

Text typologies as guides to relevance

As for many other phenomena in our world, so also for communication people have coined particular terms to distinguish between particular kinds of texts or utterances. For example, we talk about eulogies and summaries, novels and comic strips, commentaries and abstracts, text books and hymn books and so forth.

From a general communication point of view, such terms can serve a significant purpose: they can help to coordinate the intentions of the communicator with the expectations of the audience. For example, when the communicator presents her utterance as a 'report', this will trigger different expectations in the audience than if she called it a 'satire' or a 'curriculum vitae'. In this way labels referring to different kinds of communication can fulfil an important pragmatic function in coordinating the activities of communicator and audience.

From the relevance-theory point of view, by the appropriate use of such labels the communicator can guide the audience in their search for optimal relevance; for example, when given something called 'a novel' to read, one would be looking for the plot, for the way in which characters are portrayed, for values, attitudes and so forth. One would not necessarily seek the intended relevance of such a book to lie in historical accuracy, objectivity of presentation, quality and quantity of source materials used and the like, all of which would be of high relevance for a historical reference work, for example.

So, by labelling her work a 'novel' rather than a 'historical reference work', the author guides the potential audience to the ways in which she intends her work to achieve relevance. Hence, such typological labels can be helpful in guiding the audience towards the intended interpretation, and thus reducing the processing cost for the audience. In this sense, text-typological labels can serve to increase the relevance of a text or utterance, hence performing a pragmatic function.

Naturally, this relevance-increasing effect of text-type labels crucially depends on how well the types used by communicator and audience respectively agree with each other. The less they agree the less helpful they will be in the communication process. For example, if your publisher's idea of an abstract significantly differs from your own, then the chances are that the abstract you have written of a paper of yours will not be satisfactory to him and vice versa.

The notion of 'translation'

As a glance at the voluminous literature on translation shows, the term 'translation' appears to be a prime example of a text-typological label which lacks a generally agreed definition. As a result, more often than not, it has caused confusion rather than aided the coordination of intentions and expectations. Over the centuries, scholars have tried time and again to define or settle what translation is, only to find that every new proposal has been doomed to be found inadequate or simply wrong by some school of critics. The resulting state of affairs is well summarised by Söll's dictum that 'the history of translation theory [can] be thought of as a discussion of the polysemy of the word 'translation" (1968: 161, quoted in Wilss, 1982: 28).

When one meets an object of science as recalcitrant as this, an object which appears to defy all attempts at satisfactory definition or description, it may be best to stand back a little and ask some basic questions, such as what kind of reality there is in the object under investigation.

At a first glance, the answer to this question may seem obvious: there are thousands and thousands of books and articles that are all called 'translations'. So, surely, they are the reality we need to look at when we want to find out what translation is.

Unfortunately, matters are more complex than that. As soon as the scientist examines the specimens in front of him, he is likely to start sorting them out; removing some on the grounds that they are not translations and hence do not belong to the corpus. He may, on the other hand, include specimens that had not been considered part of the corpus before. In this way, the scientist finds himself in a vicious circle: his examination of the corpus will always be seen to support what his notion of translation was *a priori*.[9]

As a result, not only has no generally accepted notion of translation emerged, but it seems difficult, in principle, to define the domain of this investigation in non-circular terms. Moreover, if relevance theory is right, there are no grounds to assume that such a naturally distinct domain should exist. As previously mentioned, the core relation between the translation and the original is one of interpretive resemblance, which we further defined as the sharing of explicatures and implicatures between the two texts. As such, interpretive resemblance appears as a scalar notion, ranging from zero-shared explicatures and implicatures, at the one extreme, to the sharing of all explicatures and implicatures, at the other. To the extent that this view is correct, there is no reason to assume that somewhere on that scale there is a non-arbitrary point that would separate translations from non-translations.

However, even this scalar view is still a gross oversimplification of the real situation since there can be variation not only in the number of shared explicatures and implicatures, but also in which particular ex- or implicatures are shared. Hence, there could be a large number of translations of the same original, all of which shared roughly the same number of explicatures and implicatures with the original, but which still would be quite different from each other in content since the particular ex- and implicatures shared would be rather different from one text to another.

Against this background, there appears to be very little reason to expect that one day a reasonably well-defined and generally accepted notion of translation will emerge.

This state of affairs might look deplorable until we ask ourselves: what does it matter? As far as explaining how and why translations work is concerned, relevance theory provides a fairly explicit account of translations as instances of the interpretive use of language across language boundaries, and it does so without needing to introduce theoretical notions that would presuppose a definition of translation. The central concepts of interpretive resemblance and faithfulness already exist in the theory apart from translation.

What, then, is the significance of the term 'translation'? The way we introduced it earlier was as a potential aid to facilitate the correct interpretation of the translated product by the target audience. In this way the concept of translation is seen as playing a role similar to other text categories, such as 'novel', 'poem', 'essay', 'abstract' etc. Whatever their scientific status or otherwise might be, all these categories can be of value in pragmatic terms, coordinating the efforts of communicator and audience in their pursuit of optimal relevance — always provided that there is sufficient agreement about these terms between communicator and audience.

What successful communication does require is consistency with the principle of relevance and, as part of that, the use of the right contextual information when processing the utterance. The assignment of a particular act of communication to some category can be of help with this, but it is not a necessary condition for communicative success; there are other ways in which the communicator can inform her audience of how she intends her text to be understood, for example, by means of introductory remarks, comments or the like. When there is any doubt whether the translator's notion of translation is sufficiently similar to that held by her audience, she would do well to state clearly at an appropriate place how she has understood her task as translator.

Context-based Problems in Translation

Another primarily pragmatic aspect of translation has to do with context. It was shown earlier that the same utterance can have opposite interpretations, depending on the context in which it is processed. This means that the correct, that is, the speaker-intended, interpretation of an utterance, is highly context-dependent. The reason for this strong context-dependence lies in the inferential nature of human communication. Against this background, it is easy to understand why a change of context can change the whole meaning of an utterance and why, therefore, 'quoting someone out of context' can be a rather serious matter.

Unfortunately, the process of translation often, though not necessarily always, involves this very situation: by translating a text for a target audience with a cultural background other than that envisioned by the original writer, the translator is, in effect, quoting the original author 'out of context'. Since the notion of 'quoting out of context' usually has a negative ring to it, I prefer to call all instances where a text is presented to an audience with a context different from the one originally envisaged as 'secondary communication situations' (cf. Gutt, 1991: 72ff).

The problems arising from differences in context have not gone unnoticed in the literature on translation. Best known is perhaps Schleiermacher's often-quoted distinction:

> The translator can either leave the writer in peace as much as possible and bring the reader to him, or he can leave the reader in peace as much as possible and bring the writer to him. (Schleiermacher, 1838: 47, as translated in Wilss, 1982: 33)

'Bringing the reader to the original text' would correspond to requiring him to process the translation in the context of the original: '[The translator] thus tries to transport [the reader] to its location, which, in all reality, is foreign to him' (Schleiermacher, 1838: 219, as translated in Wilss, 1982: 33). By contrast, 'bringing the writer to the reader' would correspond to adapting the text to the context of the target readers.

While the difference between these two approaches to translation has been recognised, it seems that the nature of the problem and some of its ramifications have not been well understood.

Thus the supposed dilemma of translation, that it can either be faithful without being beautiful or beautiful but not faithful, is not limited to translation but can, in principle, affect all instances of the interpretive use of language. The use of verbally accurate quotations out of context, that is, in a context not envisaged by the original communicator, can occur, whether language barriers are crossed or not.

It may thus be helpful for the translator to realise that not all the problems she encounters in translating a text are problems peculiar to translation. Indeed, any text transferred from its original context to a different one is likely to be affected in its meaning by that change, even when there is no change of language involved. For example, when reading literature in our own language from a time period or setting other than our own, problems can arise due to differences in context.

We may then ask how such problems are usually addressed when they occur within the same language. With quotes out of context, the remedy is mostly to point out what the right context was. With problems in literary writings, it is usually seen as the reader's responsibility to familiarise himself with the historical and cultural background of a particular piece of literature to ensure correct understanding. This is one of the skills taught at school when dealing with literature. Sometimes the publisher intervenes and provides various explanatory notes to the text to help the reader overcome the problems. Very rarely, however, is the publisher expected or prepared to alter the text itself when it seems that the modern context could lead to a wrong understanding. Such alterations of the text are usually limited to special editions for children or other specified audiences, but then it is normally indicated that one is dealing with an adaptation of some kind rather than with the original itself.

Once made aware of the difference between context-based problems, on the one hand, and language-based problems, on the other, the translator may be in a better position to judge what a suitable solution might be.

When encountering a problem due to linguistic or lexical differences, these are peculiar to translation, arising when language barriers are crossed.[10] Assuming that a central part of the translator's task is to help the audience overcome the language barrier, these problems need to be dealt with in the text by the translator. If the reader is expected to figure out problems in the translation that require knowledge of the lexicon or linguistic structure of the original language, then the question arises as to what the point of translating the text is.

However, when dealing with a problem caused by contextual differences, the translator should ask herself whether she could or even should address this problem by amending the translated text or whether other means need to be sought. This is especially true when the differences in context are extensive and would require major reworking of the text.

More importantly, perhaps, without a clear understanding of the nature of communication problems in translation, the translator may not be aware that significant mismatches in contextual information can not only lead to wrong meaning here and there, but can jeopardise the communicability of substantial parts of the original or even of the original as a whole.

The reason for this risk lies in the principle of relevance, which for successful communication requires consistency with the requirement of optimal relevance; such consistency, however, is always context-dependent. The writer of the original was concerned for her text to be optimally relevant in the context which she assumed the original audience to have. She would not normally be concerned with the question of whether her text would be optimally relevant in any other context.

To take a fairly drastic example, in the Bible the writer of the Epistle to the Hebrews devotes the first two chapters almost completely to the question of the position of Jesus Christ relative to that of the angels. From the evidence we have, this was apparently an important issue for the audience he was writing for at that time. It provided them with answers to burning questions they had in their day and age. Transfer this text to a present-day, Western-type audience, and most of them will find it difficult to process this text, no matter how well it is translated, the main reason being that the information provided there does not readily link up with the contextual information they bring to this text, and hence may not seem worth their while spending effort on. In this sense, the whole text may not be communicable to the receptor audience.

This is not to say that the text cannot be *made* sufficiently relevant to such an audience. Relevance can be increased, for example, by providing further background information, that is, by making accessible to them enough of the context of the original for them to appreciate its relevance. However, without such help the content of the original may well remain largely incommunicable.

Once aware of the problems arising in secondary communication situations, translators can anticipate them and look for appropriate means to overcome them, which may well go beyond the usual task of translation and may require strategies for widening the contextual knowledge of the target audience by additional means.

As a caveat, I would like to point out clearly that this does not mean that it is possible in every case to draw a sharp distinction between communication problems as against language-based ones, just as it is not always possible to distinguish cognitive content from context.[11] There will often be an overlap. Nevertheless, a greater awareness and better understanding of the different aspects of problems encountered while translating should help the translator to deal more appropriately with them.

Conclusion

To sum up, the two main claims made are, first, that translation itself is primarily a pragmatic notion, used to indicate the kind of communication intended by the communicator. Its communication-facilitating role will depend on how similar the notion of translation held by the translator and the notion held by the audience are to each other. If necessary, the translator may have to consider measures to bring those notions closer together.

Second, one of the main difficulties faced by the translator is again a pragmatic one: the fact, that very often in translation there is a difference, not only of language, but also of context. This problem is not peculiar to translation but occurs in all secondary communication situations. The translator needs to be aware of it in order to judge the degree of its effects correctly and to look for appropriate solutions.

It is hoped that a better understanding of these pragmatic problems will enable translators to increase the likelihood of success in their work.

Notes
1. Following the convention of Sperber and Wilson (1986), 'she' refers to the communicator or translator in general and 'he' to the addressee in general.
2. In their revision of 1995, Sperber and Wilson have generalised the first condition as follows: 'the ostensive stimulus used is the most relevant one compatible with the communicator's abilities and preferences' (1995: 270). However, since that

revision does not affect the main argument of this paper, the condition has been kept here in its old and more familiar form.

3. In Sperber and Wilson (1995) a 'cognitive effect' is defined 'as a contextual effect occurring in a cognitive system (e.g. an individual) and a *positive cognitive effect* as a cognitive effect that contributes positively to the fulfilment of cognitive functions or goals' (1995: 265; italics as in original).

4. In their revised version (1995: 260ff), Sperber and Wilson have renamed this principle the 'Second Principle of Communication'; since this does not involve a difference in substance, for simplicity's sake I shall continue here to refer to the 'Principle of Relevance'.

5. For a more detailed and technical introduction to these notions, see Sperber and Wilson (1986: 224ff).

6. See Sperber and Wilson (1986: 228f) and Gutt (1991: 44).

7. This claim is understood to hold within the limits of her own 'abilities and preferences' (Sperber and Wilson, 1995: 270).

8. For further discussion, see Gutt (1991: 100ff).

9. See also Gutt (1991: 5f) for the problem of defining the domain for a science of translation.

10. Since the notion of 'translation' is not theoretically significant, little depends on the exact definition of 'language' against, for example, 'sociolect' or 'dialect'. As long as communicator and audience agree on this usage, interpretive use between dialects could usefully be accommodated within the concept of 'translation'.

11. See Sperber and Wilson (1986: 89).

References

Gutt, E.-A. (1991) *Translation and Relevance: Cognition and Context.* Oxford: Blackwell.

Schleiermacher, F. (1838) Über die verschiedenen Methoden des Übersetzens. In H. J. Störig (ed.) (1969) *Das Problem des Übersetzens* (pp. 38–70). Darmstadt: Wissenschaftliche Buchgesellschaft.

Söll, L. (1968) Sprachstruktur und Unübersetzbarkeit. *Neusprachliche Mitteilungen* 3, 161–7.

Sperber, D. and Wilson, D. (1986) *Relevance: Communication and Cognition.* Oxford: Blackwell.

Sperber, D. and Wilson, D. (1995) *Relevance: Communication and Cognition*, 2nd edn. Oxford: Blackwell.

Wilson, D. and Sperber, D. (1988) Representation and relevance. In R.M. Kempson (ed.) *Mental Representations: The Interface Between Language and Reality* (pp. 133–53). Cambridge: Cambridge University Press.

Wilss, W. (1982) *The Science of Translation: Problems and Methods.* Tübingen: Narr.

Chapter 4

Politeness and Translation

JULIANE HOUSE

I want to explore the relationship between translation and politeness. To this end, I will first discuss the sociocultural phenomenon of politeness and critically review a number of recent conceptualisations with a view to their applicability to translation studies. Second, I will address the issue of cross-cultural and cross-linguistic differences in politeness norms; I will here concentrate on the description and explanation of differences in German–English norms as they have emerged from my own work. Third, I will bring together politeness and translation by presenting a particular model of contextual translation analysis with which to demonstrate how equivalence of politeness can be achieved and assessed.

Politeness — Different Approaches

Politeness is a sociocultural phenomenon, roughly to be defined as showing, or appearing to show, consideration of others. Politeness can thus be seen as one of the basic social guidelines for human interaction. The goal of politeness can then be described as reflecting or realising the social or interpersonal function of language with politeness being 'a system of interpersonal relations designed to facilitate interaction by minimising the potential for conflict and confrontation inherent in all human interchange' (Lakoff, 1990: 34). While politeness concerns human communicative behaviour in general, I will here be concerned only with linguistic behaviour.

For many researchers, politeness is a feature of language in use. Thus Brown and Levinson (1987) and Leech (1983) stress the importance of politeness as a contextualised phenomenon (although they use decontextualised sample sentences to illustrate their theories). Further, it is generally accepted that politeness is a pervasive feature in human communication. Despite the recognised importance and omnipresence of politeness in day-to-day discourse, it has proved enormously difficult to describe and explain the operation of politeness. As Thomas (1995: 149) points out, there has been a lot of confusion in the vast literature on politeness over the past 15 years or so, and it has been discussed with reference to a number of phenomena that must be kept separate conceptually, such as (1) politeness as a real-world goal, (2) politeness as reflecting social norms and (3) as a pragmatic phenomenon. I shall discuss each of these in turn.

Politeness as a real-world goal

As a 'real-world goal', politeness is interpreted (psychologically) as the genuine desire to be 'nice' to others. It relates to the speaker's personal motivation and psychological state and is, as such, both inaccessible and uninteresting to linguists who have access only to what speakers say and how their hearers react. This view of politeness is therefore obviously of no relevance to translation theory and practice.

The social-norm view of politeness

The social-norm view of politeness (Fraser, 1990: 220ff) reflects certain social and behavioural norms and rules (embodied, for instance, in manuals of etiquette) holding in a given society, which one must observe in order to be 'polite' in the sense of displaying good manners. Politeness is here intimately connected with the realisation of speech styles and formality, and is often equated with deference. Deference is also part and parcel of certain languages such as Japanese, whose speakers are forced to make certain choices; it is, however, also built into the system of languages characterised by a 'T/V subsystem', e.g. 'du' and 'Sie' in German. Fraser claims that the social-norm view of politeness has few adherents among current researchers. However, Watts *et al.* (1992) point out that a substantial body of recent non-Western (especially Japanese) research into politeness (see, e.g. Ide *et al.*, 1992) corresponds to this view of politeness, and should thus not be dismissed prematurely. Watts *et al.* (1992) further point out that looking at politeness as a set of behaviour patterns preprogrammed as social norms leads us to consider the wider social functions of politeness, e.g. in educational systems, prescriptive grammars and translation practices. This is why I think this view of politeness is important for translation theory and practice.

The pragmatic view of politeness

There are two major pragmatic views of politeness: politeness in terms of principles and maxims and politeness as the management of face.

Politeness explained in terms of principles and maxims

One of the earliest proponents of this philosophical approach to describing and explaining politeness is Robin Lakoff (1973). Lakoff posits two basic 'interests' or strategies in human communication, first a strategy of 'clarity' (captured by the maxims of Grice's [1975] Cooperative Principle as a blueprint for 'rational language use'), which guides the transmission of information, and second a strategy of 'rapport' (captured by Lakoff's politeness rules). These two strategies are reminiscent of the two basic functions of language, the cognitive-referential and the interpersonal one, which have been suggested by many different linguists and philosophers of language as characterising the two fundamental uses of language. On the basis of these two strategies Lakoff suggests two rules of pragmatic competence: (1) Be Clear (essentially Grice's maxims) and (2) Be Polite, which are often in conflict but can also reinforce one another. The maxim 'Be polite' consists of three 'rules of politeness (or rapport)', later referred to as 'politeness strategies' (Lakoff, 1990: 35): (1) Don't impose (Distance), (2) Give options (Deference) and (3) Be friendly (Camaraderie).

The second major proponent of the philosophical, maxim-and-principle approach to politeness is Leech (1983). Leech locates politeness inside his schema of 'Interpersonal Rhetoric' where the four Gricean maxims and the Cooperative Principle as 'mega maxim' form one part of goal-directed linguistic behaviour, and the Politeness Principle as well as the Irony Principle making up another. Leech divides the Politeness Principle into six different maxims, among them the *Tact Maxim* (minimise the hearer's costs and maximise her benefits) and the *Agreement Maxim* (minimise disagreement between yourself and others, maximise agreement between yourself and others). Leech further suggests a number of different scales along which each maxim operates, such as, e.g., the *Cost–Benefit Scale* or the *Indirectness Scale*. The social goal of the complex interaction of the six maxims is to reach 'comity' between the interactants at maximum benefit and minimum cost for speaker and hearer, with comity being related to different types of politeness such as *Collaborative Politeness* or *Conflictive Politeness*.

However insightful, Leech's conceptualisation of politeness seems difficult to apply to concrete instances of discourse. As Thomas (1995: 167) points out, Leech's approach is inelegant and unfalsifiable as there seems to be no restriction to the number of maxims, i.e. it would, in theory, be possible to produce a new maxim to explain every newly perceived regularity in language use. Despite these inherent problems, Leech's approach may still be useful for generating hypotheses explaining cross-cultural differences in politeness. For translation theory and practice, however, Lakoff's simpler and more elegant approach seems to me more immediately applicable.

Politeness and the management of face

The face-saving view of politeness is above all associated with Brown and Levinson (1987). Theirs is essentially a biological, psychosocial theory in that it both distinguishes and identifies the language-user as an individual and as a member of a group, i.e. it is a theory explaining the well known drives: 'Keep your distance' and 'Come together'. Given this biological basis, the theory will be universal, premised as it is on the claim that all humans belong to one species biologically and that the roots of social organisation and structuring are not themselves derived from existing institutions, norms and structures.

Brown and Levinson's influential theory is based both on Grice's maxim theory and on Goffman's concept of 'face' as 'the positive social value a person effectively claims for himself by the line others assume he has taken during a particular contact' (Goffman, 1967: 5). Face can be likened to a person's public self-esteem or self-image, which can be damaged, maintained or enhanced in interaction with others. Brown and Levinson extend Goffman's notion of face dividing face into positive face, which is similar to Goffman's face, and negative face according to interactants' wants. A person's positive face is reflected in his desire to be liked and appreciated by others; his negative face equals the desire for freedom of action and freedom from imposition. Deviations from Gricean maxims are motivated by employing strategies to counteract so-called 'face-threatening acts' (FTAs). By using these 'politeness strategies', speakers communicate both their primary message and also the message that they intend to be polite, which has the status of a Gricean conversational implicature.

Since nearly every speech act constitutes in a specific way a threat to the positive or negative face of either of the two interactants, certain linguistic strategies must be chosen from an elaborate repertoire of positive and negative politeness in order to provide redressive action. The choice of strategies depends on the speaker's judging the size of the FTA, which is assessed on the basis of the dimensions of Power, Distance and Imposition.

However, Brown and Levinson do not provide any indication as to how speakers are to assess the values of these dimensions in any individual act. Further, the notion of face seems to be derived from an Anglophone individualistic notion of face closely linked to status and implying competition and prestige. Watts *et al.* (1992: 9–10) remind readers that the English language has a revealing metaphor 'to put on a good face', and that, in a less competitive and individualistic social group, status or prestige may either be less important or be assigned to a person through the status she occupies in the group. Still, on a basic biological level the universality claim is fully justified.

Brown and Levinson's view of politeness as biologically anchored and linked to the social-psychological concept of face is, it seems to me, not easily or usefully applied to translation, where the interaction between the human beings involved (author, readers, translator) is hidden and indirect such that psychosocial inferential processes are extremely difficult, if not impossible, to assess.

Conclusion

Despite their surface differences, the approaches to politeness discussed here seem to be essentially compatible in that they capture different levels of a comprehensive theory of politeness. This theory would explain the tension between universal aspects of politeness and specific culture- and language-conditioned aspects. It would operate on three levels: (1) a biological, psychosocial level based on well-known animal drives; (2) a philosophical level seeking to capture the biological drives in terms of a finite number of principles, maxims or parameters; and (3) an empirically descriptive level concerned with the fact that in cultures 1-n politeness operates in terms of a particular (open-ended) set of norms, tendencies or preferences.

Viewed in such a way, the universalist stance can be upheld if it refers to levels 1 and 2 — an important conclusion for translation and translatability. At level 3, one might wish to distinguish between relatively open-ended negotiable rules relating to the philosophical principles accepted at level 2 and other normative rules that are relatively closed/fixed. The distinction relates to the question how far the language system itself decrees or imposes certain politeness norms or choices (e.g. honorifics in Japanese). Working top-down, then, one might wish to pose an intermediate level between levels two and three which one might call 'Negotiability'. This 'mega-parameter' determines how flexible a culture is in terms of degrees of freedom concerning the realisation of certain maxims and principles; it is designed to explain why a particular parameter appears to be so linguistically differentiated in culture A but inflexibly hide-bound in culture B.

If one works bottom-up, one may well arrive at principles and maxims that do not have universal validity. In practice, then, one may well need a theory akin to Chomskyan principles and parameter theory, which would explain how 'exotic' a given culture may be. Given this (admittedly sketchy) first attempt to outline a theory of politeness which is particularly relevant for translation in that it is capable of capturing both the universal aspects of politeness and the possibility of cross-cultural variation, we are now in a better position to make meaningful statements about the relationship between politeness and translation. Before bringing together politeness and translation in a more systematic way, it is necessary, however, to look at some empirically established (level 3) cross-cultural differences in politeness in terms of social norms and maxims/principles, as these assume special relevance in the practical business of translation.

Cross-Cultural and Cross-Linguistic Differences in Politeness Norms

Politeness as social norm viewed cross-culturally

Early pragmalinguistically oriented cross-cultural studies were conducted, e.g., by Fraser (1978) and Walters (1979), as well as by House (1979) and House and Kasper (1981). In these studies, the realisation of certain speech acts as well as the perception of politeness by native-speakers and learners of particular languages (English and Spanish or English and German) were compared and related to underlying societal norms of usage. While Walters and Fraser worked with largely decontextualised data, the data used in House and House and Kasper consist of contextualised discourse data. In both approaches, surface linguistic forms were used as indices of politeness norms.

Later studies include data-based cross-cultural investigations of the impact of isolated social and context variables on norms of politeness. Thus 'Social Distance' was examined and found to influence politeness in the realisation of speech acts in a complex way (Wolfson *et al.*, 1989). 'Social Power' consisting of different culturally and situationally variable factors was investigated not only under the rubric of interactants' relative position in the social hierarchy (e.g. Takahashi & Beebe, 1993), but also with respect to other factors such as gender (e.g. House, 1986, 1989a).

Apart from these cross-cultural investigations of the influence of social variables on the enactment of politeness, specific features of speech acts such as 'the imposition' incurred through the act have been contrasted: e.g. for requests (Blum-Kulka & House, 1989; House, 1989a); for apologies (House, 1989b); for complaints (Olshtain & Weinbach, 1993).

The complex interaction of the various contextual and participant variables has also been contrasted: with reference to the realisation of requests, for instance, Germans, Israelis and Argentinians were found to perceive participants' rights and obligations, the difficulty in performing the speech act and the likelihood of the interlocutor's compliance in markedly different ways (Blum-Kulka & House, 1989). Moving away from isolating contextual variables, researchers have increasingly concentrated on exploring the enactment of politeness in different discourse environments, such as, e.g., everyday face-to-face interpersonal talk (e.g. House, 1996) or workplace communication (Clyne, 1994).

Massive criticism has recently been directed at the universalist claims of politeness inside the cross-cultural paradigm, e.g. by Ide *et al.* (1992), who contrasted Japanese and English politeness norms claiming that there is in some non-Western languages an obligatory choice of 'formal' linguistic forms and 'discernment', forcing speakers to use 'polite' expressions because of certain social conventions, this being very different from the Anglo-Saxon freedom of choice ('Volition'). However, given the three-level theory of politeness suggested earlier, the universalist stance can be upheld for the biological and philosophical levels of politeness, and divergence of norms and preferences across cultures is explainable at the empirical-descriptive level. In considering politeness at this third level, however, a deeper knowledge and understanding of what needs to be, and actually is, communicated, and what is considered important in different languages and cultures is absolutely essential, as is a recognition of the variability of motivations for making politeness manifest. Recognition and knowledge of these phenomena are also essential in translation.

Politeness in terms of maxims and principles cross-culturally

The general framework provided in the maxim-and-principle view of politeness is useful for explaining cross-cultural differences in the enactment of politeness. Thomas (1995) gives a number of examples of culture-specific realisations of Leech's politeness maxims. The Tact Maxim, for instance, seems to be central to Western notions of politeness in that there is routine mitigation of speech acts such as requests by offering optionality. This is very different in the Chinese conception of politeness (Spencer-Oatey, 1992: 17). Further, reference to the Agreement Maxim, which is related to 'indirectness' in speech act and discourse behaviour, can generate hypotheses explaining empirically established differences in indirectness and politeness (see, e.g., House & Kasper, 1981 and House, 1989a, b; 1996). However, the relationship between indirectness and politeness was found to be more complicated than had been predicted by politeness models: while conventionally indirect requests realised by preparatory strategies (such as *can/could you* . . . and their German translational equivalents) were rated as most polite, non-conventionally indirect requests i.e. hints, although clearly much more indirect, were rated less polite, presumably due to the high processing load imposed on the receptor (cf. House, 1986).

In order to exemplify both cross-culturally divergent social norms and negotiable realisations of maxims and principles, and to provide a better basis for linking translation and politeness later, I will briefly summarise my own cross-cultural work involving such a relatively 'close' language pair as German and English.

An Example of Cross-Cultural Difference in Politeness in Terms of Social Norms and Maxims/Principles

In a series of empirical contrastive pragmatic studies comparing the discourse of German and English native speakers (for overviews see Blum-Kulka *et al.*, 1989; House, 1996), data were collected in open dyadic role-plays often followed by retrospective interviews, and discourse completion tests combined with metapragmatic assessment tests. Four different discourse phenomena were analysed yielding the following results:

(1) *Opening and closing discourse phases*: German subjects tend to use fewer conversational routines and there was less reciprocity in the use of phatic moves.

(2) *Discourse strategies*: German subjects tend to use more content-oriented strategies, e.g. introducing topics explicitly and expanding them; they also use fewer interpersonally active strategies such as anticipatory moves, e.g. availability checks or disarming moves. Germans also prefer moves with explicit reference to self e.g. *Kann ich . . .* versus *Would you like me to . . . .* Further, there is more ad hoc formulation in German and more reliance on conversational routines in English.

(3) *Gambits*: Germans tend to prefer content-oriented and self-referenced gambits (e.g. 'starters' prefacing a speaker's message or 'underscorers' used to emphasise the content of a message), whereas English speakers prefer gambit types with which to explicitly address conversational partners (such as 'cajolers' used to coax interlocutors into heightened attention or sympathy).

(4) *Speech acts*: Requests, complaints and apologies were compared, and different 'levels of directness' were suggested. German subjects were found to prefer more direct expressions.

From these results derived from a series of cross-cultural German–English pragmatic analyses based on different data and subjects, in a variety of everyday situations, a consistent pattern emerges: German subjects tend to interact in ways that are more direct, more explicit and verbose, more self-referenced and more content-oriented; they are also less prone to resort to using verbal routines than English-speakers. The consistent pattern of cross-cultural differences in communicative norms emerging from these analyses can be displayed along five dimensions, as in Table 1. The oppositions represent end-points on different clines, with German subjects tending to give preference to positions on the left-hand side of these dimensions.

Table 1 Dimensions of cross-cultural difference (German–English)

Directness	↔	Indirectness
Orientation towards self	↔	Orientation towards others
Orientation towards content	↔	Orientation towards addressees
Explicitness	↔	Implicitness
Ad-hoc formulation	↔	Verbal routines

Given these cross-cultural differences in social norms which reflect politeness standards, one can hypothesise that the Gricean Maxims of Quantity and Relation tend to be interpreted differently in the German and Anglophone linguacultures, i.e. supplying just as much and no more information as the occasion requires and being 'relevant' to the perceived purpose of the discourse tends to vary across these two linguacultures in my samples. The tendency in German to explicate content may then well set up different conditions for the performance of inferencing operations, i.e. the mechanism of 'conversational implicature' that interprets utterances deviating from the maxims.

Within the frame of reference provided by Lakoff (1973; 1990), it seems to be the case that all three rules of politeness are interpreted differently in the German and Anglophone linguacultures: the politeness rule 'Don't impose' is given different values in German due to a preference for higher directness levels in the realisation of certain speech acts. The Rule 'Give options' is also interpreted differently due to a preference for higher directness levels and explicitness of content in German. The rule 'Be friendly' in particular is interpreted and realised differently in the German linguaculture given a preference of (explicated) content over addressees, self-referencing over other-referencing, reduced reliance on conversational routines and greater directness in speech-act realisation (House, 1996).

Differences in linguistic and cultural norms of usage and politeness as exemplified for the case of German and English are immediately relevant for translation theory and practice, as will be demonstrated in the next section.

Politeness and Translation

How can one make sure in translation that politeness as exhibited in the original is 'carried over' in the translation? How can one go about reaching 'politeness equivalence' in translation? Given a theory of politeness in which — along the levels suggested earlier — both the universality stance and cross-cultural variation in the realisation of politeness are accounted for, the concept of politeness most useful in translation studies must be a broad and general one, which will cover not only the concepts of politeness deemed relevant for translation, but will also be extended to capture the broader perspective of language functions, specifically the interpersonal function as suggested by Halliday. Extending the notion of politeness such that it embraces the Hallidayan interpersonal function is compatible with the scope of a translation theory (House, 1997) which I will now briefly describe.

Translation is a cross-linguistic sociocultural practice, in which a text in one language is replaced by a functionally equivalent text in another. The fundamental characteristic of a translation is therefore that it is a text that is doubly bound: on the one hand to a text in the source language, the 'source text' or the original and, on the other hand, to the communicative-linguistic conditions holding in the culture to which the addressees belong. This double bind is the basis of the equivalence relation which, in turn, is the conceptual basis of translation. It has been an important aim of linguistic-textual approaches to translation to specify the equivalence relation by distinguishing a number of different frameworks of equivalence (cf. Koller, 1996), such as, for instance, extralinguistic circumstances, connotative values, audience design or norms of usage that have emerged from research in contrastive rhetoric, contrastive pragmatic analyses, and from empirical investigations of pairs of translations and originals and parallel texts in different languages. Equivalence is thus never to be conceived as absolute but rather as inherently relative emerging 'from the context of situation as defined by the interplay of many different factors and has no existence outside that context' (Ivir, 1996: 155).

In my own theory of translation (House, 1997), I assume that the most important requirement for translation equivalence is that a translation have a function equivalent to that of its original, and that 'functional equivalence' (in its different forms and types) can be established and evaluated by referring original and translation to the context of situation enveloping the two texts, and by examining the interplay of different contextual factors both reflected in the text and shaping it. One of these factors to be taken into account in making and evaluating a translation is 'politeness' — an important element in achieving 'interpersonal equivalence'. Interpersonal equivalence must not be equated with what Tabakowska (1989) has referred to as 'attitudinal translational equivalence', i.e. the rendering of the original author's attitude to the propositions that make up his text. Interpersonal equivalence (which together with ideational equivalence makes up functional equivalence) in translation should be conceived as more comprehensive than merely relating to authorial stance: rather the operation of a number of pragmatic dimensions is to be seen as contributing to interpersonal functional equivalence with politeness being relevant on several of these dimensions.

The dimensions are used to 'open up' the original text such that its textual profile which characterises the function of the text can be revealed. In order to determine the function of a text — consisting of an ideational and an interpersonal functional component — which must be kept equivalent in translation, the original text is analysed at the levels of Language, Register and Genre. The relationship between these three levels can be seen in terms of semiotic planes which relate to one another in a Hjelmslevian 'content-expression' way with genre being the content-plane of register, and register being the expression plane of genre. Register, in turn, is the content-plane of language, and language is the expression plane of register. Register is divided into Field, Tenor and Mode.

The dimension *Field* refers to the subject matter and the nature of the social action that is taking place. Along the dimension *Tenor*, the author's temporal, geographical, and social provenances are analysed, as is the author's intellectual and emotional stance (his 'personal viewpoint') vis-à-vis the content he is portraying and the communicative task he is engaged in. Tenor also captures the social role relationship both between author and addressee and between fictive characters in the text as well as the 'social attitude', i.e. formal, consultative and informal style levels. Mode refers to both the channel — spoken, written and transitions between the two- and the degree to which potential or real participation is allowed for between author and addressee(s). Along Mode, the distinctions between involved versus informational text production, explicit versus situation dependent reference, and abstract versus non-abstract presentation of information are further taken into account.

The establishment in the analysis of linguistic-textual correlates of Field, Mode and Tenor and the Genre they realise yields a textual profile of the original, which characterises its textual function (ideational and interpersonal), which is to be kept equivalent.

Equivalence of function differs markedly in the two types of translation, *overt* translation and *covert* translation, posited in the model. An *overt* translation is (normally) called for whenever the original is source-culture linked and has independent status in the source-language community; a covert translation is (normally) chosen when neither condition holds. In the case of overt translation the translation embeds the text in a new speech event in the target culture, with the translation operating in a new frame, a new 'discourse world'. An *overt* translation is a case of 'language mention', similar to a citation or quotation (see Gutt: this volume). An original and its overt translation are equivalent at the level of Language and Register as well as Genre. At the level of the individual textual function, however, functional equivalence, while still possible, is of a 'removed' nature: it enables access to the function which the original text has (had) in its discourse world or frame. As this access is realised in the target linguaculture via the translation, a switch in the discourse world becomes necessary, i.e. the translation operates in its own discourse world and can thus reach only what I have called a 'second level equivalence'. This type of functional equivalence is achieved through an equivalence at all three analytic levels (Language, Register and Genre), which together facilitate the co-activation of the original's frame and discourse world. In this way, members of the target linguaculture may eavesdrop, as it were, i.e. be enabled to appreciate the original textual function, albeit at a distance.

In overt translation the work of the translator is of crucial importance, as her work is clearly visible or 'marked' in the sense posited by Hickey (this volume), i.e., the translation is quite 'overtly' a translation. It is the translator's task to allow persons in the target culture access to the original and its cultural impact on source-culture members; the translator must therefore manage to put target-culture members in a position to observe and be worked upon by the original text's function.

In terms of politeness as evidenced in the original, specifically along the dimension of Tenor, the translator cannot but leave the original linguistic-textual choices as 'intact' as possible given the transfer operations necessary in translation, i.e. whatever the politeness portrayed in the original, communicatively equivalent choices must be made. Cross-cultural differences in politeness norms are thus not relevant in this type of translation as the original is, in a sense, 'sacrosanct'.

The situation is quite different in the case of *covert* translation: here the translator attempts to re-create an equivalent speech event and to reproduce or represent in the translation text the function the original has in its linguistic-cultural framework, i.e. 'real' functional equivalence is aimed at. A covert translation operates quite 'overtly' in the different frame and discourse world set up by the target culture without wishing to co-activate the discourse world in which the original had unfolded. Covert translation is thus at the same time psycholinguistically less complex than overt translation and more deceptive. The translator's task is, in a sense, to cheat, and remain hidden behind her feat of deception, the transmutation of the original. She employs a 'cultural filter' with which she makes allowances for differences in social norms and differences in politeness norms. The cultural filter is often so expertly integrated into the fabric of the text that the seams do not show. Since functional equivalence is aimed at, changes at the levels of Language and Register may, if necessary, be undertaken, and the result may well be a very real distance from the original, which is the reason for the fact that covert translations are often received as though they were original texts.

For covert translation, the notion of a cultural filter is crucial, and it is essential that the cultural filter be based on empirical research of the type described earlier. In the case of the language pair German–English, the filter has been given some substance in my own work on communicative and politeness norms. In the following I will give some examples of the operation of this filter demonstrating how politeness is affected in English–German translations.

In the case of a commercial circular written by the president of an investment consultancy firm — later revealed as fraudulent — (cf. House, 1981; 1997), the president informs the shareholders about changes in the company that will not exactly be to their advantage. Dimensional changes on the parameter Tenor transform the English original's carefully orchestrated evasive and distantly polite tone into a more direct and undiplomatic tone in the German translation. The analysis revealed that the translation frequently fails to contribute to the interpersonal functional component in a manner equivalent to the original, e.g. *as you know* is rendered as *bekanntlich* — which avoids addressing the recipients of the circular personally and has a different value with regard to the politeness principle 'Be friendly, make A feel good'.

Compare the following:

> In order to avoid the possibility of accidental misdirection of your certificate . . . your assistance is required. We have enclosed a 'Dividend Instruction Form' for your completion; this should be returned in the pre-addressed envelope

Um zu vermeiden, daß Ihre Zertifikate versehentlich fehlgeleitet werden . . . bitten wir Sie, das beigefügte Dividendenzustellungsformular auszufüllen und in dem ebenfalls beigefügten adressierten Umschlag zurückzuschicken . . .

In the German translation, the addresser appears to be more forceful, active and direct, while the original expresses the action to be done by the addressees more abstractly and indirectly (nominally). The utterance in the English original seems to have the illocutionary force of a subtle suggestion: in the translation it has become a request. And while the original tries to suggest that it is not the company that wants something done but rather some external necessity proposes a course of action to the shareholder, the translation is less subtle and more explicit. The German translation of *Your bank (or broker) should indicate* as *Sie müssen die Bank (oder einen Makler) bitten* confirms this analysis: the translation is more direct, more explicit than the original. The social-role relationship between author and addressee(s) is also changed, so is the politeness portrayed in the original; all three of Lakoff's maxims: Don't impose, Give options, Be friendly seem to operate differently in the role relationship created in the translation. But this difference in the translation is in keeping with the directness, explicitness and content-focus discovered in German politeness norms as opposed to Anglophone ones (as discussed earlier). In other words, in the interests of reaching functional equivalence, the translator may well have employed a cultural filter in order to accommodate in a patterned way the target group's different presuppositions about communicative norms and politeness.

To take another example: in the German translation of an English journalistic text (House, 1981; 1997) on an anthropological topic, the original is changed substantially along the dimensions of Tenor and Mode. The interpersonal functional component, which is strongly marked in the original, is considerably weakened in the translation, with the ideational functional component being strongly upgraded, such that a lightly entertaining, popularised and trivialised scientific English text is changed into a sober, serious and factual German document that is more content- and instruction-oriented and less oriented towards 'making the reader feel good'. For example: a whole paragraph, in which the reader is asked to feel around his mouth to establish differences in human and ape anatomy, is simply omitted in the translation. Furthermore, the translator often chooses neutral and impersonal German *es-* or *Mensch* constructions for English utterances featuring personal pronouns in direct address. Simple everyday words and vague phrases in the English original are consistently rendered more precise and 'scientific', as in the following examples:

This length makes an ape's face projecting . . .
Die Länge der Molaren bedingt . . .

Anything on the human side
Arten mit Ansätzen von menschenartigen Merkmalen.

In producing a covert, functionally equivalent translation, the translator of this journalistic article has evidently applied a cultural filter making allowances for the differences in German and English politeness norms: Lakoff's Camaraderie principle (Make A feel good) is clearly interpreted and realised differently in the German translation, as the translation is clearly interpersonally far less potent (i.e. the original's popularisation and dramatisation of the scientific material, which makes the text interesting and easily digestible for its readers, is not realised in the translation to the same degree because the German text concentrates on the transmission of scientific facts. These changes in the translation are, however, in keeping with the empirical findings with regard to German and English differences in interactional and politeness norms (see earlier).

In the case of texts suggesting an overt translation, the cultural filter and changes in politeness norms have, as I have previously argued, no place. An example of what I would consider a 'misplaced filter' is to be found in the translation by Harry Zohn of Walter Benjamin's famous essay 'Die Aufgabe des Übersetzers'. Analysis of original and translation (see House, 1997) has revealed that there are changes along the parameter Tenor, which result in differences in the social role relationship between author and addressees. The role relationship in the original is highly impersonal and characterised, for instance, by the total absence of first and second person personal pronouns. The translation is often rendered less impersonal through the use of personal pronouns as in the following examples:

[Der Zusammenhang] darf ein . . . natürlicher genannt werden
We may call this connection

Die Geschichte der großen Kunstwerke kennt . . .
The history of the great works of art tells us about . . .

The interpersonal functional component is altogether more strongly marked in the translation than in the original, and the politeness principle 'Don't impose' (Distance) is given a different value in the English translation. Further, the distantly formal style of the German original is less formal in the English translation due, not only to the use of personal pronouns, but also to a lack of syntactically complex focusing devices such as the placing of subordinate clauses before main clauses, as in the following example:

Daß eine Übersetzung niemals etwas für das Original zu bedeuten vermag, leuchtet ein

It is plausible that no translation . . .

These changes might have been made due to the application of a cultural filter, which would in this case also be in line with the empirical findings about cross-cultural differences in communicative preferences and politeness norms. However, if one believes, as I do, that Benjamin's essay is a case for overt translation (i.e. providing readers of the translation with an unadulterated view of the original), then such cultural filtering is to be avoided.

Another example (see House, 1997, for details) of what I believe should be treated as a text for overt translation is Daniel Jonah Goldhagen's bestselling *Hitler's Willing Executioners: Ordinary Germans and the Holocaust*. In the original, the author clearly demonstrates his strong personal involvement in the subject he is treating: he frequently uses intensifiers, superlatives, emotive-expressive metaphorical lexical items, as well as structures featuring multiple repetition, iconic linkage and foregrounded rhematic structures for strong rhetorical effects. The text's Medium is 'written to be read', and although 'explicit' and 'abstract', it is also characterised — which is marked for this medium — as 'highly involved'. The text has therefore both a marked ideational functional component and a strong interpersonal one. The translation retains the ideational functional component but substantially changes the interpersonal one because the devices used to mark the original interpersonally are not rendered equivalently in German. In particular, the haunting repetition of the word *German* and the various collocations with *German* such as *ordinary Germans* are not kept up in the translation, and other key terms such as *antisemitism, genocide, eliminationist* are not repeated with the same frequency. The style level in the German translation is more formal, the social distance markedly greater, and along the parameter Medium the translation is much less involved, considerably toned down, flattened in its perlocutionary force and altogether more sober and factual than the original. Due to a lack of those emotive and rhetorical devices characterising the original, the translation is also more monologous.

One might put forward the explanatory hypothesis that we are here again confronted with a legitimate application of a cultural filter in which (empirically established) cultural differences between English and German communicative and politeness norms are taken into account transforming a strongly interpersonally active English text into a more content-based, academic-scientific German one, with the politeness maxims 'Don't impose' and 'Give options' being allocated different values in the German translation. However, in view of the particular meaning this text has for German readers and their particular involvement, consideration of their reactions may have played a role in toning down the unbearably strong accusatory light the author throws on them.

On the other hand, given the status the author and his work have acquired, one might argue, as I certainly would, that an overt translation is clearly more appropriate in this case. Such a translation would give the German readers direct access to the original, enabling them to judge for themselves. The changes imposed on the original Goldhagen text may, however, also have altogether different reasons (see House, 1997, for a discussion), i.e. political and marketing reasons, which it is not the place to discuss here.

These examples of covert and overt translations and the differential legitimacy the application of a cultural filter has in these two translation types have shown that politeness is an important component of cross-cultural differences. I have demonstrated the role politeness plays in translation using German–English translations, because my own English–German contrastive research can most fruitfully be applied in these cases. However, as far as the model for translation analysis and the two translation types are concerned, I believe the remarks here are generally applicable. Still, there is a great need for empirical cross-cultural research into communicative and politeness norms and preferences involving different language pairs. Only a solid basis of cross-cultural empirical studies can provide translators with the instruments necessary to transcend accidental intuition and personal prejudice.

References

Blum-Kulka, S. and House, J. (1989) Cross-cultural and situational variation in requesting behaviour. In S. Blum-Kulka, J. House and G. Kasper (eds) *Cross-Cultural Pragmatics: Requests and Apologies* (pp. 123–154). Norwood, NJ: Ablex.

Blum-Kulka, S., House, J. and Kasper, G. (eds) (1989) *Cross-Cultural Pragmatics: Requests and Apologies*. Norwood, NJ: Ablex.

Brown, P. and Levinson, S. (1987) *Politeness. Some Universals in Language Usage*. Cambridge: Cambridge University Press.

Clyne, M. (1994) *Intercultural Communication at Work. Cultural Values in Discourse*. Cambridge: Cambridge University Press.

Fraser, B. (1978) Acquiring social competence in a second language. *RELC Journal* 9, 1–21.

Fraser, B. (1990) Perspectives on politeness. *Journal of Pragmatics* 14, 219–36.

Goffman, E. (1967) *Interaction Ritual: Essays on Face to Face Behavior*. New York: Anchor.

Grice, H.P. (1975) Logic and conversation. In P. Cole and J. Morgan (eds) *Syntax and Semantics vol. 3: Speech Acts* (pp. 41–58). New York: Academic Press.

House, J. (1979) Interaktionsnormen in deutschen und englischen Alltagsdialogen. *Linguistische Berichte* 59, 76–90.

House, J. (1981) *A Model for Translation Quality Assessment* (2nd edn). Tübingen: Narr.

House, J. (1986) Cross-cultural pragmatics and foreign language learning. In K.-R. Bausch *et al.* (eds) *Probleme und Perspektiven der* Sprachlehrforschung (pp. 281–95). Frankfurt: Scriptor.

House, J. (1989a) Politeness in English and German: The functions of 'please' and 'bitte'. In S. Blum-Kulka, J. House, and G. Kasper (eds) *Cross-Cultural Pragmatics: Requests and Apologies* (pp. 96–123). Norwood, NJ: Ablex.

House, J. (1989b) Oh Excuse me please . . . apologizing in a foreign language. In B. Kettemann *et al.* (eds) *Englisch als Zweitsprache* (pp. 303–29). Tübingen: Narr.

House, J. (1996) Contrastive discourse analysis and misunderstanding: The case of German and English. In M. Hellinger and U. Ammon (eds) *Contrastive Sociolinguistics* (pp. 345–61). Berlin: de Gruyter.

House, J. (1997) *Translation Quality Assessment: A Model Revisited*. Tübingen: Narr.

House, J. (forthcoming) *Cross-Cultural Pragmatics and Translation*.

House, J. and Kasper, G. (1981) Politeness markers in English and German. In F. Coulmas (ed.) *Conversational Routine* (pp. 157–85). The Hague: Mouton.

Ide, S., Hill, B., Carnes, Y.M., Ogino, T, and Kawasaki, A. (1992) The concept of politeness: An empirical study of American English and Japanese. In R. Watts, S. Ide and K. Ehlich (eds) *Politeness in Language. Studies in its History, Theory and Practice* (pp. 281–297). Berlin: Mouton de Gruyter.

Ivir, V. (1996) A case for linguistics in translation theory. *Target* 8, 149–57.

Koller, W. (1995) The concept of equivalence and the object of translation studies. *Target* 7, 191–222.

Lakoff, R.T. (1973) The logic of politeness; or, minding your p's and q's. *Papers from the Ninth Regional Meeting of the Chicago Linguistics Society*, pp. 292–305.

Lakoff, R.T. (1990) *Talking Power*. New York: Basic Books.

Leech, G. (1983) *Principles of Pragmatics*. London: Longman.

Olshtain, E. and Weinbach, L. (1993) Interlanguage features of the speech act of complaining. In G. Kasper and S.Blum-Kulka (eds) *Interlanguage Pragmatics* (pp. 108–122). New York: Oxford University Press.

Spencer-Oatey, H.D. (1992) Cross-cultural politeness. British and Chinese conceptions of tutor–student relationship. PhD Thesis, University of Lancaster.

Tabakowska, E. (1989) Lexical markers of subjective modality and translation equivalence in English and Polish. *Multilingua* 8, 221–236.

Takahashi, T. and Beebe, L.M. (1993) Cross-linguistic influence in the speech act of correction. In G. Kasper and S. Blum-Kulka (eds) *Interlanguage Pragmatics* (pp. 128–57). New York: Oxford University Press.

Thomas, J. (1995) *Meaning in Interaction*. London: Longman.

Walters, J. (1979) Strategies for requesting in Spanish and English: Structural similarities and pragmatic differences. *Language Learning* 9, 277–94.

Watts, R., Ide, J. and Ehlich, K. (eds) (1992) *Politeness in Language: Studies in its History, Theory and Practice*. Berlin: Mouton de Gruyter.

Wolfson, N., Marmor, T. and Jones, S. (1989) Problems in the comparison of speech acts across cultures. In S. Blum-Kulka, J. House and G. Kasper (eds) *Cross-Cultural Pragmatics: Requests and Apologies* (pp. 174–96). Norwood, NJ: Ablex.

Chapter 5

Text Politeness: A Semiotic Regime for a More Interactive Pragmatics

BASIL HATIM

The aim of this chapter is both to look back on the way pragmatic inquiry has evolved and to assess some of the new ways in which certain pragmatic questions have been formulated. This is a fairly wide remit, hence the need to limit ourselves and to focus on recent proposals for a pragmatic theory of politeness. This will be set against the background of how Austinian speech-act analysis has over the years given way to the notion of the 'text act', and how the Gricean Cooperative Principle has likewise gradually accommodated beyond-the-sentence phenomena such as the norms which govern entire actions, activity types and so on.

But to home in on politeness, this has seen some interesting developments which have taken the notion of 'causing offence verbally' away from an almost exclusive focus on dyadic face-to-face encounters towards concern with entire monologic structures and (more recently) with the politeness of writing. In fact, having restored to writing its essentially dialogic and optimally interactive nature, the new trend is not content simply to study politeness *in* texts, but insists on extending the idea to include the politeness *of* texts. That is, in describing 'face-threatening action', we have gone beyond what normally happens in selected 'bits and pieces' of interaction to what can arguably amount almost to an entire mapping of linguistic form on to rhetorical macro-function.

Given the complexity of the task, the need for a framework within which the portrayal of this highly variable linguistic behaviour may comprehensively be seen has never been more urgent. With the communication explosion we witness as each day goes by, and with message construction becoming so closely bound up with new communicative exigencies, a scheme which captures the intricacies of what we do with words as part of highly sophisticated systems of what I will call *socio-textual practice* has become crucial to an understanding of the way text-users cope with new realities. It is the ways in which such schemes have been formulated which will occupy our attention here, focusing as we intend to do on testing the various insights against real data. Choosing translation as the applied linguistic arena within which to operate should prove instructive in making our models of description more interculturally sensitive.

From Speech Act to Text Act

It is now commonplace in studies of intercultural communication to suggest that 'pragmatic' meaning is not only negotiable but also highly variable across both linguistic and cultural divides. From the perspective of orality versus literacy, for example, Ong (1981) has drawn our attention to the fact that promising, responding, greeting, asserting, threatening, commanding, protesting and other so-called illocutionary acts can mean totally different things in literate cultures, on the one hand, and orate cultures, on the other. This is at the root of cross-cultural pragmatic failures resulting in well-known stereotypes which have perpetuated myths such as the dishonesty characteristic of certain 'peoples', say, in fulfilment of promises or in responses to queries. Korn and Korn (1983) illustrate this with their fascinating description of how 'promising' as we know it is not only missing in Tonga, but is also incompatible with the Tongan view of the future and with the Tongans' conduct of social relationships.

The move to develop speech-act theory in a number of directions has thus been necessitated not only by the need to look again at oral communication in face-to-face encounters but also by the need to attend more reflectively to textual communication precisely as 'textual'. The written mode which has, for a long time, been systematically neglected in mainstream pragmatics has attracted particular attention in this regard. Horner (1975), for example, incisively suggests that the act of writing a 'composition' as an academic exercise is a special kind of pragmatic act (which she calls a 'text-act') and must be approached in such terms in our analysis of pragmatic meaning.

These insights into the scope of speech 'acting' have been of immense interest to those of us involved in the practice and theory of translation. Let us look at a practical example which illustrates both the intrinsically seamless nature of the communicative act and the futility of a restricted view of speech acts in coping with such exigencies. In an on-sight translation exercise from English into Arabic done under normal conditions for this kind of activity in real-life interpreting, the stretch of text that proved to be particularly difficult to process in the news report being tackled is:

Sample (A)

She noted that her entire budget for foreign aid and diplomacy and the United Nations and all the other international organizations to which the United States subscribes, amounted to *barely 1 per cent of the federal budget* — '*but that will be used to write 50 per cent of the history and legacy of our time*'. (*The Guardian* 21 January, 1997; emphasis added)

The bewildering nature of the elements underlined stems from the fact that, from amongst a number of likely readings, the most natural interpretation for *barely 1 per cent* is 'too little' (i.e. deplorable etc.). The 'deplorable' scenario makes the element which follows about the 'writing of history' either an expression of 'irony', or indeed a self-congratulatory 'pat on the back' (with 'deplorability' becoming 'possibly a petty sum, but we're doing wonders with it'). The first scenario of 'deplorable' followed by irony amounts to a statement of denunciation; the second (i.e. we are doing so much with so little) yields 'prudence' as an overall reading.

The first ironical reading was the one favoured by the majority of those who participated in the on-sight exercise. Those who made this choice are to be commended for the sophisticated level of textual competence which they have shown in processing an opaque use of intentionality and appreciating the rhetorical edge which the statement could conceivably have. Moreover, to relay the irony in Arabic, the 'adversative' gloss has to be suppressed and the mood perhaps changed from an assertive statement to a tongue-in-cheek interrogative. Thus, credit must go to those who made this choice for their skill in exploiting texture to identify complex rhetorical functions, and for doing so entirely within the overall drift of the argumentation in the source text. Heeded are the various textual manifestations of attitudinal meanings such as irony and evaluativeness, cued by key phrases scattered throughout the entire news report (e.g. *despite yesterday's grand rhetoric at the inauguration*), and by the general air of intransigence on the part of a congress where the Republicans are clinging to their majority.

Regrettably, there is more to the context within which the sequence in Sample A is embedded than that which caught the students' attention, adequately appreciated as it was. The utterances cited are made by a member of the Clinton team and are embedded within a sequence intended to use rhetoric to best effect ('Clinton and his team see the next four years in equally ambitious terms') and to shake off an otherwise hostile congress. Sample (A) is introduced in this way:

Madeleine Albright, the new secretary of state, set the tone by telling the senate last week that 'more than audience, more even than actors, we must be the authors of the history of our time'.

This puts a different slant on both of these readings (the deplorable/ironical and the self-congratulatory). Coming from a member of Clinton's new team, it is up-beat and self-confident: the '1 per cent may indeed be a petty sum but it is going to be managed so dexterously that history will be shaped as a result'. While superficially leaning towards both the deplorability and the self-congratulatory readings, Albright skilfully combines these two perspectives and makes a statement which is both 'interesting' and 'self-serving'. The ultimate effect is highly persuasive and the theme of prudence is broached most subtly.

The purpose of this illustration is merely to demonstrate how pragmatics at work defies restricted views of speech-act theory (and, as we shall see, of the so-called Cooperative Principle). The example shows that the sentence or the conversational equivalent (the speaker's turn) cannot convincingly be the standard unit of pragmatic meaning, be this speech act or implicature. Furthermore, it is a misconception to hold that speech acts are discrete entities meshed together to form a whole which invariably equals the sum of its parts. This analysis also shows that, in the absence of empirical research into authentic discourse, there is no basis for specifying, say, how many speech acts are needed to achieve a pragmatic goal.

It is the latter problem of goals and ways of pursuing them within texts that has exercised the thinking of pragmaticists in the last 20 years or so. Ferrara (1980 a, b) has pioneered the study of 'speech-act sequence' and has successfully attempted to introduce an interactive dimension to pragmatic meaning. Building on the assumption that communication is not realised by isolated linguistic elements but rather by utterances in discourse, Ferrara poses a number of thought-provoking questions: does being part of a sequence affect the appropriateness conditions which, in some decontextualized fashion, obtain for individual speech acts and, if so, how? And, when sequences are involved, are appropriateness conditions for the isolated speech acts to be upheld, abandoned or re-evaluated in the light of the unfolding textual evidence?

As I hope to make clear in the course of the following discussion, it is the re-evaluation option which predominates in our day-to-day experience with texts: a speech-act sequence will fasten on and further develop original appropriateness conditions. The assumption implicitly entertained in this kind of analysis must be that some of the acts in the sequence will be treated as 'main', others as 'subordinated'. But what are the criteria for assigning a particular status to a given act within a sequence? To answer this question, we must first learn to deal with an essentially hierarchical text design concealed by a seemingly linear order of textual elements. And, within this hierarchic organization, we must also learn to cope with whatever it is that holds the sequence together within what must ultimately be a finite set of activity types, speech events etc.

Ferrara broaches some of these questions and illustrates his pragmatic model of speech act sequence with an example from conversational data:

Sample (B)
There are 30 people in here. Could you open the window?

As we pointed out earlier, one basic organisational principle at work is that of dominance versus subordination: a 'main' point (to have the window open) and a 'subordinate goal' (to provide a good justification for the request). Ferrara argues that, applied to subordinate speech acts in a sequence, standard conditions of appropriateness may well be necessary but are not sufficient. To be non-defective, an assertion (e.g. 'there are 30 people' or indeed 'barely 1 per cent') must be seen in terms of what follows ('the desire that the window be opened' or 'this is simply not good enough'). Given the same context, these assertions could not have been performed appropriately in isolation, because they would not have fulfilled the 'non-obviousness' condition. But, together with what follows them, the assertions point to a 'perspective' from which the propositional content becomes 'non-trivial'. As Ferrara (1980a: 238) puts it, 'without this *relevance* criterion, explicitly suggested by another sentence in the sequence, the propositional content is simply too obvious and brings no information to the hearer' [italics added].

The implications of these views for the analysis of written texts or spoken monologues in domains such as translation and interpreting are obvious. If we cast our minds back to the kind of difficulties encountered in dealing with a sample of writing such as the news report (Sample (A)), we find that hearers are able to maintain relevance mainly by seeking to uphold principles such as non-obviousness or non-triviality, and thus conceive of the utterances within a particular perspective. In dealing with a sequence of sentences, text-users generally seem to work to an intentional 'plan' comprising goals and the means to achieve them. Producers and receivers of texts negotiate this conceptual order through 'shared beliefs' as well as 'norms' in operation.

To cast this in terms of speech-act theory, 'plans' are essentially large action structures in terms of which given illocutionary forces are evaluated and their contribution assessed as a means of achieving ultimate perlocutionary effects. It is this context-bound potential displayed by a given speech act for entering a certain kind of relationship with the main speech act (justification, explanation etc.) which ultimately seems to determine the appropriateness or otherwise of both the individual act and the entire sequence (and the sequence of sequences). We will shortly have an opportunity further to tighten this analytic apparatus and envisage it within what we shall refer to as 'socio-textual practices'. But before we can do this, it might be helpful to build on the extremely interesting notion of 'relevance' touched on above and reassess recent developments within the Gricean framework of the Cooperative Principle.

Extending the Boundaries Beyond the Cooperative Principle

What forms a crucial part of the quest for an optimally effective, efficient and appropriate use of language, then, is not

> some huge set of *ad hoc* rules for constructing and interpreting [. . .] speech acts but a small but powerful set of general principles of inference to interlocutors' communicative intentions in specific contexts (Levinson, 1981: 481–2)

In this respect, Grice has made a valuable contribution, raising a number of exciting questions which have remarkably influenced our whole attitude to language use. According to Grice, meaning is not determined beforehand but is negotiated only while utterances are made. Indeed, meaning may well become fixed in the process, but all the way, this is informed by a variety of contextual factors, including hearer's cognitive processing abilities to infer meaning from context.

The Gricean scheme hinges on the so-called Cooperative Principle and a set of Maxims regulating how knowledge is conveyed when people imply, suggest or mean something distinct from what they say. This is important since the text-user is not seen as constantly committed to acting under conventionally established conditions. True, the text user is essentially someone who is 'merely trying to communicate with a minimum of needless efforts and disturbances', but this is not always straightforward and producers' intentionality itself may lead them to violate the maxims when it seems expedient (Beaugrande & Dressler, 1981: 123).

This point has been recently reiterated by critical linguists who specifically target the notion of individualism perpetuated by much of pragmatics. As Fairclough (1989: 9) points out, conventionalised ways of speaking or writing are not internalised intact to be called up every time an occasion arises which requires their use. Nor is it plausible to promote the attitude that we are all engaged all the time in 'cooperative' interactions in whose ground rules we have an equal say. In reality, interaction can be and often is socially constrained by diverse social struggles and inequalities of power. This leads to an element of creativity in the performance of text-users which can be adequately accounted for only by a theory of 'action' envisaged in terms of 'social practice'.

The Gricean scheme has certainly presented us with fewer holes to plug than, say, speech act theory. However, notions such as 'expedience' and 'language use as action' within 'social practice' do not seem to be adequately catered for by concepts such as maxim flouting. Take, for example, the Albright extract cited as Sample A. This cannot be said to be entirely 'cooperative' in the crisply Gricean sense, but it is highly 'informative' (i.e. engaging): with the *barely* element, the speaker has hijacked the way those who 'whine' operate or how the opposition might feebly question Clinton's foreign policy card. In this way the expectation is set up for a rebuttal which might run along the following lines: 'but this is hardly a sensible way of conducting foreign policy'. Indeed, as I pointed out earlier, a more devious tactic from the opposition could have been to use exactly the same wording as Albright but ironically: 'but that will be used to write 50 per cent of the history and legacy of our times!'. The way Albright intended her text to read, however, is one which is suffused with self-denial, self-sacrifice and, as mentioned earlier, prudence and good management.

In processing a text like Sample (A), the question essentially becomes: how do we know that a particular maxim has been flouted and an implicature generated in the first place? And assuming that an implicature is identified, how do we know which particular maxim has actually been infringed — Quantity, Quality, Manner or Relevance? Is what has hap-pened a 'flout' (producing genuine implicatures) or some other form of non-observance (mere violation or infringement of the maxims)? And, assuming once again that more than one maxim is implicated and that the various maxims are not of the same conceptual order, can a ranking order or a scale of predominance be established? These and a host of other questions have recently been raised by commentators on the Gricean model (e.g. Thomas, 1995). The answers, however, can be found neither in Grice nor in the work of those who have subsequently popularised the scheme. Nonetheless, these are real questions facing language-users and analysts alike. What do we do when we encounter a politician insisting on borrowing from legal language or English for science only to relay racist attitudes, as Sample (C) shows?

Sample (C)

Let us take as our starting point the calculation of the General Register Office that by 1985 there would be in this country 3.5 million *coloured immigrants and their offspring* — in other words, that the present number would have increased between two- and three-fold in the next seventeen years on two assumptions — current *rate of intake* and current *birthrate*. (Enoch Powell, cited in Sykes, 1985 [italics added])

Or when we come across a working class housewife who, only to relay resentment, borrows the precise wording of the police or experts in health care, as Sample D and E show?

Sample (D)

Woman interviewed: a *domestic* they call it; they don't give a stuff! (From a documentary on 'violence to women')

Sample (E)

Woman interviewed: She is *sectioned* for 28 days and became one of those they call *specialed* which means you have a nurse following you everywhere you go. (From a documentary on 'mental health care')

To salvage what is otherwise a viable framework, we might perhaps look again at the Cooperative Principle and the notion of implicature and consider alternative models of implied meaning. The maxim of relevance will feature prominently, but before we outline the main proposals in this area of cognitive communication studies, it is important to distinguish two levels of pragmatic meaning related to 'relevance': one deals with relevance in terms of text organisation (i.e. in terms of the contribution which a given text element makes as a 'step' in an argument or an 'event' in a narrative and so on); the other related yet distinct sense of relevance is closely bound up with effectiveness and efficiency at the level of propositional content (i.e. ideational investment and returns). While not strictly adhering for the moment to the precise context of text politeness in which Sell (1992) uses the terms, it is tempting to refer to the first sense of relevance as 'presentational' and the second as 'selectional'. The Sperber and Wilson model of relevance (1986) may usefully be seen as catering for the domain of the latter 'selectional' manifestations and it is to these that we shall now briefly turn.

The Gricean scheme has been taken to task by a number of theorists within pragmatics for the way the maxims are formulated and how this leaves a number of questions unanswered. For example, Grice does not explicitly say what is precisely meant by 'relevance'. The term is so ill-defined that a spate of theories have subsequently appeared with the disturbing conclusion that all maxims can be reduced to the single arch-maxim of relevance. To rectify what is certainly unwieldy as a domain of inferential communication, Sperber and Wilson (1986) put forward a number of proposals and start from the central premise that the basic aim of communication is to engender a change in the hearer's assumptions about the world, to change a situation in a way that would not have been possible otherwise, in von Wright's (1967) terms. For this to be achieved, information must be new or newly presented, and this would normally be processed in a context of existing assumptions.

New information is said to carry so-called 'contextual effects'. Blakemore (1987: 53) lists three ways in which a contextual effect is achieved: new information may lead to the formation of a new assumption; it may strengthen an existing assumption; or it may lead to the abandoning of an existing assumption. In each case the hearer is left with a modified set of background assumptions which are available for use in assessing the effect of the next proposition, which itself contributes to the background of the next, and so on. In this cyclical fashion, new information would be seen as being 'relevant'. And it is here that Sperber and Wilson's relevance principle properly comes into effect: communication operates in terms of cost and benefit, a balance between processing effort and pay-off, with the contextual effects yielded constituting the profit side. Relevance, then, is the number of contextual effects gained divided by the cost of the effort expended, thus:

$$R = \frac{E(\text{number of contextual effects})}{C(\text{cost of effort involved in obtaining } E)} \qquad \text{(Levinson, 1989: 459)}$$

This is the inferential mechanism of relevance in a nutshell. While the 'presentational' (organisational) criteria are obviously catered for, albeit by implication, the model focuses on the 'selectional' (propositional) side of relevance. However, it is only when we turn our attention to the presentational aspects that we can begin to see text relevance as a macro-level phenomenon specifically related to text organisation (i.e. the contribution which a given text element presentationally makes to prop up, say, an 'argument' or sustain a 'narrative'). Blakemore (1987) touches on this dimension of relevance when, in dealing with how contextual effects are generated, she speaks of the availability of accruing background assumptions for use not only in assessing current propositions but also in seeing how this benefits from, and at the same time contributes to, the background of propositions yet to unfold. This also neatly ties in with speech acting as part of a 'plan': to maintain relevance is to uphold principles such as non-obviousness or non-triviality, and conceive of utterances within a particular perspective (Ferrara, 1980, discussed in the previous section).

This text-level 'staging', however, implicates not only relevance but all the other Gricean maxims. As Green (1989: 101) observes:

> One consequence of the Cooperative Principle, and the maxim 'be relevant' in particular, that Grice never discussed, is that it provides the basis for a natural account of the problem of the coherence of texts.

However, if they are to be plausible, accounts of coherence must build on a conception of cohesion which goes beyond a narrow focus on the 'linguistic' properties of sentences (e.g. Halliday & Hasan, 1976), and certainly away from spurious comparisons with the grammaticality of sentences. What is needed is a theory of cohesion and coherence as two intimately related aspects of text constitution working in harness and firmly based on the assumption that a sequence of sentences hangs together by virtue of the text-user's compliance with the Cooperative Principle or motivated departures from it. Within such a scheme envisaged at the level of text, individual sentences would be seen as intended to say something necessary, true and relevant to accomplishing some objective in which (it is mutually believed) the text producer and the intended audience are mutually interested. A coherent text is one where the interpreter can readily reconstruct the speaker's plan with reasonable certainty, by inferring the relations among the sentences, and their individual relations to the various subgoals in the inferred plan for the enterprise understood to be at hand (Green, 1989: 103).

This does not only bring together the various strands of speech acting and cooperativeness under the umbrella of textuality but also holds good for the process of translation. To make texts more coherent, the tendency among translators, particularly in the Anglo-American tradition of literary translation and when working into the more prestigious 'literate' languages, say, from a predominantly orate tongue, has invariably been to impose order on a seemingly chaotic source text. This is sometimes achieved by spelling out the connections that could well have been deliberately left implicit. As we will make clear in a later part of this chapter, such translator decisions, even if well-meant, are risky: interventions of this kind could distract the attention of the target reader away from the author's point and towards issues that could potentially be marginal.

From Socio-cultural Values to Socio-textual Practices

So far, we have sought to see the entire pragmatic enterprise in a new (and hopefully refreshing) light. Speech acting involves more than the identification by a speaker or a hearer of a collection of neatly delimited linguistic elements each of which carries its own 'illocutionary' and 'perlocutionary' tags, and which are ultimately strung together in the realisation of texts. Nor is cooperativeness always conventional and unconstrained. To be viewed more realistically, doing things with words which, other things being equal, must be necessary, true and relevant, can only be pursued adequately when seen in its natural habitat — the text in context. This is not always a straightforward matter, with intentionality more often than not turning out to be particularly opaque and with the result that we are required to invoke a number of other communicative systems which define and are in turn defined by context.

One such communicative set of parameters is that related to the register membership of the text. Here, we certainly talk about aspects of the message such as field or subject matter, tenor or level of formality and whether texts are in the spoken or written mode. But we also and perhaps more meaningfully see field of discourse as home to intense ideational activity, tenor of discourse as a site of conflict and harmony, and mode as the mainstay of textualisation — the way sequences of sentences exhibit a structure and a texture which together contribute to the ultimate effect of texts being cohesive and coherent. Consider, for example, how the idea of social institutions and social process, on the one hand, and power and solidarity, on the other, have respectively proved to be crucial ideational and interpersonal resources in processing Albright's contribution in Sample A.

Granted, this is all underpinned by intentionality but, for intentions to be pursued properly, we are inevitably pointed in the direction of language use as a social semiotic. Here, what we may refer to as the 'sociocultural' dimension becomes a factor to be reckoned with. It does indeed matter what 'honour' can mean to an Englishman or to an Argentinean, or that the needs of the group, say, in Chinese receive greater emphasis than in English. Ultimately, however, these socio-cultural values become meaningful only when deployed in sequences of utterances serving particular rhetorical purposes such as arguing or engaging in detached exposition (i.e. become what we shall now technically refer to as 'texts').

Texts are not processed in a vacuum but rather in terms of certain norms conventionally governing given communicative events (or what we shall call 'genres'). Recall how the 'deplorable + irony' reading in the Albright Sample (A) above was worked out essentially as a 'textualisation' procedure motivated by the 'political polemic' as a genre. By the same token, the rival reading of 'mildly deplorable + good management' is also possible when a 'yes-but' textual strategy is activated within the 'political manifesto' or the 'inaugural address' as a genre.

However, genres and texts cannot function alone. Albright could indeed be said to have mastered the relevant genres and texts, but the effect which she has achieved on this occasion is, I suggest, ultimately related to her mastery of the discourse: the confidence-inspiring, non-whining, upbeat tempo of someone who believes in the American way, who was there 'at the creation' in the postwar years, and so on. Discourse, then, is an all-encompassing aspect of what we have been referring to as 'sociotextual' practice subsuming the expression of particular attitudes in the service of given social institutions, social processes and a dominant ideology. Here, our speech acting and explicatures or implicatures are seen within a discursive plan implemented through a strict adherence to the rules of both the genre and the text as communicative occasion and rhetorical purpose respectively. Inter-discursivity will be the framework within which text politeness and other related aspects of intentionality will now be seen, as the following schematic representation of text in context in Figure 1 shows.

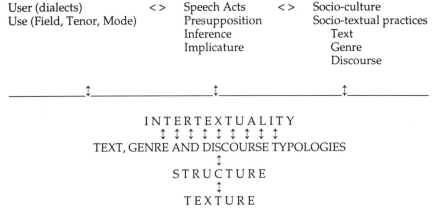

(Adapted from Hatim & Mason, 1990)

Figure 1

Politeness: A Discoursal Perspective

The story of politeness, about which we will have to be fairly brief, strikingly parallels that of much of pragmatics, and specifically the way theories of the speech act, implicature and indeed relevance have evolved.

Atomism

Let us start with how analytic atomism characterised the early approaches to the study of the subject. Politeness was, for a long time, treated as an utterance-level phenomenon and the diverse realisations were almost exclusively seen in terms of 'speech-act strategies' and from the standpoint of how these are perceived by native- and non-native-speakers (Walters, 1979). In fact, Walters' experiments, using a 'standard lexical context' for the language pair English–Spanish, specifically instruct informants to ignore context as much as possible. In these and similar studies, comparative/quantitative analyses were systematically conducted yielding conclusions such as 'in X language 12 forms are available for the polite performance of a given speech act, while only 6 are at the disposal of speakers from Y language'.

But, as Thomas (1995: 156) points out, such approaches to politeness suffer from a number of serious shortcomings. One has to do with confusing pragmatic with sociolinguistic analysis. In the latter, it is indeed legitimate to list all the forms used in the performance of a given function, speech act or whatever. But taxonomies become pragmatics proper only when the formal distribution of a particular use is seen in terms of strategic deployment of a given form in an attempt to achieve a speaker's goal.

The second weakness of utterance-level approaches, Thomas observes, relates to the requirement of context which is crucial and which is invariably glossed over in predominantly formal analyses of politeness. The myth perpetuated by some of the 'descriptive' studies of politeness is that some connection necessarily exists between linguistic forms and polite function. This may indeed be borne out by decontextualised data, but as soon as contextual specifications are restored, such a linkage all but disappears.

Atomism, then, is the root cause of the problem in a great deal of work on politeness, precisely as was the case with speech act theory under the Austin/Searle regime. This criticism is levelled by Sell (1992) even at early formulations of politeness within a Brown & Levinson (1978) framework: here, like speech acts, certain expressions are said to have certain effects (polite or impolite) on people. But, as Sell (1992: 213) incisively asks:

> What about all the other expressions and all the other things? Can linguistic form not be mapped on to interactive moves *more closely and more comprehensively*? In particular, can one really isolate FTAs (face-threatening actions) and politeness from everything else?

The socio-cultural bias

In charting the routes which present-day notions of politeness have traversed over the years, another striking feature (in addition to the atomism and the sociolinguistic tendency previously discussed) has been the undue focus on matters sociocultural. We start at the beginning and recall how, in certain quarters, politeness was seen as a 'real world phenomenon'. Thomas (1995: 150) defines this trend in terms of the way 'politeness [was] interpreted as a genuine desire to be pleasant to others'. This harks back to how, once again like speech acts, politeness was, at one stage, seen as the underlying motivation for linguistic behaviour. Such a wished-for and often contextually implausible correlation cannot be considered legitimate pragmatics.

Similarly, deference and formality of register have been invoked in an attempt to explain politeness phenomena. A great deal of effort has been expended, I might add in vain, in trying to correlate, say, T/V pronoun distribution with pragmatic politeness. However, these factors can be and perhaps often are used strategically, with speakers deliberately opting for a particular form in order to achieve a given goal. We therefore suggest that, unless this element of motivatedness is built into the analysis (in which case we are no longer in the purely sociocultural but well and truly within the sociotextual domain), deference or register has little if anything to do with pragmatic politeness as we understand it.

Undue emphasis on the spoken mode

To date, most formulations of politeness have been envisaged with spoken discourse in mind and almost exclusively within face-to-face interaction. In fact, Brown and Levinson (1978/1987) do not consider there to be a politeness dimension to written texts and, when Leech (1983) broaches the issue, he deals with writing under the so-called 'collaborative functions' where, as he sees it, the 'illocutionary' goal is indifferent to the 'social' goals and where talk of politeness is therefore largely irrelevant. True, there have been a number of studies which use the politeness framework in the analysis of written (mostly literary) texts (e.g. Wadman, 1983; Simpson, 1989 etc.). But, as Sell (1992: 217) points out, the discussion invariably revolves around politeness *in* texts and not *of* texts. That is, politeness is perceived not as part of genuine interaction between writer and reader but rather within the contrived interaction of the world of mimeses between personae and characters.

With Sell, we may ask: Is writing less interactive than speech? As far back as the 1920s, Volosinov (1921) argued for the need to see the written text as 'a vitiated dialogue worked into the body of a monologic utterance'. This has recently been echoed by a number of writers working on text structure and pragmatics. From the perspective of applied linguistics and speech-act theory, Flowerdew (1990: 93) observes that, in addition to the locutionary and illocutionary acts which utterances convey, a third, more interactive component may be identified, namely the 'interactional' act. This conveys how one utterance relates to the other utterances in the discourse.

Two approaches to the analysis of pragmatic meaning are thus in evidence: one focuses on the communicative intent and relates to the illocutionary act performed; the other, in the words of Widdowson (1979: 2),

> would not focus so much on *what* communication is achieved, [but] is directed at the interaction management aspects of use . . . [i.e.] with reference to their function as elements of discourse structure (e.g. agreement, disagreement, initiation).

In the same vein, Edmondson (1981: 82) suggests that:

> A communicative act has a function with respect to both the structure of the interaction of which it forms a part and with respect to the attitudes, feelings and beliefs of the speaker making it. It is both an *interactional* and an *illocutionary* act [italics added].

More specifically, Hoey (1983, 1988) focuses on the means by which writers establish a dialogue with their readers, anticipating their reactions and building this into the constitution of their texts. It is this dialogic nature of the written text which has particularly caught the attention of Literary Pragmatics: of course, speech is more personally evaluative than writing, but some speech can be as analytic and objective as any written text designed with these communicative aims in mind. By the same token, it is argued, writing can be casual and unceremonial and always capable of interacting with human beings sometimes more fundamentally than any speech (Sell, 1992: 218).

This can now shed some useful light on the dynamics of the written text. Sell (1992: 219) lists a number of interesting phenomena and convincingly shows that writers are just as keen to hold the floor as any speaker, a source of utter disquiet particularly when mutual communicative access is blocked as a result. Sell (1992: 220) accepts the notion that compromising particles, for example, are less in evidence in writing than in speech, but goes on to point out that writers hesitate just as often as speakers and the need of (cooperative) writers constantly to justify every move can only point to a genuine desire to resist rejection.

Writing, then, is dialogic and interactive. This has obvious implications for the study of politeness and has been admirably explored by what has come to be known as the 'conversational contract view', proposed by Fraser (1990). Here, the basic idea is that of 'rights and obligations' and of how interaction is invariably constrained by an awareness of the norms obtaining within the interaction and of the rights and obligations entailed by it. Thomas (1995) welcomes the trend as fitting in well with the idea of the 'activity type' — those goal-directed and socially-constituted events which control what can or cannot be done by a conventionally established set of participants, setting and so on.

In sociotextual practice terms, the earlier discussion of the 'interactional' versus the 'informational' and of the way this relates to politeness (in written or spoken exchange) all raise issues which can be adequately settled only by reference to what we shall call 'text', 'genre' and 'discourse', to be dealt with from a translation perspective in greater detail shortly. However, let us briefly return to the politeness of the written text seen from the standpoint of Literary Pragmatics. Here, the sense of politeness relayed by distinctions such as illocutionary versus that which focuses on interaction management has been captured by an interesting scale of values suggested by Sell (1992: 221) in terms of 'choice and cooperativeness in interpersonal relations': among other things, politeness would be 'a matter of choosing subject matter and language, and . . . a matter of helpfulness'.

The 'choice' element in both style and substance is labelled 'selectional politeness' and involves text users in observing all the taboos and conventions of social and moral decorum operative within their culture (Sell, 1992: 222). Note in passing that this must also subsume what we have so far referred to as locutionary/illocutionary, communicative intent, 'what' communication is achieved, that aspect of the message which tends to be information-based, and even that which is related to attitudes, feelings and beliefs.

The cooperativeness element, on the other hand, yields so-called 'presentational politeness' involving the text-user in varying degrees of compliance with the cooperative principle to ensure that the reader is reasonably guided through what is happening, what is meant, or why something is said when it is said in a particular form and not another' (Sell, 1992: 222). Here, we must also include what we have referred to as the interactional, the interaction management aspect, the function of elements in discourse structure, the broadly function-based which, in the words of Thompson and Thetela (1995: 104), is said to concentrate:

> on the ways in which writers more or less overtly conduct interaction
> with their readers, particularly by assuming for themselves and

assigning to the readers roles in the interaction [. . .] and by intruding in the message to comment on and evaluate it.

Politeness of Texts

For our purposes, we shall here borrow and slightly modify the basic parameters originally worked out for politeness by Brown and Levinson (1978, 1987). Their Model Person (and ours) is a language-user with two endowments: practical reasoning which provides a basis for the identification of ends and the means to achieve them; and face. Face involves the desire on the part of the text-user to be left alone (negative face) and the wish to be approved of (positive face). Thus, writers who, as Thompson and Thetela (1995) observe, manage the interaction properly and who intuitively know when to intrude in the message for a comment or an evaluation, assume for themselves and their readers appropriate roles in the interaction and could be said to uphold principles of text politeness in the sense in which we are using the term. That is, as part of their 'practical reasoning' (or what we would rather call 'textual competence'), they are able to see beginnings, middles and ends to texts and, through what they do with language, value the freedom to do as they want and appreciate such a desire in others (negative face). Moreover, they like to feel 'included' and appreciate that others wish to feel the same (positive face).

Against this background, distinctions outlined above such as information versus function, communicative versus face managing, illocutionary versus interactional, become particularly meaningful. To uphold politeness norms, writers resort to a variety of textual resources in order to make sure that the content of what they say is sensitive to face needs and that this is supportively negotiated, in such a way that face damage is minimised. In other words, they operate the 'politeness' mechanism at both the level of selection and of presentation (Sell, 1992). Along similar lines to the relationship suggested between selectional, propositional matters, on the one hand, and the information-based, illocutionary, communicative side of message construction, on the other hand, I wonder if a similar relationship could not be envisaged between the selection aspect and sociocultural values, leaving us with some kind of relationship between presentation (organization) and sociotextual values.

That is, while not wishing to equate too strictly the socio-cultural domain with the 'selectional' and the socio-textual with the 'presentational' (after all these values are emphatically envisaged on a scale, a continuum), it is nevertheless tempting to view selectional manifestations in terms of politeness as an utterance-level phenomenon or as a real-world phenomenon (deference, formality etc.). Consider, for example, how choice of subject matter, helpfulness, taboos, social and moral decorum and so on, all form part of the cultural milieu within which text-users operate and negative and positive face work is conducted.

However, selectional politeness and sociocultural values, important as they are in their own right, will in effect be dormant (some lapsing into dead metaphors or clichés or, worse, into stereotypes) unless and until they acquire varying degrees of sociotextual significance when 'presented' in a particular manner and for a particular purpose. The 'yes-but' straw man gambit is a rhetorical purpose around which texts become cohesive and coherent; the mean sheriff in Cowboy films or the half-human howl in horror movies is an important ingredient of the genre functioning as a viable clue to conventionally recognised communicative events; and addressing a black audience with the infamous *you people* (which allegedly cost Ross Perot the candidature for the presidency of the USA) is a feature of discourse, where language becomes the mouthpiece of social institutions and social processes (e.g. racism). To put this slightly differently, our selections and the cultural values they relay become genuinely communicative only when viewed as part of the sociotextual practices of text-users. This has obvious implications for the way politeness is perceived, practical reasoning is carried out and face work managed. To expand on some of these issues and to focus properly on the notion of text politeness, let us consider one or two text samples.

Sample (F)

Department of . . .

Announcing a special lecture by our most distinguished guest

Dr . . .

All are welcome and admission is free. This is one of Dr . . . 's rare public appearances in the UK. In order to secure your place at the lecture, we would ask you to register in advance by filling in the form below and returning it before 24 February. The venue for the lecture . . .

This text appeared on a flyer issued by a British university department announcing a lecture by an internationally renowned guest-speaker. Sociocultural and selectional problems relating to face and politeness are certainly manifest here, but these are ultimately explainable in terms of sociotextual practices customary for this kind of writing. More specifically, it is genre which is infringed. The genre problem does not only have to do with the conventional profile of the 'academic announcement', but also, perhaps more seriously, with the 'other' genre hijacked and misappropriated, namely that of show business publicity material. True, academic life has in recent years seen a great deal of what Fairclough (1992) calls the 'commodification' of higher education (e.g. universities advertising their wares on TV). But for a daring example of intertextuality like that triggered by Sample (F) to pass muster, it must be properly negotiated (i.e. presented with subtlety) which, I suggest, is not the case here. The socio-textual *faux pas* involved may partly be due to the fact that we seem to know a great deal about both the genre of the academic announcement (actually present) and the genre of show business publicity material (virtual and invoked). For English at least, these are surrounded by a fairly strict and deep-rooted set of dos and don'ts. There is also the issue of the source of the advertisement, the absence of commercial pressure or economic imperative etc.

Assessing samples of writing such as (F) in terms of text politeness and socio-textual practice is necessarily a matter of focus. For example, genre is singled out as the socio-textual aspect most at risk in Sample (F). But text and discourse are also implicated. Sample G demonstrates this overlap more clearly.

Sample (G)

A soaking on the beach . . . a snub by the Left

CANUTE KINNOCK

By GORDON GREIG, Political Editor

NEIL KINNOCK, just elected Labour's youngest leader at 41, saw an old party tide threaten to swamp his new beginning last night.

Once again, the nightmare question came up. How far are you going to dismantle Britain's nuclear defence shield?

The answer helped Michael Foot lose the last election and from the way the argument was boiling at Brighton, it clearly threatened to help Mr Kinnock lose the next one.

His induction to the mantle of leadership began with a soaking on Brighton beach as he stumbled and fell at the sea's edge while posing for photographers. But the embarrassment of the Canute-like ducking was nothing to the problem of a backroom row between Labour's Left and Right over the rising tide of pacifism and one-sided nuclear disarmament in the party.

Suicide

An angry session of the National Executive provided a curtain-raiser to a debate on Wednesday which may nail young Mr Kinnock more firmly than ever to getting rid of all nuclear weapons.

It saw the novice leader frantically buttonholing colleagues in an attempt to avert what he sees as political suicide. It also saw Denis Healey angrily pounding the table and warnings from Anthony Wedgewood Benn and Ken Livingstone that Mr Kinnock could blow it in the next year if he does not stick to left-wing policies.

And there was a blunt message to Mr Kinnock from veteran Left Winger Joan Maynard at a fringe meeting: 'If you don't walk with your shoes straight we'll have you next year'.

But for a few moments the trendy new leader enjoyed the razzmatazz of an election night with an overwhelming victory for the 'dream ticket' — Mr Kinnock plus Roy Hattersley as his deputy.

The result of the leadership ballot, with Mr Kinnock streets ahead of his nearest rival Mr Hattersley and Peter Shore and Eric Heffer nowhere, produced an explosion of cheers.

Mr Kinnock clenched his hands above his head boxer-style and gave his wife and inspiration — Glenys — a hearty kiss. (*The Daily Express*, 8 October 1983)

This text is normally processed against the background of a set of expectations which may be summarised as follows. The register member-ship of the text (field, tenor and mode) is assumed to be least hybrid (straightforward, albeit front-page, news reporting). Intentionality is similarly expected to be least opaque (to inform with minimal expenditure of unnecessary effort), and semiotics least turbulent (integrity of the signs 'discourse', 'genre' and 'text'). Consider, however, how register member-ship is irreparably shifted in the actual text: huge headline, huge photo-graph to reinforce a Tory pseudo-sympathy towards a 'misfortune' of Labour; a mock-heroic tone and a comic dissimilitude (which both conspire to underline the opponent's predicament); the logical and rhetorical sophistry in *Canute Kinnock* (with the two words linked by similarity of sound and stress pattern to prop up the comic tone).[1]

As for intentionality, this has also been perniciously shifted to relay sentiments serving a single overarching theme: undemocratic instability and the consequent unelectability of a Labour government. This global thematic thrust is facilitated by numerous local intentions utilizing a variety of pragmatic resources such as irony (e.g. Michael Foot 'helped' Labour in losing the last general elections). The element of pragmatic 'purposeful-ness' involved eventually seeps into the semiotic constitution of the text and acts on 'signs', producing in the process an interaction that is blatantly biased to say the least: 'young' is stripped of its positive connotations to acquire distinctively negative values (e.g. unfit to govern); and semiotic constructs such as *old party tide, dream ticket, trendy, razzmatazz*, through *novice*, enhance the overall effect of 'youthful irresponsibility'.

Texture responds to and manifests these shifts in register, intention and semiotic sign. Within register, a number of linguistic resources have been fully tapped: ideational choices (e.g. non-core vocabulary and metaphoric expression), interpersonal choices (the formality of *mantle of induction* lapsing into 'rows' and 'ducking') and textual choices (through-argumentation with a text producer rarely pausing to consider alternative views). Through the kind of intentionality described earlier, the normalcy of the sign has been tampered with at both micro- and macro-level (socio-cultural and sociotextual practices respectively). In the latter domain, the text, the genre and the discourse are all cast in a mould totally counter to expectations.

This is the kind of writing which we shall describe as 'done in blatant contravention of the norms of text politeness'. In translation, as I shall explain later, this infringement becomes part and parcel of meaning-making and, all things being equal, must be preserved warts and all in the target language. In dealing with this kind of text, it is a matter solely for readers of the source text within the source language and culture to complain about the 'offence', if so felt, by writing to the editor, cancelling subscriptions to the paper or even leaving the Conservative Party; it is not an issue we could do much about in translation. That is, it is not for us as translators to right the wrongs of politeness when the object of the exercise in the source language (target language *skopos* permitting) is not merely to impart information but to be deliberately devious.

To return to the mechanics of text politeness, the concept can now be defined in the following terms:

> *Texts are said to be upholding norms of politeness when in terms of both their micro- and macro-structure they are seen to fulfil expectations regarding all or some of the normal and customary contextual requirements in the following domains: register membership, intentionality and both the socio-cultural and socio-textual practices involved. The latter semiotic dimension pertains to the discourse, genre and texts felt to be appropriate within the communicative event or speech activity in question.*

> *Texts which uphold norms of politeness would also include those which systematically defy expectations on all or some of the grounds previously identified provided that such departures are rhetorically motivated and adequately negotiated, securing uptake and gaining the acceptance of textually competent users of the language. Otherwise, texts would be deemed 'impolite' incurring damage to face both negative and positive.*

Cast in a Gricean framework, this hypotheses could now read: texts deemed 'impolite' would include those elements which, at sequence-level, violate any of the Cooperative Principle maxims (Quantity, Quality, Manner and Relevance). Seen particularly from the vantage point of relevance, 'impolite' texts would thus be those which piecemeal or collectively fail to yield sufficient contextual effects to justify the expenditure of processing effort in terms of accruing returns. Finally, with speech acts in mind, 'impolite' texts would be those in which the sequential order of elements does not readily yield a hierarchic organization and which thus fail to deploy cohesion in the service of coherence, making the retrieval of plausible text worlds unnecessarily difficult. All these 'impoliteness' conditions could be reversed and rendered advantageous (interesting, engaging, creative etc.) *if and only if* violations are rhetorically motivated and adequately negotiated securing uptake and gaining the acceptance of textually competent users of the language.

To conclude this section, it is perhaps worth noting that the socio-textual dimension (with varying degrees of socio-cultural input) and the presentation aspect (with varying degrees of selectional input) are particularly privileged in the way we relay or perceive text politeness. Consider the list of features which Sell (1992) provides in the context of discussing writing as a phenomenon which is just as interactive as speech and which we present here as features of 'polite' writing:

- expressing reservations by means of inverted commas or phrases such as 'so to speak' and 'as it were';
- using the resources of modal expressions to the same effect;
- explicitly forestalling objections or resorting to hedging by means of what can still conveniently be called indirect speech acts;
- resorting to metatextual comment, summaries, headlines and structural parallelism or antithesis, to point up an argument;
- deciding on stylistic embellishment, or plainness, as more likely to hold attention;
- including overt or covert evaluations of our subject matter, so as to prevent the reaction most dreaded by writers or speakers alike, 'So what?'

The textual enterprise

But who is it that ultimately oversees this complex machinery for the construction of meaning? To answer this question we must first enquire into how communities of text users go about their textual business. This seems to be conducted through what may be described as an incessant quest to achieve effectiveness, efficiency and appropriateness. Modifying de Beaugrande's (1980) terminology slightly, effectiveness is achieved when a group of language users negotiate and agree on conventional ways of directly catering for:

(1) the cultural codes which adequately serve the mores of the diverse institutions and social processes at work;
(2) the communicative events which collectively make up the 'life-world' (to use Ong's, 1983, term) of the community in question;
(3) the variety of rhetorical purposes whose pursuance guarantees that verbal or non-verbal output is both cohesive and coherent (i.e. commensurate with accessible text worlds).

We have referred to these elements of the semiotic regime as discourse, genre and texts respectively. But to secure efficiency, the principle of recurrence enters the equation: we tend to do things not only in an orderly fashion but also within a system of expectations which can be flouted only for a good reason. This conventional pattern underpins appropriateness and basically determines what can or cannot be done with language, given the stringent dos and don'ts negotiated by generations of speakers of a given language and evolving against a backdrop of both tradition and modernity.

Now to answer the question of who looks after this gigantic textual enterprise, adjudicating as it were over what is polite and what is not, we must recognise that a variety of sources are involved, the most important of which is the mass media and those men and women who work on the output, readers who write in and so on. To illustrate how powerful and authoritative this can be in a language such as English, let us take what we have termed politeness of texts as the specific area of pragmatic meaning, and focus on non-verbal signs as a socio-cultural dimension of semiotic meaning. In an article for *The Sunday Times*, Hugh Pearman argues for the need to adopt a coherent design policy to sort out the civic muddle displayed on Britain's city streets. Pearman is worth quoting at some length:

> Today, however, not only has the red gone, but the new BT style just doesn't work as well. The current virtually invisible style of the BT phone box is even worse, when it comes to spotting one, than the better-looking glass and aluminium sub-high-tech image of the French PTT. BT's rival, Mercury, has a clearer understanding of the importance of colour, but unfortunately has opted for a hideous turquoise to do the job. Both logos — BT's prancing fairy and Mercury's zappy M — are equally nasty, and both are amateurish, compared with the cool, rational design of, for instance, the Dutch PTT...
>   ... But so what? Why shouldn't public service companies louse up their image if they want to? Are these not mere incidentals to life, no more important than the design of cornflakes packets?

Individually, they may be incidental, but collectively they matter a great deal . . . ('Signs of the time', *The Sunday Times*, 27 September 1992.)

Our aim in citing this piece of applied semiotics is simply to show that today's hunch is tomorrow's norm which in the fulness of time becomes inviolable, something we live by. To return to politeness of the written word, a similar act, this time of institutionalizing language use, is effected by letters to the editor (themselves a genre with its own discourse and typical text formats). Martin (1985) discusses ideology in discourse and suggests a scheme within which text producers may be 'for' or 'against' an issue (e.g. Should Australia mine and export uranium?). Within either camp we encounter the radicals of the Left and the conservatives of the Right (with some obviously more radical or more conservative than others).

On the subject of 'killing kangaroos', *Habitat* (a magazine of conservation and the environment produced by the Australian Conservation Society) published an editorial. *Habitat* typically expresses the views of the 'less' radical (the resolvers) within the anti-camp. The editorial, however, was untypical and the discourse had an unfamiliar edge to it. This was immediately spotted by the readers of the magazine and letters flooded in, decrying the way the editorial specifically used 'a little too much of the language of the [ultra radicals] for their liking' (Martin, 1985: 38).

This is politeness of texts at work: BT, Mercury, *Habitat* and the *Daily Express* front page news editor have all been ticked off by self-appointed (but effective) guardians of felicity for overstepping some mark and thereby infringing 'politeness'. Face is implicated and the text receiver is either thwarted or insulted. But we are nowhere nearer to answering the question we set out with. At this stage of ethno-semiotic research, we simply do not know enough about what keeps this textual machinery running and, in the case of languages with a respectable measure of literacy, smoothly I might add. Thankfully, the translator who would no doubt benefit from this discoursal awareness is not in a hurry to know, as we will make clear in the following section.

The Translator's Angle

When we closely examine the phenomena cited here, we see that they all involve socio-textual practices recognized by given language communities and sanctioned by the rhetorical conventions at work. This leads us to question the 'universality' thesis of politeness as far as texts are concerned. Of course, like 'promising' or generating an implicature or approaching issues related to relevance, politeness is a universal in the sense that we all have 'face' of some kind and practical reason to go with it. And certainly there will be many areas of textual activity across the languages and cultures of the world where the ground rules are almost universal.

When it comes to (a) the availability or otherwise of a given politeness strategy, (b) the incidence and frequency of such strategies and (c) the realization in linguistic form of such strategies, that is, when it comes to how we actually go about our textual business, these pragmatic constructs will invariably turn out to be unique to us and to the culture (and subculture) to which we belong. In fact, this also goes for micro-level speech acting (e.g. some languages do not promise or are more likely to promise differently), generating implicatures (e.g. the Quantity maxim is problematic in certain languages which value prolixity) and as far as relevance is concerned, one man's meat is certainly someone else's poison.

In the maze of this textual activity across diverse cultural and linguistic boundaries, the translator truly functions as a mediator. In the area of text politeness, for example, the translator would have to appreciate source-text politeness within the norms and conventions operative in the source language and culture. He or she would then have to anticipate how politeness in the relevant area of textual activity would be handled in the target language and culture.

It is the latter procedure of assessing how a given rendering can secure optimal reception in the target language which would most certainly take precedence over all other criteria. This scenario, however, is valid only for highly stable contexts and only when information-imparting is the basic function of both source and target texts. Consider the following sample as an illustration of the kind of difficulties encountered in this domain of cross-cultural communication, particularly when working from languages with a certain measure of what Ong (1983) calls 'residual orality':

Sample (H) (back-translation from Arabic)
This study aims to attain goals which quantitatively go beyond the number of pages it contains. For it is essentially intended to embark on a general and comprehensive assessment of all of the studies which have been conducted so far in the field of Islamic Civilization, and to expose the ad hoc, intuitive nature which, in those rare studies which are somewhat objective, can only reflect a low level of awareness of the value of this civilization and its role in the present and future existence.

In the absence of the translator's much-needed intervention here, Sample (H) (regrettably a published abstract of an academic article) would by all the criteria discussed above be deemed to have contravened norms of text politeness in English. In addition to the selectional and socio-cultural aspects of message construction, presentational politeness has suffered badly due to a blatant flouting of what constitutes the genre 'abstract', the text format 'conceptual exposition' and indeed the analytical, detached discourse of academic abstract writing. This is not the case in Arabic (the source language) and, for text politeness to be restored in translation, target language norms in operation within the socio-textual practices customary in this kind of context will have to be heeded and the elements underlined perhaps doctored accordingly.

But, as pointed out earlier, this is not always the case. When source-text function is not purely information-imparting but, say, persuasive, departures from norms of politeness (be these socio-cultural or socio-textual) must be appreciated for what they are and rendered intact, if only to draw attention to them or even to shock the target reader. An example of text politeness compromised, predominantly due to socio-cultural factors, is taken from a novel by the Moroccan writer M. Shukri:

Sample (Ia) (back-translation from the Arabic)
There were three men smoking *kif* around the card table. I asked Mr Abdullah if I could leave my bag with him till the following day. He wanted me to show him what was in it: two large framed pictures, a pair of trousers, two shirts and a pair of socks. (Shukri 1990, *zaman al-akhta'*: 19)

The published translation into English misleadingly re-negotiates predominantly socio-cultural politeness of text (or the deliberate absence of it) along the following lines, closing the gaps deliberately left for the reader to work out:

Sample (Ib)
I asked Mr Abdullah if I could leave my bag with him till the following day. He *said it would be alright, but* he wanted to check what was in it, *so I had to show him* — two large framed pictures, a pair of trousers, two shirts and a pair of socks. (Emery [1995] *Streetwise* p. 11; material in italics added or modified by the translator)

What the translation in Sample (Ib) has irredeemably lost is the atmosphere ('at the end of one's tether) which is characteristic of the genre, the discourse and the text format of the source text. It is this kind of loss which domestication invariably inflicts on source texts and cultures (Venuti, 1995).

To illustrate the issue of uninvited interventions predominantly involving needless restoration of deliberately fractured socio-textual patterns in translation, consider the following text sample:

Sample (Ja)
I was 24 years old and I was enamoured of gambling. The matter like so many things in life started with small easy things, such that one never dreams that one's whole life would change. At first we would play for walnuts, then we began to play for poultry, and then came the day when I played for the three calves I had. Finally, I played for the trees. (Munif, 1973)

Here, a number of features contribute to a residually oral narrative where aspects of text constitution such as repetition are part and parcel of literary meaning-making. The translation into English took similar liberties as Sample (Ib) and we end up with the following flawed target version:

Sample (Jb)
I was 24 years old *and fond* of gambling. *Like so many things in* this world, *the whole thing started* in a very small way. *In such cases* you never dream that your whole life is going to change *as a result*. At first we *used to gamble with* walnuts, then we began to *play for* poultry; and then came the day when I *gambled with* the three calves I had. Finally, I *threw the trees in*. (The Iraqi Cultural Centre *The Trees;* material in italics added or modified by the translator)

No doubt, the target renderings in Sample (Ib) and Sample (Jb) are models of text politeness (selectional and presentational, respectively) in English. The reader would not be interested so much in models of English on this occasion as in the way politeness is skilfully flouted. The comic effect generated as a result of this misapplied domesticating strategy in these target renderings (as opposed to a more appropriate foreignising strategy — Venuti, 1995) is certainly not what the source texts are about.

Two important points must be underlined at this juncture: one is to do with the literal versus free distinction which has been erroneously invoked and more or less equated with foreignising and domesticating strategies respectively. It is indeed tempting to equate foreignising with a more literal mode and domesticating with a freer mode and this is more or less how it is in most cases. But, as Venuti (1992, 1995 and personal communication) stresses, the literal-free line of attack is just one part of the overall strategy of foreignisation or domestication. Of considerable importance in this regard is source-text 'strategic design' or the 'falling into dialogue' which the author would have initiated with the reader and which the translator must heed and present intact to the target reader.

The other point emerging from this discussion of domestication is that the 'strategic design' of texts, which is the mainstay of a foreignising strategy, is by no means restricted to literary expression. Along a continuum of evaluativeness for both fiction and non-fiction, the more dynamic a text is, the more profound (and consequently the more foreignizable) its strategic design will be. To illustrate this from a non-fictional text, consider Sample (K):

Sample K
It was through the war that we unveiled the deceitful face of the World Devourers. It was through the war that we recognized our enemies and friends. It was through the war that we concluded that we must stand on our own feet. It was through the war that we broke the back of both Eastern and Western superpowers. It was through the war that we consolidated the roots of our fruitful Islamic revolution. It was through the war that we nurtured a sense of fraternity and patriotism in the spirit of all the people. It was through the war that we showed the people of the world — in particular the people of the region — that one can fight against all the powers and superpowers for several years . . . (Translated by the BBC monitoring service and published in *The Guardian*, 1989)

The translator has no doubt foreignized (Hatim & Mason, 1990), but is this done consciously and methodically or is it merely blind literalism? It is probably the latter option if we consider how the strategy badly misfires later on in the translation of the same speech:

Sample L
Of course this does not mean that we should defend all clergymen. Dependent, pseudo and ossified clergy have not been, and are not, few in number. There are even persons in the seminaries who are active against the revolution and against pure Mohammedan Islam. There are some people nowadays who, under the guise of piety, strike such heavy blows at the roots of religion, revolution and the system, that you would think they have no other duty than this . . .

The sentence-initial, text-initial *Of course* in Farsi is a rhetorical device which ushers in a through-argument: a thesis is cited then extensively defended. The English surface equivalent to such a textual design performs an entirely different function: it is a so-called straw-man gambit, a counter-argumentative format in which an opponent's thesis is cited, then opposed (with *however, but* etc.). That is, when the Ayatollah said that 'not all clergymen are trustworthy', this was a statement of conviction which he then went on to support and substantiate. The way this came across in English (signalled by an English rhetorical *of course*) can only be seen in terms of the straw-man gambit: paying lip-service to some proposition only to oppose it subsequently ('but the majority of clergymen are good, righteous men who must be given every possible opportunity'). The latter reading is nowhere in sight and textual evidence to that effect is not forthcoming, a source of immense frustration for the English reader, hence the text's intrinsic 'impoliteness'.

To round off the discussion of politeness, both Samples (K) and (L) have infringed norms of text politeness. The English reader might justifiably feel harangued and thwarted. In the case of Sample K, however, the infringement is motivated since it reflects source text rhetorical mores in a context which calls for the use of, say, parallelism. Sample L, on the other hand, infringes politeness for no apparent reason and the English reader might justifiably feel like crying out aloud 'So what?'

Summary

In this chapter, the overall aim has been to restore an element of interactiveness to the analysis and appreciation of a number of pragmatic strategies (speech-acting, implicature, relevance etc.). The focus has been on the study of politeness and on how the concept originally formulated in Brown and Levinson (1978/1987) could be usefully extended to cover politeness of texts. This is defined in terms of factors regulating text register membership, intentionality and intertextuality. In the latter domain of semiotic activity, two basic phenomena may be identified, one catering for the socio-cultural objects which given linguistic communities and cultural groups live by, the other for what we actually do with words, with the way we pursue rhetorical purposes in texts, perform efficiently within the conventions governing certain communicative events or genres and, finally, relay attitudinal meanings through our discourse. This study concludes that to contravene the dos and don'ts of these socio-textual constructs is to commit a face threatening act vis-à-vis texts as holistic, cohesive and coherent plans of action. It is this sense of text integrity and the situations in which it is threatened either for a reason or sometimes for no reason that have proven to be a stumbling block in the work of the translator of fiction and non-fiction alike.

Note

1. In the discussion of this sample, I draw heavily on the excellent analysis presented in Carter (1988).

References

Blakemore, D. (1987) *Semantic Constraints on Relevance*. Oxford: Blackwell.

Brown, P. and Levinson, S. (1978) Universals in language usage: Politeness phenomena (pp. 56–288). In E. N. Goody (ed.) *Questions and Politeness: Strategies in Social Interaction*. Cambridge: Cambridge University Press.

Carter, R. (1988) Front pages: Lexis, style and newspaper reports. In M. Ghadessy (ed.) *Registers of Written English: Situational Factors and Linguistic Features*. London: Pinter.

Edmondson, W. (1981) *Spoken Discourse: A Model for Analysis*. London: Longman.

Fairclough, N. (1989) *Language and Power*. London: Longman.

Fairclough, N. (1992) *Discourse and Social Change*. Cambridge: Polity.

Ferrara, A. (1980a) An extended theory of speech acts: Conditions for subordinate acts in sequences. *Journal of Pragmatics* 4: 233–52.

Ferrara, A. (1980b) Appropriateness conditions for entire sequences of speech acts. *Journal of Pragmatics* 4: 321–49.

Flowerdew, J. (1990) Problems of speech act theory from an applied perspective. *Language Learning* 40 (Mar): 79–105.

Fraser, B. (1990) Perspectives on politeness. *Journal of Pragmatics* 14 (2): 219–36.

Green, G. M. (1989) *Pragmatics and Natural Language Understanding*. Hillsdale, NJ: Lawrence Erlbaum.

Halliday, M. A. K. and Hasan, R. (1976) *Cohesion in English*. London: Longman.

Hatim, B. and Mason, I. (1990) *Discourse and the Translator*. London: Longman.

Hoey, M. P. (1988) Writing to meet the reader's needs: Text patterning and reading strategies. *Trondheim Papers in Applied Linguistics 4*: 51–73.

Horner, W. B. (1975) Text act theory: A study of non-fiction texts. Unpublished PhD thesis, University of Michigan.

Korn, F. and Korn, S. R. D. (1983) Where people don't promise. *Ethics* 93 (Apr.), 445–50.

Leech, G. N. (1983) *Principles of Pragmatics*. London: Longman.

Levinson, S. C. (1981) The essential inadequacies of speech act models of dialogue. In H. Parret *et al.* (eds) *Possibilities and Limitations of Pragmatics: Proceedings of the Conference on Pragmatics at Urbino, 8–14 July 1979*. Amsterdam: John Benjamins.

Levinson, S. C. (1989) Review of relevance. *Journal of Linguistics* 25, 455–72.

Ong, W. (1982) *Orality and Literacy: The Technologies of the Word*. New York: Methuen.

Sell, R. D. (1992) *Literary Pragmatics*. London: Routledge.

Simpson, P. (1989) Politeness phenomena in Ionesco's *The Lesson*. In R. Carter and P. Simpson (eds) *Language, Discourse and Literature: An Introductory Reader* (pp. 171–93). London: Unwin Hyman.

Sperber, D. and Wilson, D. (1986) *Relevance: Communication and Cognition*. Oxford: Basil Blackwell.

Sykes, M. (1985) Discrimination in discourse. In T. Van Dijk (ed.) *Handbook of Discourse Analysis, Vol. 4: Discourse Analysis in Society* (pp. 83–101). New York: Academic Press.

Thomas, J. (1995) *Meaning in Interaction: An Introduction to Pragmatics*. London: Longman.

Thompson, G. and Thetela, P. (1995) The sound of one hand clapping: The management of interaction in written discourse. *Text* 15 (1), 103–27.

Venuti, L. (ed.) (1992) *Rethinking Translation: Discourse, Subjectivity, Ideology*. London: Routledge

Venuti, L. (1995) *The Translator's Invisibility*. London: Routledge.

Volosinov, V. N. (1921) *Marxism and the Philosophy of Language*. Translated by L. Matejka and I. R. Titunik. New York: Seminar Press, 1973.

Wadman, K. (1983) Private Ejaculations: politeness strategies in George Herbert's poems directed to God. *Language and Style* 16, 87–106.

Walters, J. (1979) Strategies for requesting in Spanish and English — structural similarities and pragmatic differences. *Language Learning* 9 (2): 277–94.

Widdowson, H. G. (1979) *Explorations in Applied Linguistics*. Oxford: Oxford University Press.

Wright, G. von. (1967) The logic of action. In N. Rescher (ed.) *The Logic of Decision and Action* (pp. 121–36). Pittsburgh: University of Pittsburgh Press.

Chapter 6

'New' versus 'Old'

FRANK KNOWLES

Linguists and philosophers have never cast serious doubt on a finding of the ancients that human utterances are — in their overwhelmingly vast majority — structured in a fashion which takes proper account of one of the prime logical and existential realities. This is that utterances are intended to communicate information. *Communicate*, of course, means to make something common property between two or more interlocutors. *Information*, on the other hand, is something — rounded? — to which intellectual shape or form can be given.

The process of communication is simple if the addressee already has the information on offer and needs only to activate it by retrieving it from memory in accordance with some sort of cue. However, the purpose of a particular act of communication may be to 'transmit' to somebody a message which results in the incrementation of the recipient's knowledge. In this case a clue is needed rather than a cue. This is because the number of informational possibilities is so large that ready comprehension is impeded by the operational demands of testing and rejecting as many of these numerous possibilities as necessary, until the correct or most plausible one is identified and selected. The point is that — without any delimitation of the message's 'domain' — there is no basis or stratagem available to a recipient for dividing and conquering. In order to solve this problem humankind has developed and refined, since the earliest days of communication by language, a method of providing supplementary detail sufficient to delimit the context of the substantive message to follow.

This method — dictated analytically by logic but pragmatically subliminal in many, perhaps most, communication contexts — is adapted to the apparent needs of human psychology in that utterances routinely have a bi-partite structure in existential terms. Listeners/readers, in normal circumstances, wish to apprehend the messages that are directed at them. However, in order to maximise the probability of receiving a message and successfully apprehending its content, they require some information about the context of the message, which can 'anchor' it and, in so doing, preclude the need — as noted earlier — to consider many logically imaginable but, in the event, redundant contingencies.

All human languages hence need and have systems for assisting speakers and writers to communicate pragmatically important information, such as focus and emphasis, in addition to strictly referential content. The most basic ways of doing this do not differ extensively from one language to another: for example, phonetic emphasis in communication by speech is a ready option frequently resorted to by speakers of all languages. However, typological divergency across languages does mean that the mechanisms that need to be activated in order to successfully place and signal what is 'old' and what is 'new' differ from one language to another.

In this paper reference is made to English and Russian. The latter is a 'synthetic' language with a very rich declensional and conjugational morphology. The effect of this is that the various words which combine to create utterances change their shape but not necessarily their sequence. Inflection carries the greatest burden in the configuration of utterances. A possible figurative analogy would be to say that Russian words wear military uniforms, with badges of rank and function, as it were. Part of speech is virtually 100% detectable by appearance and a type of syntactic 'connectionism' enables and facilitates the correct configuration of utterances.

Let us take a simple example:

koshka ubila krysu
cat has-killed rat

This could be interpreted, depending on any greater context, as:

a cat has killed a rat
a cat has killed the rat
the cat has killed a rat
the cat has killed the rat

If, however, we take this statement, alter the case markers of the nouns but leave element order unchanged, thus:

koshku ubila krysa

we obtain the opposite meaning: the rat has killed the cat. Yet this re-alignment introduces a different perspective, the answer to a different hypothetical question: 'What is it that the rat has killed?'

It can now perhaps be seen, to pursue the analogy, that English words wear civilian clothes rather than military uniforms: their function depends on their micro-environment. This factor severely limits remote syntactic linkage. There are not many options to exercise and translators, in particular, are frequently forced into large-scale syntactic reformulation when working from Russian into English. Conversely, those translating in the opposite direction often need to go to unusually great lengths in order to detect and isolate the logical thrust of the propositions they encounter. Unless they do this deliberately and conscientiously they can never achieve translational adequacy, never mind true equivalence.

The discussion so far has, in fact, been about subject and predicate. 'Subject' — in this technical sense — is the topic about which a speaker or a writer wishes to make a statement. It is something which is 'placed under' discussion. 'Predicate', on the other hand is what is actually said or asserted about the subject. It is important to make a very clear distinction between *logical* subjects and predicates and *grammatical* subjects and predicates. There is no necessity whatsoever for a logical subject to be a grammatical subject as well! It is also helpful to recognise other terminologies used in discussions of this general matter: Theme and Rheme, Topic and Comment, Given and New, Old and New. *Theme* [something 'put' or 'placed' (in the mind)] and *rheme* [something stated/asserted about the theme] are the Greek equivalents and progenitors of the Latin *subject* and *predicate*. *Given* and *New* and *Old* and *New* are positioned the furthest away from grammar and logic. They are encyclopaedic and existential as opposed to linguistic and they seem to place the accent on ontology rather than on logic. Because the theme is a signal or an 'indicator', pointing forward to the climax of an utterance, it is clear that a certain tension of expectation is created in the interim and relaxed only at the moment when what was previously unknown or uncertain is finally revealed. This momentary uncertainty evokes psychological and/or intellectual interest and curiosity and, above all, it creates a focus for the imminent disclosure.

A simple proposition or assertion is hence universally held to be bi-partite, consisting of a logical subject and logical predicate. Copular mechanics do not need any discussion here. The logical subject is the 'old', 'given', topic, or theme — usually already previously established. The logical predicate is what is asserted about the subject, the comment made about it, the new information made available, the rheme. The identification of the rheme is often patently obvious, but there are occasions when it has to be brought out into the open with some subtlety. One technique for doing this is to take an assertion and mentally ask what question it could be the answer to. In this way an informational, theme–rheme profile emerges, sometimes immediately, sometimes after deeper reflection or even after the mental posing of a lengthier series of Socratic questions. This process cannot side-step the realia of linguistic formulation but its fundamental purpose is the *logical* separation of subject and predicate.

Once the theme and rheme of an utterance/assertion have been identified, attention can then be directed to the details, often the intricate and difficult details, of linguistic formulation. Each language has its own mechanisms for communicatively profiling utterances. In the case of some languages the arsenal may be full of ready-made tools for the job, whereas others have to make do with a much more limited and clumsier tool-kit.

Let us 're-run' and develop a couple of examples from Shevjakova (1976). She first analyses the 'simple' two-word Russian sentence: *Dokladchik prishël*, which in translation means: *The-speaker has-arrived*. This is the answer to the hypothetical question: Has the speaker arrived? If the word order of the question is reversed to *Prishël dokladchik*, then this can only be the answer to the question: *Who has arrived*?

More generally, element order — following Shevjakova *passim* — may and normally does fulfil a number of functions with regard to the operational deployment of a given language system's resources for creating meaning. It can be used to highlight the communicative core of an utterance. It can be employed to express grammatical relationships between the constituent members of a sentence. It can modulate the communicative content of an utterance. It can be used to establish linkage between sentences and to set up communicatively significant juxtapositions or adjacency relationships. Various types of element-order relationships can be exploited to create differential emphases. Not least, element order can be deliberately controlled in order to mark preferences, to communicate euphony, rhythmicality and pace. By extension, it can be made to enhance style by creating an aura of, say, cohesion, symmetry, parallelism, unity and balance.

It follows that, as a text develops, one of the major ways in which development occurs must be with respect to 'Old' versus 'New'. The basis of this is the notion that 'New', once uttered, must by definition immediately become known or 'Old'. A totally regular — but in practice artificial — development would exhibit a set of sentences (both logical and grammatical) in which current rheme transmogrifies into new theme as each sentence passes the baton on to its successor. This configuration might not achieve a high rating from an aesthetic point of view but it is a valid and extant way of proceeding for certain types of functional-stylistic purpose. Much more frequent, however, is the case where a given theme is maintained over sentence boundaries until the set of rhemes allocated to it or mentally associated with it is exhausted.

Two other contingencies must also be noted: first, that rheme may precede theme for reasons of emphasis and, second, that a theme may be maintained in force explicitly or even implicitly across grammatical sentences.

Different languages, naturally, have different degrees of flexibility in terms of permissible or normal — i.e. not marked — element order and overall sentence configuration. They also have very considerable constraints. The syntactic structuration of utterances in a given language is dependent on the degree of flexibility within that language with respect to the operation and cooperation of the three basic structuration mechanisms extant in human language: inflection, function words and element order. A highly inflected language (such as Russian) offers considerable latitude with regard to element order, whereas — conversely — zero or residual inflection (as in English) imposes severe constraints on liberty with regard to element order. The implication of this is that, in any translation context, the most important macro-task the translator needs to achieve successfully is to mirror in the target text the theme–rheme structure of the source text. If this task is not carried out properly then the attempt at translation will fail, because emphases will be miscued, coherence will be ruptured and the demands of cohesion will not have been fulfilled.

English does not — because its morphology is 'residual' — possess a high degree of flexibility in the area of element order. To compensate for this, English has developed a small but useful number of devices for allocating appropriate prominence to rhematic material.

The chief devices are:

(1) inversion accompanied by initial 'there' — *there are many interesting mysteries in the world of nature;*
(2) inversion not accompanied by initial 'there' — *behind the government's press-releases lies a very different story;*
(3) double inversion for emphasising the subject — *included in the text is a long excursus on macro-economic theory;*
(4) clefting via the pronoun 'it' — *it was the Great Depression that originally helped Hitler to commence his journey to power;*
(5) passivisation — *the modern world is seriously threatened by rampant overpopulation;*
(6) pseudo-clefting — *what this country needs is a totally new transport policy.*

The degree of difficulty encountered in accomplishing a good translation hence depends to a very considerable extent on the typological-cum-genealogical degree of affinity existing between the source and target languages.

More generally, the two questions that need to be asked about any translation prior to its creation are:

(1) What resources — such as clefting, extrapositioning, fronting and inverting etc. — does the target language have with respect to the flexibility of information placement in sentences?
(2) Do the target language's resources need to be unduly strained for the purposes of the translation process or can a reasonably flowing target text be produced without excessive risk of confusion in the recipients' minds by reason of faulty or 'jerky' theme–rheme structuration?

During the translation process itself the translator must isolate the individual 'messages' which are normally reflected by grammatical sentences. Each individual message is a construct which needs to be segmented into its component parts, that is, into its atomic idea units. These units then need to be re-arrayed in the target language according to two fundamental but obvious criteria: the idea units need to be sequenced correctly and they need to somehow become environmentally imbued with the correct prominence, so that the illocutionary force of the target language rendering is maximally close to that of the original speech act. This is a very intricate task for a translator to perform, because the engineering of equivalence in matters of focus and tone units often involves a struggle and possibly a compromise.

The next issue to give some brief consideration to is the permissible variety of element orders (and their associated statistical frequencies and qualitative emphases) in the given target language. Then comes the task of achieving a good fit between the source text utterances and their rendition in the target language. The degree of fit hinges materially on three factors:

(1) replication in the target text of the source text's theme–rheme structure, with its associated perspectives and emphases;
(2) lack of infringement of any of the target language's grammatical and stylistic norms — this includes any innovation which attracts attention in its own right;
(3) reprojection in the target text of the source text's communicative value, message and thrust.

The actual dynamics and mechanics of utterance specification represent a conundrum which has been mulled over by many scholars down the years, the centuries even. The 'either–or' conundrum is concerned with whether logic or grammar should ultimately have primacy when it comes to formulating statements. It was noticed very early that logic, as a formal system, is universal, whereas the grammar confronting people is usually 'local' in the sense that it is perceived and learned via a particular national language rather than by reference to any other — foreign — human language generally familiar to an educated stratum in society. This does not gainsay what might, reasonably enough, be called the moral authority of the classical languages, plus, possibly, Hebrew and Sanskrit.

The first — in terms of age — notable surviving treatise on word order, entitled 'On the arrangement of words', comes to us from the pen of Dionysius of Halicarnassus in Asia Minor who was active circa 20BC, having previously migrated to and settled in Rome. According to Pumpjanskij, Dionysius surveyed the ideas broadcast by previous thinkers on the doctrine of parts of speech, noting that arraying them in groups produces the members of the syntactically constituent parts of sentences and that grouping these constituent parts finally produces sentences themselves. More interestingly, Dionysius voices the opinion that, although philosophers and rhetoricians had hitherto not paid any attention to word order, the placement of words nonetheless exercises a similar influence on speech as the utilisation of different materials in architecture or in weaving textiles — *nota bene* the close etymological, for us perhaps more metaphorical, relationship between 'textile' and 'text', the latter being something that has strands, fabric and is or should be 'woven' with great care and artistry. The almost explicit claim here — carrying the analogy over to language — is hence that although the materials — the clay — are first selected and deployed where needed only subsequently, basic meaning is created precisely by the final distribution pattern of this initial material.

Dionysius' treatise was subsequently held in high regard by the so-called Solitaires of the Port Royal school of grammarians in France, notably Arnault, Lancelot and Nicole. Their main aim was to produce an idealist philosophy of logical grammar, emphasising the 'universal' order of subject followed by predicate, to which linguistic communities — like their own — might well aspire but which they admittedly could not really find reflected to any significant degree — never mind overwhelmingly — in daily or even in learned discourse.

Over the last 300 years many other scholars — such as, to name only 19th and 20th century luminaries, Blinkenberg, Firbas, Halliday, Gabelentz, Ginneken, Jakobson, Jespersen, Marouzeau, Mathesius, Sechehaye, Weil — have devoted their efforts to the intricacies of word order. Empirical studies of word order in various languages demonstrated easily enough that the 'universal' order of subject followed by predicate was far from universal. Inversion was seen to be a regular pattern in discourse, both written and spoken. The trigger for inversion is the need felt, and acted on, for a psychological rather than a logical focus but the quest for stylistic adornment is also part of this. Pumpjanskij (1974) describes the situation thus:

> An excited and a calm person do not expound their thoughts in an identical manner. The former describes things by proceeding from his perceptions and feelings, the latter expresses an attitude to them. Both subject themselves to the law of maximum connectivity between ideas but they use different syntactic constructions. If thought represents a judgement, it is sufficient to have a command of the rules of grammar to express it. But feelings, just like a picture, demand a different word order. The various parts of a good picture are subordinated. First the main [physical] object appears, accompanied by the circumstances of time and place. The remaining parts follow according to the strength of their linkage with the main object and our eye perceives them in this natural order and has no difficulty in grasping the whole picture. The artist uses three methods: the drawing, the colour of the paints, and chiaroscuro. The writer also has three methods: the accuracy of syntactic constructions corresponds to the drawing, ornamented and figurative expression(s) correspond to the paints, word order corresponds to chiaroscuro'.

Shevjakova notes (see pp. 10–11 of her 1980 monograph) that among experts working on theme/rheme, new/old etc. there is no consensus about a whole series of important matters. Let us list the following dozen cruces:

(1) The terminology of logico-grammatical categories.
(2) The question of an 'extra-contextual subject'. Is it possible to assign theme or 'given' status to the subject of a thought, the 'given-ness' of which does not proceed from the situational or verbal content of previous sentences? What is the theme or 'given' in the first sentence of a narration, for example?
(3) Does English actually have a rheme-marking position and, if so, what is it: initial or final?
(4) How is the functional sentence perspective (FSP) of interrogative statements arrived at?
(5) Is there logical emphasis in all sentences or only in some?
(6) What is the actual rheme-marking role of articles?
(7) What is the theme–rheme structure of passive sentences in English and in sentences with various types of element order inversion?
(8) What is the theme–rheme structure of English sentences such as 'There's an interesting programme on TV'?

(9) What actually creates new information? Is it the rheme alone or the statement as a whole, representing the combination of theme and rheme?

(10) What are the precise theme–rheme problems caused by ellipsis?

(11) Should sentences, if their structure suggests it, be classifiable as di- or even poly-rhemic?

(12) Does intonation have a differential effect in different languages?

What, at first sight, might appear to be 'deviance' in an isolated sentence — as in the statement *And very interesting it was too!* — can usually be explained and justified on what might be called holistic grounds by reference to the larger context or even to 'existentiality'. Be that as it may, willingness to deliberately risk deviance of this sort — and of other sorts — is precisely the criterion which distinguishes good writers and speakers from poor writers and speakers. The same is equally true with respect to translators and interpreters. In this important connection, it is currently not clear what precise arrangements institutions concerned with the training of translators and interpreters are offering to their trainees in the area of theme–rheme analysis and synthesis skills. Is there any systematic instruction in this 'make-or-break' training area? And if there is, where are the textbooks and reference manuals associated with this endeavour? Such 'confrontative' study and reference literature is needed, of course, for discrete language 'pairings' and — woe betide! — for the different sub-language varieties used by members of the constantly evolving and self-reconfiguring myriad of discourse communities — à la Swales — in existence.

Pumpjanskij and Shevjakova have set an enviable precedent in their separate studies of the informational role of word order in Russian and English scientific and technical literature. Pumpjanskij, furthermore, has developed an analytical apparatus of eight clusters of directional logico-grammatical formulae for the translation from English into Russian of scientific (including medical) and technical literature. The minute analysis of source text utterances was felt to be the crux of the translators' task, to be followed by the relatively easier step of invoking the appropriate 'algorithm' in order to complete the discrete translation task in hand. Pumpjanskij's materials were conceived as priming material for the creation of working tools and skills for both expert and apprentice translators.

There is, in sum, no escape from the conclusion that the royal — but probably undoubtedly still stony — road to success for translators and interpreters must be to accord their highest priority to the resolution of all cruces appertaining to 'old' versus 'new'.

Bibliography

Agricola, E. *et al.* (1969) *Die deutsche Sprache. Vol. I and II.* Leipzig: Bibliographisches Institut.

Arnauld, A. and Lancelot, D. (1675) *Grammaire générale et raisonnée.* Amsterdam: Publisher unknown.

Arnauld, A. and Nicole, P. (1665) *La logique ou l'art de penser.* Paris: Publisher Unknown.

De Beaugrande, R. (1980) *Text, Discourse, Process.* London: Longman.

Brömser, B. (1982) *Funktionale Satzperspektive in Englischen.* Tübingen: Narr.

Daneš, F. (ed.) (1970) *Papers in Functional Sentence Perspective.* Mariánské Lázně: Publisher Unknown.

Firbas, J. (1992) *Functional Sentence Perspective in Written and Spoken Communication.* Cambridge: Cambridge University Press.

Givon, T. (1993) *English Grammar: A Function-Based Introduction, Vol. I & II.* Amsterdam: John Benjamins.

Halliday, M. A. K. (1985) *Introduction to Functional Grammar.* London: Arnold.

Halliday, M. A. K. and Martin, J. R. (1993) *Writing Science: Literacy and Discursive Power.* London: Falmer Press.

Heidolph, K. *et al.* (1984) *Grundzüge einer deutschen Grammatik.* Berlin: Akademie-Verlag.

Hoberg, U. (1981) *Die Wortstellung in der geschriebenen deutschen Gegenwartssprache.* Munich: Hueber.

Hoey, M. (1991) *Patterns of Lexis in Text.* Oxford: Oxford University Press.

Kovtunova, I. I. and Russkij, J. (1976) *Porjadok slov i aktual'noe chlenenie predlozhenija [Russian Word order and functional sentence perspective].* Moscow: Prosveshchenie.

Krylova, O. A. (1984) *Porjadok slov v russkom jazyke [Word order in Russian].* Moscow: Russkij Jazyk.

Lambrecht, K. (1994) *Information Structure and Sentence Form.* Cambridge: Cambridge University Press.

Leech, G. and Svartvik, J. (1975) *A Communicative Grammar of English.* London: Longman.

Łuszczyk, S. *et al.* (1981) *Gramatyka języka niemieckiego.* Warsaw: WSiP.

Malone, J. L. (1988) *The Science of Linguistics in the Art of Translation.* New York: SUNY.

Pumpjanskij, A. L. (1974) *Informacionnaja rol' porjadka slov v nauchnoj i tekhnicheskoj literature [The Informational Role of Word Order in Scientific and Technical Literature].* Moscow: Nauka.

Quirk, R. *et al.* (1985/1989) *A Comprehensive Grammar of the English Language.* London: Longman.

Shevjakova, V. E. (1976) *Aktual'noe chlenenie predlozhenia [Functional Sentence Perspective].* Moscow: Nauka.

Shevjakova, V. E. (1980), *Sovremennyj anglijskii jazyk — Porjadok slov, aktual'noe chlenenie, intonacija [Modern English — Word Order, FSP, Intonation].* Moscow: Nauka.

Swales, J. (1990) *Genre Analysis.* Cambridge: Cambridge University Press.

Thein, M. L. (1994) *Die informationelle Struktur im Englischen.* Tübingen: Niemeyer.

Tomlin, R. (1986) *Basic Word Order.* London: Croom Helm.

Uszkoreit, H. (1987), *Word Order and Constituent Structure in German*. Stanford: CSLI.

Van Dijk, T. (1977) *Text and Context: Explorations in the Semantics and Pragmatics of Discourse*. London: Longman.

Whitehall, H. (1958) *Structural Essentials of English*. London: Longman.

Chapter 7

Presupposition and Translation

PETER FAWCETT

The study of presupposition, of the background assumptions made in the
process of communication, can be a highly technical subject, involving
subtle (not to say arid) logical distinctions. Experts in these matters are
dreadfully keen to find out, for example, what kind of person would say
'The King of France is bald' when, as everybody knows, there is no such
person and so the presupposition of his existence cannot hold. Presupposition is not only a potentially complex object of study, but also one where
explanatory theories have been supported and attacked by example and
counter-example, with the 1970s seeing most of the battle. As Hickey (1993:
89) says, echoing Levinson (1983: 167), 'virtually everything written about
presupposition is challenged or contradicted by some authority on the
subject', a condition which can be said to hold true of much of pragmatics.
(For a brief discussion of the subject-matter of this chapter, see Fawcett 1997:
123–6.)

The literature on presupposition has been to some extent concerned with
matters of categorisation, with the question of whether the phenomenon is
amenable to a purely logico-semantic analysis arising out of stable,
word-internal meaning and grammatical relationships or whether it can
only be adequately dealt with by a pragmatic approach. In a semantic
analysis we would expect to be able to describe the phenomena involved
as constant, context-independent meanings which can be judged to be
either true or false, which can be assessed without reference to anything
other than the semantic features of the linguistic items which give rise to
presupposition, and which would not, in particular, require us to resort to
notions of variability of use in context. Since it can be demonstrated quite
easily that context can cancel presuppositions (a standard kind of example
here is 'Charlie didn't fail his driving test because he didn't even take it')
and that presuppositions in utterances may be neither true nor false but
simply not applicable (the 'King of France is bald' is a case in point), the

view generally taken now is that the phenomenon requires a pragmatic approach, in other words an approach that links linguistic utterances to the context of use and user. Even if we accept that presupposition is a part of pragmatics, there remains a further discussion as to whether or not presuppositions as pragmatic phenomena can be described purely in linguistic terms (conventional presuppositions) or whether they involve non-linguistic knowledge about how the world functions. Grundy (1995: 78) takes another classic example (He died before he made a will) as proof that world knowledge (what we can and cannot do after dying) combines with linguistic form to produce presuppositions. Restricting the discussion to the purely linguistic produces an approach which Levinson himself admits will seem narrow and disappointing to many people (1983: 168) and will also, it should be added, be of less interest to the subject of translation.

Clearly, presupposition is a complicated and, as Levinson admits, frequently sterile area of linguistics where many translators, being essentially practical people who may not be enamoured of logical notation, would be unwilling to tread, so let us begin with a simple example to make the concept clear before moving on to a brief description of the theory of presupposition and a discussion of how the phenomenon might be of interest to the subject of translation.

If I ask 'Have you got any children?', I am obviously presupposing that there is somebody there to answer (I won't say 'another person to answer' because I could, of course, be talking to myself). I am also presupposing that the somebody in question understands English. I am further presupposing rather less obvious things, such as the ability of the other person to respond (I'm not likely to ask the question of someone who is lying face down at the bottom of a swimming pool), and the willingness of the person to respond (I'm not likely to ask it of somebody who has just been fitted with a pair of concrete shoes and has other things on their mind). I am also presupposing their willingness or predisposition to answer questions of a personal nature.

I can derive the first and second of these presuppositions from the language used: the word 'you' implies the existence of another and the sentence is in English. It might also be possible to derive at least some elements of the other presuppositions from the language used since my utterance takes the form of a question, which presupposes answers. These are presuppositions which are triggered by the actual language used, in other words there are linguistic items which act as 'presupposition triggers'.

There is a long list of such triggers in language. It includes such things as:

- verbs of change of state (asking somebody to stop or start doing
  something presupposes that they were/were not doing it in the first
  place, just as telling somebody to 'get a life' presupposes that they
  lead a boring existence);
- iteratives (asking somebody if they have done something again
  presupposes they have done it before);
- temporal clauses (telling somebody 'after you've done that, do this'
  presupposes they will do 'that');
- definite descriptions (expressions which refer to entities supposed to
  exist in the real world).

However, at least some elements of the presuppositions in our sentence
'Have you got any children?' will be related not to the linguistic items which
go to make up the question but to the context of situation, and beyond that
to knowledge and culture: I am unlikely to ask the question if I am in
possession of information that would make it unwise or unwelcome. I will
not , for example, ask the question of somebody who is putting flowers on
a grave marked 'In loving memory of X, the only child of . . . ', and I won't,
more generally speaking, ask questions of a personal nature if I know my
interlocutor comes from a culture where people exercise discretion when
talking about themselves and others, as in the Japanese culture, where they
practise *enryo*, an attitude of personal reserve in social relationships
(Simeoni, 1993: 176). There are, of course, people who will do both of these
things, either because they are ignorant, insensitive, offensive and/or cruel
or because they get paid to do it (working against the grain of presupposition is one of the elements of comedy and satire).

In other words, presuppositions can also be triggered by discourse
elements other than the actual language used. This makes the phenomenon
more difficult to theorise from a linguistic point of view, in the same way
that semantics seemed initially difficult to theorise because it appeared to
cover phenomena not embraceable by purely linguistic concepts. However,
to omit these other sources of presupposition from a discussion on
translation would be to make the mistake of assuming that translation can
be treated as a purely linguistic act, an assumption once dominant but now
widely and rightly challenged, and to leave out of the discussion what are,
in fact, the most interesting elements from the point of view of translators.

If I pursue my dialogue about my interlocutor's children and take my
questioning one stage further to ask 'How often do you take your children
to the zoo?', I am making yet more presuppositions, most notably this time
that the person *has* children (the word 'your' is the give-away) and that the
person is in the *habit* of taking his or her children places (the words 'how

often' let this particular cat out of the bag, but note yet again how context can modify presuppositions since the question might fit into a sequence such as: 'You never take your children anywhere. How often do you take them to the zoo, for example? Never.'). Again I am making other presuppositions of a personal and cultural nature. I am probably assuming that taking children to public places is a thing that people do, and I am assuming that zoos are seen as a place of enjoyment and a fit place for impressionable young people (although a more information-rich context might yet again throw up entirely different presuppositions).

In fact, when one starts taking an utterance apart to find out just what presuppositions it contains, there turn out to be a lot of triggers, both linguistic and non-linguistic (contextual and cultural), which show that when we talk or write we make a very large number of presuppositions, a state of affairs which is inevitable because it allows for economy of communication.

There are several features which are claimed to define presuppositions and to delimit them from other forms of inference. The first is that they remain 'constant under negation' (Kiparsky & Kiparsky, 1971: 351). In other words, whether I say 'She loves her job' or 'She doesn't love her job' does not alter the presupposition that 'she' has a job (always assuming that the words 'she' and 'her' refer to the same person).

The second feature of presuppositions is that they are 'defeasible' (Levinson, 1983: 186), which means that they can be cancelled out by either the immediate linguistic context or by some wider context or mode of discourse. If we say 'The committee failed to reach a decision', it presupposes that they tried, but we can cancel out that presupposition if we add 'because they didn't even get round to discussing it'. Similarly, we can argue presupposition out of the way by a variant on the *reductio ad absurdum* mode of discourse: 'He didn't do it, and she didn't do it . . . In fact, nobody did it'.

A third feature of presuppositions according to Levinson (1983: 186) is that they are tied to particular aspects of the surface structure of an utterance, and it is on this basis that Karttunen (1973) has proposed to deal with what happens to presuppositions in complex sentences by classifying them as holes, plugs or filters, where the first allow presuppositions in a subordinate clause to apply to the whole sentence, the second restricts them only to the subordinate clause and the third either blocks or lets them through in specific technical conditions which are theoretically interesting but of no real importance from the point of view of translation.

There is a problem, however, with wanting presuppositions to be tied to surface structure. It would clearly be useful for the linguists if they were, because the problem would then be amenable to purely linguistic analysis, whereas otherwise a study of the subject would have to deal with disparate phenomena irreducible to propositional terms (Palmer, 1981: 172), but attempting to define items in the lexicon in such a way that the presuppositions to which they can give rise are a part of the word's meaning to be filtered in or out as appropriate, as in Gazdar's approach (1979), rather than a part of our internalised encyclopedia, could prove to be a daunting task and raises questions about the often narrow line between a dictionary and an encyclopedia. One reason for making the distinction between linguistic and non-linguistic presuppositions and for not excluding the latter from the discussion is also, as I stated earlier, that ultimately it is precisely the latter which are of most interest to translators. Presuppositions triggered by the kind of linguistic categories and structures listed here are unlikely to be affected in translation. Levinson (1983: 216) makes the point that, even in languages from very different families, the linguistic items which give rise to presuppositions seem to be precisely parallel.

If I have to translate a sentence like 'After the emergency meeting, NATO took prompt action', the presupposition that the committee met should come out in the translation as clearly as it does in the original, just as any translation of 'The boy's done it again' will retain the same presupposition, even if the target language has a different set of words when the phrase is being used idiomatically, as in the French *'il a encore fait des siennes'*. Similarly, translating a counterfactual such as 'If only I hadn't done that' (which presupposes that I did the thing in question) into a language which uses some other grammatical form (such as a subjunctive) will not destroy the presupposition. And the same largely holds true for the other linguistic triggers which give rise to presupposition. Taking any of the sentences used in any of the standard discussion of presupposition and translating them into another language will leave the presuppositions intact. 'She regrets drinking the beer', *'Elle regrette d'avoir bu la bière'*, *'Sie bedauert, daß sie das Bier getrunken hat'*, *'Ona cozhelaet, shto vypila pivo'* all presuppose the same thing. And the same holds true for the once classic but now rather dubious example of presupposition, 'When did you stop beating your wife?' / *'Quand avez-vous cessé de battre votre femme?'*, and so on. Even where languages do not have the same linguistic means (stress, most notably), there will be some structure (cleft constructions, for example) which will convey the presuppositions. Thus, the use of the French conditional and the German subjunctive to make allegations will correspond to other presuppositional trigger forms in other languages.

There are occasionally situations when this does not work, however. A trigger such as the 're-' morpheme does not always serve to indicate repetition of an act, as in the French *'La Résistance française réunit des hommes et des femmes'*, where the verb *'réunir'* does not mean 'to bring back together', presupposing a previous union, but simply 'to bring together'. This is clear from the context of the sentence but that does not prevent student translators from producing a literal and therefore wrong translation. And there are cases where the presupposition disappears or becomes retrievable by other means because the target language uses a different collocation. The 're-' morpheme again provides an example: the French expression *'pour reprendre le terme des experts'* conveys the conventional presupposition associated with 're-', whereas the English translation equivalent ('to use the experts' terminology') does not.

This area of collocation or selection restriction, the semantic rules which allow words to cohabit with some but not others, is one of the main situations in which linguistically triggered presuppositions may not survive, although Palmer (1981: 170) is unhappy at the idea of including selection restrictional meaning under the heading of presupposition, unlike Leech (1981: 286), who admits that the kind of information imparted in such cases may not be 'earth-shatteringly novel' but is still *bona fide* presupposition. Similarly, if, as some experts claim, connotational meaning can be included under the heading of presupposition, then cross-language transfer may well have the results of destroying that kind of presuppositional meaning on a large scale, but this is an area where much more research is needed, especially since there is still no universally accepted definition of what constitutes connotational meaning.

Nida's famous example (1969: 4) of 'white as snow' being translated as 'white as the feathers of' whatever bird happens to be readily accessible in the target culture lies at the boundary between connotational presuppositions of 'good/bad' etc. and the presuppositions associated with definite descriptions, which probably form the vast bulk of problems a translator is called on to deal with, and which take the problem of presuppositional meaning across the border between lexicon and encyclopedia.

Outside of a restricted geographical area, few people will be able to make any sense whatsoever of the sentence 'We need Mohács', with the definite description of the proper noun, because they do not share the cultural knowledge presupposed by the author. It is for that reason that the English translator wrote 'We need defeat' instead (Radó, 1979: 191), even though there is considerable loss in the translation.

Similarly, a literal translation of *A force de voir des Budapest sur nos écrans de télévision* [By dint of seeing Budapests on our television screens] can safely carry the presuppositions about television ownership, viewing habits and the existence of a place called Budapest, but will overlook the fact that most of those reading it are unlikely to know without research what Budapest symbolises in this particular case, just as the student who produced the translation 'He "dies without a sound" like Alfred de Vigny's wolf' was daringly presupposing a fair cultural baggage on the part of the reader: who was Alfred de Vigny and what exactly was his relationship with wolves (not to mention the question of why and how the wolf died and why part of the sentence is in quotation marks)? Such pragmatic problems assume increased acuity when the text to be translated includes deictic references to 'we' and 'us' — '*Wir Deutschen haben immer geglaubt*', '*Notre attitude en tant que Français*' — which presuppose an involvement which the target-language reader will probably not have or feel.

Very few texts will not be affected by this kind of presupposition, which is perhaps best handled by the concept put forward in German translation theory, by people like Reiß, Vermeer and Nord, of a text as an '*Information-sangebot*', an economics-based viewpoint which sees a text as a supply of information for which there is presumed to be a demand. The point of presupposition is that you save time by not supplying information for which there is no demand, since you believe it to be shared. This approach also covers situations in which knowledge which could have been presupposed is made explicit because the situation demands it, as well as the linguistic act of provocation in which the speaker unilaterally assigns presuppositional status to knowledge in an act of power over the listener. We need presupposition, of course, because without it we would not get out of the house in the morning, but it poses acute problems in translation. Most Hungarians do not have to be told that Mohács was the site of a military defeat, just as most French people do not have to be told about a certain minor difficulty at Alésia. A writer in these languages can call up powerful complexes of knowledge and feeling very economically. Transfer these to another culture, however, and the presupposed supply of information may not be there. The problem then becomes one of assessing the likely state of affairs and the possible solutions, with each step of the way fraught with difficulties.

As a first question, we have to ask whether the translator shares the presupposed knowledge or not and, if not, how he or she is to find it. The answer to this question is not necessarily obvious, since so much presup-posed knowledge is not included in the reference books (how far would a person have to look to find the information needed to understand Vigny's wolf?). Nor are native informants always reliable, since they may not in the event possess the presupposed knowledge that the author of the original assumed them to have, a point made by a number of writers on translation theory in the argument against the 'equivalent effect' concept of translation. The present author once attempted to find the meaning of an unfindable acronym by telephoning the author of a book he was translating, only to find that he had himself long forgotten. Another related question is whether one actually agrees with Durieux when she says (1990: 671) that 'the translator must, in any event, possess the knowledge which the author presupposes his readers to have', even though a lot of translation is done without such knowledge. Does a translator need to know, for example, that the sentence '*Offrez-vous le luxe d'une journée beauté-calme-volupté*' may be intended to presuppose familiarity with the work of Baudelaire?

If we cannot be sure that the readership of the original possessed the presuppositions required to make sense of the text, then how can we begin to be sure to what extent the *target* audience is likely to share it? This is a difficult judgement to make except in specific instances when the translator can know with some precision just who will be reading the translation. If it is assumed that the presuppositions are *not* shared, that will lead to the need for a delicate balancing act. Either the translator will patronise the target audience by treating them as if they know nothing and lack the means to find out, or the translator leaves them in the dark by not supplying what is needed to make sense of the text in a situation where the target reader is unlikely to have the means or the inclination to pursue their own research.

If the target audience is assumed not to have access to the presuppositions which will enable them to understand what is being talked about and if the translator decides in consequence that they need to be told, then the next question becomes: what is the best way, in other words the optimal translation technique, to pass on the information with a minimum of disruption if at all possible. Katharina Reiß (1971: 79) would relate this to the type of text being translated, so that footnotes, for example, would not normally be used in the translation of literary texts in order to avoid the kind of frustration experienced by people attempting to read an annotated classic.

Sometimes, the presuppositional knowledge forming the background to a text may prove to be problematic, conveying, as it does, information of a 'sensitive' nature which may possibly even require suppression, or some other radical irruption into the text as a translation strategy. As a trivial example, take the word 'April' as a homophoric reference which may begin to pose problems if you have to translate the words of a popular song such as 'Though April showers May come your way, They bring the flowers That bloom in May' for a culture where April presupposes anything but rain. In cases like this, it is the expected function of the translation in the target culture which becomes paramount in deciding strategy.

As a non-trivial example take the case of the translation of an Inuit legend (Ireland 1989) in which the translator decided to translate a word meaning 'skins from seals less than a year old' as simply 'sealskins' because the seals in question were being killed for food and because the idea that the Inuit might kill and take the skins of baby seals would put them in a bad light with a Western audience which selectively sentimentalises the natural world. This is where the translator needs to know not just what presuppositional information may be *lacking* in the target culture, but what presuppositions *exist* in that culture which may 'proactively' influence the translation.

A case where the original text was altered for the target-language culture with rather less sinister motives is quoted by Ehrman (1993: 165) in relation to a translation of the theologian Paracelsus. The 16th century philosophies behind the argument were considered by the translator not to convey the intended presuppositions because the philosophy was no longer prevalent and so not known in the 20th century. In this case also, the translation technique used was one of omission rather than rewriting or annotating.

Even when the translator has identified possible problems of a presuppositional nature, they may still get the translation wrong; or they may decide that there is no problem but go ahead and make changes anyway. Thus, the economics textbook by Samuelson (one of the best known in the world) uses the image of a tennis ball and a wad of gum to make a point about economics: 'Like a tennis ball (and unlike a wad of gum), [economic growth] is likely to bounce back from the full-employment ceiling into a recession' (1970: 246–7). Presumably judging that 'wad of gum' was less obviously comprehensible (or perhaps an example of cultural imperialism) to nations for whom the substance was not a part of national identity, both the French and German translators decided to replace it, but they both got it wrong: neither the French object (ball of wool) (1972: 373) nor the German object (medicine ball) (1973: 328) display quite the same habit of sticking to the ceiling as does a wad of chewing gum.

In the same section, the translators had to deal with the cultural reference to 'policy makers in Washington'. The German version assumed, no doubt rightly, that 'die Wirtschaftspolitiker in Washington' would pose no problems of presupposed information, although one might wonder about the *effect* of the allusion in a textbook which, in every other respect, reads like a German original targeting a German audience. The French translator presumably also realised that the readership would have no problems with a literal translation, but thought either that the effect would not be right or wanted to combat cultural dominion and so omitted 'Washington' and inserted a specifically French allusion to 'the hero in René Clair's film *C'est arrivé demain'* (Samuelson, 1972: 374), which presupposes a different knowledge set.

Conclusion

Presupposition is a complex phenomenon for which there is still no widely accepted and adequate account, especially if the term is taken in the extended meaning of the word, but also even when the concept is taken in the restricted sense imposed by the linguists in their attempt to create an area in which there is some hope of bringing order. Ironically, however, from the point of translation it would seem that most of the phenomena delimited in this way are uninteresting because unproblematic, while the interesting elements are those which the linguists would like to put beyond the pale.

References

Durieux, C. (1990) La recherche documentaire en traduction technique: conditions nécessaires et suffisantes. *Meta* 35(4): 669–75.

Ehrman, J.F. (1993) Pragmatics and translation: the problem of presupposition. *Traduction, Terminologie, Rédaction* 6(1), 149–70.

Fawcett, P. (1997) *Translation and Language*. Manchester: St Jerome Press.

Gazdar, G. (1979) *Pragmatics: Implicature, Presupposition, and Logical Form*. New York: Academic Press.

Grundy, P. (1995) *Doing Pragmatics*. London: Edward Arnold.

Hickey, L. (1983) Presupposition under cross-examination. *International Journal for the Semiotics of Law* 6 (16): 89–109.

Ireland, J. (1989) Ideology, myth and the maintenance of cultural identity. *ELR Journal* 3, 95–136.

Karttunen, L. (1973) Presuppositions of compound sentences. *Linguistic Inquiry* 4, 169–93.

Kiparsky, P. and Kiparsky, C. (1971) Fact. In D. Steinberg and L. Jakobovits (eds) *Semantics* (pp. 345–69). Cambridge: Cambridge University Press.

Leech, G.N. (1981) *Semantics*. Harmondsworth: Penguin Books.

Leech, G.N. (1983) *Principles of Pragmatics*. Harlow: Longman.

Levinson, S. C. (1983) *Pragmatics*. Cambridge: Cambridge University Press.

Nida, E.A. and Taber, C.R. (1969) *The Theory and Practice of Translation*. Leiden: E.J. Brill.

Palmer, F.R. (1981) *Semantics* (2nd edn). Cambridge: Cambridge University Press.

Radó, G. (1979) Outline of a systematic translatology. *Babel* 25 (4): 187–96.

Reiss, K. (1971) Möglichkeiten und Grenzen der Übersetzungskritik. Munich: Max Hueber.

Samuelson, P.A. (1970) *Economics*, 8th edn, Vol.1. New York: McGraw Hill. Translated into French by G. Fain (1972) as *L'Economique: Introduction à l'analyse économique*. Paris: Armand Colin, and into German by U. Schlieper (1973) as *Volkswirtschaftslehre: Eine Einführung*. Cologne: Bund.

Simeoni, D. (1993) L'institution dans la langue: lexique et pensée d'État. *Traduction, Terminologie, Rédaction* 1(1), 171–202.

Chapter 8

Deictic Features and the Translator

BILL RICHARDSON

Pragmatics and Deixis

Deixis appears to be a universal feature of human communication (Kryk, 1990), linking utterances to the contexts in which they are produced via the three fundamental deictic dimensions, viz., the spatial ('Beethoven lived *here*'); the temporal ('They *went* to Paris) and the personal ('*I* love Jane'). Although there is great variety in the approaches adopted to analysing the theoretical underpinnings of this area of language study (see, for example, Rauh, 1983; Levinson, 1992; Jarvella and Klein, 1982; Green, 1995), deixis is generally interpreted as being a subcategory of reference (Nuyts, 1987), and one which, in the words of Levinson (1992: 55) 'straddles the semantics/pragmatics border'. Deixis is frequently treated as one of the core areas within pragmatics (Levinson, 1992; Nuyts, 1987; Parret *et al.*, 1980; Hickey, 1993); at the very least, in works on pragmatics, deictic notions will be implicit in discussions of context and language use, even if these are subsumed under headings other than deixis itself.

Thus, a consideration of deixis leads us to focus on the variety of ways in which texts interact with their contexts, both exophorically (in terms of referring to the features of the situation in which utterances are produced) and endophorically (i.e., with reference to features of the text within which the utterance is produced). This chapter is aimed at exploring such interactions and their relevance to the area of translation. The examples given are drawn from instances of translation between Spanish and English.

While deixis may be principally a pragmatic phenomenon, its relationship to translation can be perceived through at least four domains of language: the morphosyntactic, the semantic, the pragmatic and the discourse domains. For example, at the morphosyntactic level, deictic reference may, on occasion, give rise to changes in word class in translation (for instance, when a Spanish pronoun is rendered in English as a noun which has been mentioned previously in the text); at the semantic level, basic lexical distinctions between two languages, for example, can bring about differences in the patterns of expression of similar concepts, as is the case with the lexicalisation of expressions of motion in Spanish and English; pragmatic differences between languages can result in differences of usage, as, for instance, in the distinction between formal and familiar pronominal address patterns in languages such as French, German, Spanish etc., when this distinction does not exist in English; finally, at the level of discourse, the arrangements of features of the text which bear deictic information may need to be altered in the transition from one language to another: such is the case, for example, with the organisation of personal and spatial information conveyed in a business letter in Spanish and English respectively.

The area of deixis implicates all four of these domains to such an extent that separating one from the other is often impossible, and the mere fact that one is likely to encounter discussions of deixis in the literature on areas as diverse as semantics, sociolinguistics, discourse analysis or literary theory is an indication of how the notion of deixis can fuse different strands of linguistic inquiry in an attempt to achieve adequate explanations of how language functions. Such a catholic approach to deixis is the one adopted here, although the fundamental emphasis is pragmatic, in the sense that is implied by Verschueren's definition of the task of pragmatics as 'tracing the dynamic construction of meaning in language use' (Verschueren, 1995: 16). Such a definition highlights the importance of understanding the role of context, and deixis, which is concerned with the ways in which linguistic utterances point to their contexts, is a fundamental factor in that process.

Deictic Perspective

Following Verschueren, we may summarise the translator's task as being the creation of a linguistic representation in the target language (TL) of the construction of meaning achieved in a particular instance of use of the source language (SL). One consequence of this process is that the deictic perspective which pervades the TL text must be structured in such a way that it is deemed coherent by the TL reader.

At the most basic level, the macro-pragmatic features associated with the production of the text will mean that the spatio-temporal parameters implicit in that text must be made to cohere. In a translation, as in most written texts, prototypical indexical items such as *I, now* or *here* do not imply reference to a personal, temporal or spatial *origo* congruent with the reader's encounter with the text; there is, rather, a deictic projection made from the situation of production of the text to the reception of that text by the reader. Beyond this normal projection, however, in a translation, a transformation is required which will lift the message away from the SL deictic perspective and orient it in accordance with the deictic necessities of a TL text. At the most fundamental level, such a deictic transformation is frequently achieved by the facts of the extra-textual context: the TL reader is often aware that the text being encountered *is* a translation, that its provenance is 'foreign' to the culture of the language in which it is written. This need not necessarily be the case: many everyday texts (for example, the instruction leaflet accompanying a toy or a bottle of Tippex) are produced in several languages, and no particular relevance attaches to what the 'original' language of the text may have been; but, probably, the majority of texts are clearly the product of a certain culture and need to be adapted — through translation — for the culture in which they are intended to circulate. One basic level on which such adaptation occurs relates to the spatio-temporal deictic features of the text.

Many types of text, not just translations, can operate transpositions on the spatio-temporal characteristics of the messages they contain. For instance, a newspaper article written on day X may make implicit reference to a temporal *origo* which is day $X + 1$, so that temporal references to day X, made on day X, will be couched in terms of day $X - 1$, on the basis that it is on day $X + 1$ that the reader encounters the text: 'Yesterday, the Minister for Tourism announced . . . ', although, as Nord (1991: 64) points out, the strategy adopted for dealing with this task will vary from one culture to another. The translator may indeed need to make adjustments of this type to particular items that actually appear in the text, or may need to add to the text information which serves to contextualise it for the target reader. Thus, a phrase in a Spanish text such as *en este país* [in this country] may well refer unequivocally to Spain in an original text, but may need to be translated as 'in Spain' in a translation destined for a foreign readership. Even a reference such as '*el ministro Vargas*', however, may require more than mere translation to 'Minister Vargas' in English, since the allusion may not be clear without expansion to something like 'the Spanish Minister for Defence, Mr Vargas'. Clearly, not all texts require such adaptation: decisions about how much adaptation is needed, if any, will depend on a variety of factors, such as the purpose of the translation, the intended readership or the characteristics of the text being translated.

In a literary translation, there will often be a tendency to avoid such contextualisation: the reader may be expected to make the necessary imaginative leap and to understand allusions which the SL reader would understand. Such a translation, more literal and less 'communicative' (in the sense of being adapted to the TL reader's perspective) may be felt to convey something essential about the author's construal of his or her message and about the uniqueness of the 'world-view' which is being communicated. Even in non-literary translations, however, it may be the case that no explicit adjustments of this sort are made, an example being the everyday business situation where letters are being translated and where references to the spatial and temporal origins of the text are left intact. As was suggested earlier, it could be argued that, in these cases, the transposition is still occurring but is invisible: it is the very context of presentation of the translated discourse which achieves the adjustment of the deictic perspective. Often, indeed, it is the overt 'foreignness' of the resultant text in itself which signals the shift being made, and the macro-level pragmatic parameters of the source text (ST) are 'translated' by means of other macro-level pragmatic parameters at the point of reception of the target text (TT) (see Hatim: this volume). The difference may usefully be viewed as a difference in emphasis relating to the respective roles of the translator, on the one hand, and of the potential readers of the text, on the other. In the former case, the translator plays an active role in transposing the text, in making it amenable for the readers; in the latter, the readers play the more active role and perform the necessary transformations at the moment when they encounter the text.

Deixis and Re-Translation

Classic literary texts require re-translation for succeeding generations for reasons related to this phenomenon: the older translations themselves become outdated and can appear no less 'foreign' than the original text. In a contemporary, early 17th century, translation of *Don Quixote*, for instance (reprinted as Cervantes, 1923), the inn-keeper's wife expresses her pleasure at her husband's obsession with listening to tales of chivalry as in example (1a):

Example (1a)
I never have any quiet hour in my house but when thou art hearing those books, whereon thou art so besotted that then only dost thou forget to chide, which is thy ordinary exercise at other times. (Cervantes, 1923: 315)

Is the system of person deictic markers evidenced here, with second-person reference indicated by 'thou' and 'thy', a reflection of the patterns of 17th century Spanish or of 17th century English? The Spanish original reads as in Example (1):

Example (1)
nunca tengo buen rato en mi casa sino aquel que vos estáis escuchando
leer; que estáis tan embobado, que no os acordáis de reñir por entonces.
(Cervantes, 1964: 234)

Clearly, the mark of the 17th century is on this text, in particular in the
use of the verb-forms employed for addressing the inn-keeper (*estáis, os
acordáis*).

The following extract (1b) is from a twentieth century translation by J.M.
Cohen:

Example (1b)
I never get any peace in my house except when you're listening to the
reading. You're so fascinated then that you forget to scold for once.
(Cervantes, 1950: 278)

This translation is written in an English which is recognisably 'modern',
not just in terms of how it handles deictic relations but also in respect of
syntax, vocabulary etc. The very fact of its modernity is itself part of its
deictic quality: a language evolves over time, varies dialectally from place
to place and has different characteristics according to who the speaker/
writer and the intended hearer/reader are. Again, however, a projection
from one deictic context to another may be necessary or desirable: in the
case of literary texts, the author may vary the deictic perspective, so that
the temporal parameters of the work, for instance, may appear to place it
in a time frame which is not that of the period when it is written. Deliberate
archaisation, while uncommon, is not unheard of, so that a modern work
such as Antonio Buero Vallejo's play *Las meninas* (Buero Vallejo, 1985), set
during the life of the painter Diego Velázquez and written in 17th century
Spanish, would presumably be given a translation which employed
appropriate archaic English forms.

Each of the two Cervantes translations cited here is appropriate to the
time in which it is produced. The author of the 20th century translation (1b)
makes no attempt to approximate 17th century English on the grounds that
this would be contemporaneous with the Spanish in which the original
work was written. Rather, as Vladova (1993: 13) suggests, what readers
normally require of the translator is that the work be 'situated' temporally
for them by the maintenance of references in the text to archaic forms and
artefacts which evoke the atmosphere of the historical setting, but that
this should be done using the language of the period when the
translation is written, thus emphasising the outdatedness of these
references. Normally, therefore, a form of language which is contempo-

rary with the reader is used, in order to 'help the reader of the translation to experience a reception of the text that approximates the reception of the original as closely as possible', and archaisation should only be employed in translation when the original author writes in an archaic form (Vladova, 1993: 13).

Spatio-Temporal Location

The contextualisation of the three basic deictic dimensions of time, place and person can present a translation problem such as that presented by the use of the expression *'nuestra península'* [our peninsula] in a chapter on prehistory in a standard textbook on the history of Spain (Ubieto *et al.*, 1977: 4). It is worth pausing to consider what the possible translations of this phrase in such a context might be. The relevant chapter sets out the major phases in the prehistory of what is today called the Iberian Peninsula, and the paragraph in which this expression occurs deals with the locations in the peninsula where a type of prehistoric axe has been found. These locations include sites in Soria, Madrid and Lisbon. A literal translation of the sentence in which the phrase occurs would be:

Example (2a)
The Acheulian period has symmetrical axes, with more regular edges. On our peninsula, they have been found in Torralba (Soria), in the terraces of San Isidro (Madrid) and in the proximity of Lisbon.

The original paragraph reads as follows:

Example (2)
El *achelense* tiene hachas simétricas, con bordes más regulares. Aparecen en nuestra península en Torralba (Soria), en las terrazas de San Isidro (Madrid), y en las cercanías de Lisboa. (Ubieto *et al.*, 1977: 4)

A translation such as (2a) would not be unacceptable, but our attention is likely to be drawn to the use of the possessive: in the context of the detached tone employed in this academic text, we may find that its use here represents an unwarranted intrusion of an overly personal voice into the discourse. In English at least, the phrase seems more personalised than we would expect, especially as it occurs in a university-level text in a chapter which is dense with technical scientific fact and archaeological terminology. It is true that part of the explanation lies in the fact that there is, in general, a difference between Spanish and English usage in such instances: first person plural reference appears to be more common in Spanish academic writing than in the equivalent English register. Thus, references to *nosotros* [we] and to *nuestro* [our] are found more frequently in Spanish academic writing, a phenomenon probably associated with the less frequent use of passive voice forms in Spanish; first person plural references are considered to be modest references to the author in Spanish and are far less pompous than the use of the 'royal we' in English (Butt & Benjamin, 1994: 127).

Nonetheless, there is a further, more concrete, explanation for the use of *nuestra* here, and it relates to both the semantics and the pragmatics of the term. Consider that the most obvious alternative strategy for the author would be to deploy an expression such as *Península Ibérica* [Iberian Peninsula], given that such alternatives as 'in our country', 'in Spain' etc. would simply be inaccurate, since (1) the division of the peninsula into Spain and Portugal is irrelevant in the context of 150,000 years ago: and (2) the sites reported on include a location in what is now Portugal. In a sense, however, even the use of 'Iberian Peninsula' would be anachronistic: the peninsula did not become 'Iberian' until the arrival of the Iberians, over 100,000 years *after* the Neanderthal period being discussed in the paragraph we are considering; although we may decide that we are simply going to use the geographical term which is current in modern times for naming the peninsula, the effect of such a term in a sentence such as (2a) would be infelicitous, given that the interpolation of 'Iberian' in this sentence would set it in a context in which several archaeological terms are being employed (in this paragraph and in others occurring before and after this one).

The question is worth asking, however: to whom does the 'our' in 'our peninsula' refer? A semantic interpretation of the term would offer us two alternatives: an 'exclusive' interpretation would have it refer to 'those [Ubieto *et al.*] who are the authors of this book' (or, given the conventions of academic usage, 'the one of us — Ubieto himself, as it happens — who wrote this particular section'); an 'inclusive' reading would interpret it as referring to 'writer(s) + reader(s)'. Pragmatically, it can be said to contribute to the sense of a shared inheritance between writer and reader, i.e. to a kind of solidarity between writer and reader. But what if the reader is Portuguese, for example? Does the reference to 'our' include him/her, on the grounds that what is being discussed is archaeological findings in places that include Lisbon? This, however, would not sit easily with the fact that the volume in which the phrase occurs carries the title *Introducción a la historia de España*. On the other hand, readers from outside the Iberian Peninsula are presumably meant to feel a kind of pseudo-solidarity on their encounter with the term.

What this example suggests is that deixis in its fullest sense embraces more than the mere abstract 'locating' of an utterance or text within spatial, temporal or personal parameters. Here, we have not only the interplay of these three dimensions, but a hint of the possible ramifications that the use of this particular deictic has on the cultural, social or political levels. To state this another way, the fact of being 'located' according to the three basic deictic dimensions carries with it implications about a diverse range of aspects of being human and about the identity of participants in an act of discourse. It also relates, in an important way, to the very nature of the verbal interaction taking place. If we reduce deixis and deictic centring to a simplistic summary of the spatial, temporal and personal parameters as they relate to an *origo* which is neatly identifiable with the ego of the speaker/writer at the moment of utterance, we fail to do justice to the richness of experience related to those parameters. In a very real way, we are *where* we are: our multifaceted selves relate in different ways to different circumstances. As Jones (1995: 27) suggests, discussions of deixis have often emphasised the 'egocentric' aspects of the concept to the detriment of the social, as if a speaker (or writer), from a position of glorious isolation, imposed a set of reference points on his or her discourse, which the reader then has the task of decoding. A more adequate analysis would see the 'deictic field', not just as a shared spatio-temporal context, but as an area of common purpose between speaker and hearer, between writer and reader. The two share knowledge of the situation of the verbal interaction, of its purpose and context, so that the 'shared, situated 'business' of the communicants' (Jones, 1995: 41) contributes to the accomplishment of the communicative act. Thus, texts with different purposes display different deictic characteristics; as Hosen-feld *et al.* (1995: 419) point out, deixis is an area of language that is particularly sensitive to context, including the discourse genre in which it appears. Consider, for example, how markers of person deixis in a 'persuasive' text such as an advertisement differ from those used in a narrative text such as a novel, and how each of these would be different from, say, a formal business memorandum; in turn, all of this would vary significantly from one culture to another. In each case, however, the selection of one rather than another option from the range of personal deictic terms (for example, the use of the informal mode of second person address using *tú* rather than the formal mode with *usted* in Spanish, or the use of 'we' rather than 'the company' etc.) is made as much on the basis of the writer's view of what the reader expects as on the basis of any characteristics we could attribute to the writer himself or herself. Thus, deictic perspective can best be viewed as the structuring of a *relationship* between writer and reader, a dynamic relationship between the multiple selves of each participant in the discourse.

Shifting Deictic Perspective Within Texts

The deictic perspective not only varies from text to text and from genre to genre but can also shift and alter over the course of the encounter between reader and text. What we are suggesting, then, is that, on a macro-pragmatic level, contextual features constrain the markers of deictic perspective in translation, but also, on a micro-pragmatic level, deictic perspective changes as the discourse progresses. This has been well demonstrated for narrative texts in the development of what has come to be called 'deictic shift theory' (see Duchan *et al.*, 1995; Zubin & Hewitt, 1995; Segal, 1995), where the aim is to develop a cognitive science perspective on (mainly fictional) narrative. In the approach adopted by these authors, the existence of a dual perspective is posited for narrative, viz. a 'focalising perspective' or origin which is a shifting localisation in time, space and person from which the story is exposed to the reader, and a 'focalised perspective' or content which is the objective of the focalising perspective as it moves along its spatial, temporal and personal coordinates through the story world (Zubin & Hewitt, 1995: 132). In other words, a mental model is constructed at the moment of the reader's reception of the text: 'the reader tends to witness most events as they seem to happen [. . .] The events tend to occur within the mental model at the active space–time location to which the reader has been directed by the syntax and semantics of the text' (Segal, 1995: 17).

What the speaker/writer does, then, is attempt to get a hearer/reader to 'build one, rather than another, mental representation of incoming information' (Payne, 1992: 2). The syntactic, semantic, cognitive and pragmatic domains are all relevant to how this is achieved, as all of these dimensions of the text impact upon the representation constructed by the reader. The translator's task in this regard can be illustrated for the case of Spanish–English translation by the following examples:

Ir/venir versus come/go

Although the usual translation for the Spanish verb *ir* is the English 'to go', and for the verb *venir* is 'to come', the way in which these verbs are used makes them sufficiently different from their English counterparts for *ir* to often be translated as 'come'. The perspective adopted by the Spanish speaker in relation to motion is such that, almost invariably, *venir* will only be used in reference to motion *towards* the speaker. Thus, an utterance such as (3), gleaned from the speech of a Spanish teenager, would have a literal translation along the lines of (3a), but would be more likely to have as an actual equivalent in English an utterance such as (3b):

Example 3
Ven a la fiesta. Estoy seguro que te divertirás si vas.
(a) Come to the party. I'm sure you'll enjoy yourself if you go.
(b) Come to the party. I'm sure you'll enjoy yourself if you come.

Now the over-extension in English of 'come/bring' to uses which might strictly be said to belong to the area of 'go/take' is a widely recognised phenomenon (see, for example, Abkarian 1983) and Indo-European languages other than English also show a tendency to over-extend the equivalent verbs. The point illustrated here, however, is that the degree to which such over-extension operates will vary from one language to another, with less of a tendency towards such over-extension in Spanish than in English. The translator has the task of ensuring that he or she avoids being influenced by the source text to the extent of adopting the pattern presented by it and employing such a pattern in the TL; in other words, the translator of (3) needs to produce (3b), not (3a).

The 'historical present'

The use of present tense forms to make reference to past events is a phenomenon common to both Spanish and English. The degree to which this device is employed, however, seems to vary from one language to the other, with Spanish showing a greater facility for employing it than English, i.e. it is likely to occur in a range of contexts and style levels in Spanish where the most likely English translation would employ a past verb form. On a pragmatic level, its use can be said to have the effect of making past events and past states seem more vivid and more 'real' by actualising them. This explanation is complemented by the account given by a semanticist such as King (1992), who speaks of the Spanish 'presente histórico' as causing a situation which belongs to the past in real time to be 'brought or 'pulled' into the present perspective of the speaker' (King, 1992: 22). Although the events may be past in the real world, they are 'simultane-ous to (included within) the speaker's perspective of the present, because tense as temporal perspective allows the speaker to associate realized events with the present and so to afford these events a status as accomplished fact: '[T]o include a past situation within the present perspective is simply the association of the occurrence in the past with the perspective of "fact" ' (King, 1992: 23). Thus, in the following simple example (4), a statement made in the present in Spanish alludes to a past reality, but the use of the present tense makes that reality more vivid or more 'actual' to the reader:

Example (4)
Iberia o Hispania [. . .] es un país de carácter muy desigual desde todos
los puntos de vista . . . (Temprano, 1988: 19)

A relatively literal translation, using the corresponding present tense in
English, would be:

Example (4a)
Iberia or Hispania [. . .] is a very varied country, from every point of
view . . .

But, as the names 'Iberia' and 'Hispania' suggest, the country being referred
to here is not modern Spain, but the Iberian Peninsula as it was thousands
of years ago; thus, normal English usage would prompt us to write:

Example (4b)
Iberia or Hispania [. . .] was a very varied country, from every point of
view . . .

Again, both Spanish and English allow the speaker/writer a choice of
perspective — the present historic is used in English also — but in many
cases where the present temporal perspective would appear in Spanish, the
English option, for reasons of style or appropriacy to the discourse context,
would be to favour a past perspective.

Entitativity and spatial concepts
There is a significant difference between the way movement is expressed
in Spanish and English respectively, and there are clear distinctions
observable also with regard to the related issue of how these two languages
establish the entitativity of spatial concepts. In Talmy's discussion of the
lexicalisation of movement in Spanish and English (Talmy, 1985), it is
suggested that the basic elements of the expression of movement are
motion, manner, path, direction and location. In a development of this
work, Slobin (1995) has shown how English tends to pay more attention to
the concepts of path and direction than Spanish. Slobin (1995: 11) offers the
following sentence (5) as typical of an English expression of movement,
with its relative richness of path description:

Example (5)
I . . . climbed up the path over the cliffs towards the rest of the people.
(du Maurier, 1938: 236)

The published Spanish translation (5a), influenced presumably by the
English original, reflects this concern with the details of trajectories to some

degree, although it does not contain the same number of path expressions as the English:

Example (5a)
Tomé el sendero que conducía al lugar donde estaba la gente.
['I took the path which led to the place where the people were.'] (du Maurier, 1959: 318)

Examination of original Spanish works, however, shows that nothing like the same degree of path elaboration occurs there, and Slobin concludes that 'Spanish writers do not seem to make full use of the devices that are available in their language' (Slobin, 1996: 12).

Thus, English has a greater facility for concatenating a series of statements about path and direction ('up the hall', 'along the corridor', 'down the stairs' etc.), while directionality in Spanish is normally expressed within the verb itself (*subir*, [to go up]; *entrar*, [to go in], etc.). Slobin and Bocaz (1988: 21) found that Spanish speakers tended to devote more effort to establishing static locations of objects and participants, and to the elaboration of circumstantial description, while English-speakers attend more to the elaboration of trajectories. On the basis of this evidence they suggest that 'there seem to be clear differences in the ways in which one's thoughts are mobilized, moment-by-moment, for purposes of speaking in one language or another' (Slobin & Bocaz, 1988: 6). Sebastián and Slobin (1994: 265) illustrate this contrast in the patterns of expression of motion with the following pair of utterances (from the speech of children who are native-speakers of Spanish and English respectively):

* He tips him over a cliff into the water.
* Lo tiró. Por suerte, abajo, estaba el río. El niño cayó en al agua.

As all these authors suggest, the choices made in the two languages respectively represent general trends, not absolute rules: more than one option is often available in each of the languages. The translator, therefore, may have to choose between following a pattern which is typical of Spanish, or re-arranging the spatial concepts to arrive at a pattern typical of English. As an illustration of this, let us compare how the movement of encroaching flames is expressed in the following two published translations (6a and 6b) of part of a sentence from J. L. Borges' story 'The Circular Ruins' (the original is given as 6):

Example (6)
el mago vio cernirse contra los muros el incendio concéntrico. (Borges, 1971: 68

(a) the wizard saw the concentric fire licking the walls. (Borges, 1993: 44)
(b) the magician saw the circling sheets of flame closing in on him. (Borges, 1973: 42)

We would suggest that there is a clear contrast here between the relatively 'static' image conveyed in (6a) and the more dynamic character of (6b). Not only does the latter provide more specification of path details than the former by employing a phrasal verb and two prepositions in the expression 'closing in on', but it also conveys a sense of movement and direction through the use of the participle 'circling'. The original Spanish (6) would appear to have influenced the author of (6a) towards a more explicit statement of the relatively static relationship between the fire and the walls. The author of (6b), on the other hand, eschews any reference to the walls themselves in this sentence (thereby omitting some scene-setting detail) and focuses instead on conveying more information on path and direction.

In a similar vein, the same pair of translations of this story offer an interesting contrast in their respective representations of the spatial concept contained in the Spanish word *recinto*. This word is difficult to translate but normally refers to 'premises' or 'space' usually perceived as enclosed or surrounded. In the context in which it occurs in the Borges story, it refers to an open area within a wood or forest where the 'ruins' referred to in the title are found. Again, there is a clear difference between the two translations as regards the perspective which is implicit in the respective versions. The original sentence and the translations read as in (7–7a–7b):

Example (7)
se arrastró . . . hasta el recinto circular. (Borges, 1971: 61)
(a) crawled . . . up to the circular enclosure. (Borges, 1993: 39)
(b) dragged himself . . . to the circular opening. (Borges, 1973: 37)

The spatial concept conveyed in (7a) implies the notion of a closed area, with the emphasis being on the limits set to that area by the surrounding forest; the concept in (7b), on the other hand, emphasises the notion of openness — an area which is a *clearing*, an area free of trees. The former (7a) is a more direct translation of (7): as suggested, the *recinto* notion normally implies spatial limits; the latter translation (7b), however, is probably a more acceptable translation in English.

This suggests that the translator's task, therefore, is to apprehend the message conveyed by the communication as it is construed in the original text, and to then re-create in the TL a similar message using a deictic perspective which is appropriate for the TL, avoiding (usually) the influence of the deictic patterns evident in the original.

Deictic Equivalence and Style

How are we to achieve this re-creation of the message contained in the ST? One answer to this question is the despairing one which suggests that true re-creation is impossible, that absolute equivalence cannot be achieved. Given that there will always be differences between the ways two languages operate — differences which are either inherent in the grammatical system or the consequence of stylistic preference — it is self-evident that a degree of 'miscommunication' will always take place in interlingual translation. But the fact is that translation (sometimes) succeeds, and the explanation of its success is the same as the explanation for the success of any communication. No two speakers of the *same* language bring to bear exactly the same cognitive, semantic, syntactic or discursive factors on an utterance in any one language which they supposedly 'share'. Some slippage is inevitable in any communicative act. The pragmaticist's classic response to this dilemma is to seek to achieve 'equivalent pragmatic effect', i.e. to make the translation 'do the same things' as the original text. But, of course, the purpose of the translation is frequently different from the purpose of the original, so that the context has changed and the characteristics of the participants and of other relevant aspects of the situation have also changed. As Robinson (1991:134) suggests, the success of translation defies logical analysis; language is too fluid, too slippery, for it to be effectively simplified or reduced.

What we can seek to do is to bear witness to the complexity of the factors involved and to the reality of the pragmatic — and deictic — factors which impinge on the text. Pierre Menard, the character in the Borges story 'Pierre Menard, author of Don Quixote', which George Steiner has called 'arguably . . . the most acute, most concentrated commentary anyone has offered on the business of translation' (Steiner, 1977: 70), recreates (or translates) *Don Quixote* by *creating it for the first time*: he imbues himself with knowledge of the historical period Cervantes lived in, and develops sensibilities appropriate to that time, to such an extent that the words he produces are identical to those of Cervantes. Borges' tongue-in-cheek comment, however, is that the *effect* (of the identical words) is different from the effect achieved by the Cervantes text, because the production of those words in the twentieth century conveys a series of ideas which are revolutionary to the 20th-century mind. The change described in this fiction is a change of deictic perspective; at a fundamental level, it is not unlike the shift in 'meaning' that occurs when the word 'now' is pronounced once and then pronounced again five seconds later. In line with deconstructionist approaches to text (cf. Tabakowska, 1993: 15) we can adopt the view that the meaning of the text, like the meaning of the word 'now', is instantiated at the moment of its reception by the reader, at which point the text enters into a complex network of relationships with other acts and entities (and other texts, and parts of texts) which contribute to the realisation of its meaning.

Such relationships are neither static nor merely physical: they exist as factors influencing the mental act that occurs when the text is read; they are fluid and dynamic, in the sense that the reader of the translation, like the reader of the original, is actively taking meanings on board and altering and adjusting interpretations of messages as these unfold. The reader, then, is constructing a 'world' in which the text will live; rather, a diffuse *set* of worlds emerges as congruent with the perspective adopted by the author's voice in the test. A Spanish text triggers relationships to a 'Spanish' world; a translation of a Spanish text triggers similar, but by no means identical, connections; a text on taxation or biology evokes connections with the relevant 'worlds' of economics or science that provide a context in which their meaning is fully realised. As Werth (1995) points out, such worlds exist as part of the real external world (for example, what we refer to in everyday speech as 'the world of high finance'), but are as much a product of our mental processes as part of that physical world. Werth defines 'world' as 'a conceptual domain representing a state of affairs' (Werth, 1995: 78). Deixis, in this view, is itself a mental construct; it 'defines the conceptual space appropriate for the processing of a particular discourse' (Werth, 1995: 79).

In translating from Spanish to English, then, we first apprehend the context-dependent conceptual space of the original Spanish text, as it relates to a Spanish 'world-view' and to a set of 'worlds' associated with various textual parameters such as text-genre, sublanguage, field of discourse etc.; we then initiate the process of constructing an English-language text with its attendant world-view and its relations to another set of 'worlds' which we deem to be equivalent to those of the original.

The new conceptual space created in the course of translation is necessarily different from that of the original but must somehow contribute to the achievement of 'equivalence' in the text. Some of the decisions made by the translator with regard to deictic features will be of an elementary nature and relatively uncomplicated, as we have seen; others, however, are quite subtle and affect precisely those qualities in the text which help to give the text an identity as a 'Spanish' or 'English' text. Thus, although the selection of appropriate deictic terms — choosing the right pronoun or the right tense, for example — may frequently be a straightforward matter of drawing on knowledge of the linguistic system of English, it is also often the case that the selection of the appropriate item is *not* a simple matter. In other words, deictic feature selection is often a *stylistic* decision rather than a *grammatical* one. The use of demonstratives in anaphoric reference is a case in point, as it represents a common problem in translating between various languages, even within language families. Note, for instance, how demonstratives and determiners are utilised differently in Spanish and English in the following sentences (8)–(10) and their translations (8a/b)–(10a/b), and how the choice of demonstrative can be less than straightforward, as the two alternative translations offered in each case illustrate:

Example (8)
Hay que movilizar las bases pulmonares a fin de que el aire alcance *los* alveolos libres de secreciones.
(a) The bases of the lungs must be moved so that the air can reach *the* alveoli which are free of secretions.
(b) The bases of the lungs must be moved so that the air can reach *those* alveoli which are free of secretions.

Example (9)
Del siglo v a 1800, Europa no consigue tener une población mayor de 180 millones. De 1800 a 1914 asciende a más de 460 millones. *El* brinco es único en la historia humana. (Ortega Gasset, 1956: 164)
(a) From the fifth century to the year 1800, Europe's population managed to reach only 180 millions. From 1800 to 1914 it rises to more than 460 millions. *The* jump is unique in human history.
(b) From the fifth century to the year 1800, Europe's population managed to reach only 180 millions. From 1800 to 1914 it rises to more than 460 millions. *This* jump is unique in human history.

Example (10)
El que solemos llamar país extranjero tiene que ser lejano, pero no demasiado, porque en *este* caso pasaría a ser un país exótico. (*El País*, June 1986.)
(a) What we call a foreign country has to be far away, but not too far away, because in *this* case it would be an exotic country.
(b) What we call a foreign country has to be far away, but not too far away, because in *that* case it would be an exotic country.

Thus, stylistic considerations are a significant factor in the translation of demonstratives and anaphoric referents, as they are in the deployment of metaphors for spatial representation and the representation of movement alluded to earlier. The practitioner of the art of translation is therefore operating with a series of factors which are bound up with the nature of linguistic representation in the mind. Varying the deictic perspective from language to language implies establishing a focus on the material being translated which is coherent with a world-view that the reader can identify with. In subtle but important ways, deixis and anaphora are aspects of that operation which touch on the very limits of translatability.

Notes

1. Some authors (e.g. Levison, 1992; Asher, 1993) discuss what they consider to be a separate category of deixis called 'social deixis', focused on the use of markers of social status in languages, especially in oriental languages such as Japanese, with its system of honorifics.
2. Laurence Venuti (1996) advocates having the style of the target text reflect the fact that the text *is* a translation and not an original (cf Hickey: this volume). The translator, in this view, has the task of valorising the language and culture of the original, as part of a democratic agenda, aimed at promoting an appreciation of other cultures in English and counteracting the ethnocentricity and cultural hegemony of English language and culture.
3. Even then, presumably, the peninsula was not 'Iberian', either in name or in reality. The Iberians occupied certain parts of the South and East of the peninsula during the First Millennium BC and shared possession of it with the Celts.
4. The complete paragraph in which this sentence occurs reads as follows:

   Iberia o Hispania, escribe don Julio Caro Baroja, es un país de carácter muy desigual desde todos los puntos de vista: los pueblos del Mediterráneo Oriental y Meridional establecen colonias desde muy antiguo en sus costas y grandes extensiones se hallan pobladas por grupos étnicos de distinto origen, con lengua, cultura e instituciones distintas. Unos viven muy aislados, como los del Norte; otros muy influidos por las grandes civilizaciones mediterráneas, como los del Sur y Levante. (Temprano, 1988: 19)

5. It is perhaps not surprising that the second alternative is a superior translation, given that Borges himself collaborated with N. T. di Giovanni on the work of translating the version published in Borges (1973).
6. The origin of this (anaphoric) usage of the Spanish definite article clearly relates to its etymological connection with the Latin demonstrative *ille*, from which it is derived (cf. Penny, 1991: 128).

References

Abkarian, G.G. (1983) Dialectic use of causative verbs: you can't 'take' it with you. *Applied Psycholinguistics*, 4, (1), 47–67.
Asher, R.E. (1993) *The Encyclopaedia of Language and Linguistics*. Oxford: Pergamon.
Borges, J.L. (1971) *Ficciones*. Madrid: Alianza.
Borges, J.L. (1973) *The Aleph and Other Stories 1933–1969*. London: Picador.
Borges, J.L. (1993) *Ficciones*. London: David Campbell.
Buero Vallejo, A. (1985) *Las meninas*. Madrid: Austral.

Butt, J. and Benjamin, C. (1994) *A New Reference Grammar of Modern Spanish* (2nd edn.) London: Edward Arnold.

Cervantes, M. de (1964) *El ingenioso hidalgo Don Quijote de la Mancha.* Madrid: Nacional.

Cervantes, M. de and Shelton, T. (trans.) (1923) *The History of Don Quixote of the Mancha.* London: Navarre Society (originally published 1612).

Cervantes, M. de and Cohen, J. M. (trans.) (1950) *Don Quixote.* Harmondsworth: Penguin.

Duchan, J.F., Bruder, G.A. and Hewitt, L.E. (eds) (1995) *Deixis in Narrative: a Cognitive Science Perspective* (pp. 129–155). Hillsdale, NJ: Lawrence Erlbaum.

Du Maurier, D. (1938) *Rebecca.* New York: The Modern Library.

Du Maurier, D. and Calleja, F. (trans.) (1959) *Rebecca.* Barcelona: Plaza & Janes.

Green, K. (ed.) (1995) *New Essays in Deixis: Discourse, Narrative, Literature.* Amsterdam: Rodopi.

Hosenfeld, C. , Duchan, J.F. and Higginbotham, J. (1995) Deixis in persuasive texts written by bilinguals of differing degrees of expertise. In J. F. Duchan *et al.* (eds) *Deixis in Narrative: A Cognitive Science Perspective* (pp. 407–20). Hillsdale, NJ: Lawrence Erlbaum.

Jarvella, R. J. and Klein, W. (eds) (1982) *Speech, Place and Action.* Chichester: John Wiley.

Jones, P.E. (1995) Philosophical and theoretical issues in the study of deixis: A critique of the standard account. In K. Green (ed.) (1995) *New Essays in Deixis.* Amsterdam: Rodopi.

King, L.D. (1992) *The Semantic Structure of Spanish: Meaning and Grammatical Form.* Amsterdam: John Benjamins.

Kryk, B. (1990) Deixis — a pragmatic universal? In J. Bechert *et al.* (eds) *Toward a Typology of European Languages.* Berlin: Mouton de Gruyter.

Levinson, S. (1992) *Pragmatics.* Cambridge: Cambridge University Press.

Nord, C. (1991) *Text Analysis in Translation: Theory, Methodology and Didactic Application of a Model for Translation-Oriented Text Analysis.* Amsterdam: Rodopi.

Nuyts, J. (1987) *A Comprehensive Bibliography of Pragmatics.* Amsterdam: John Benjamins.

Ortega y Gasset, J. (1956) *La rebelión de las masas.* Madrid: Revista de Occidente.

Parret, H. *et al.* (1980) *Le langage en contexte: études philosophiques et linguistiques de pragmatique.* Amsterdam: John Benjamins.

Payne, D. (ed.) (1992) *Pragmatics of Word Order Flexibility.* Amsterdam: John Benjamins.

Penny, R. (1991) *A History of the Spanish Language.* Cambridge: Cambridge University Press.

Rauh, G. (1983) *Essays on Deixis.* Tübingen: G. Narr.

Robinson, D. (1991) *The Translator's Turn.* Baltimore: Johns Hopkins University Press.

Sebastián, E. and Slobin, D. I. (1994) Development of linguistic forms: Spanish. In R.A. Berman and D. I. Slobin (eds) *Relating Events in Narrative: A Crosslinguistic Developmental Study.* Hillsdale, NJ: Lawrence Erlbaum.

Segal, E. M. (1995) Narrative comprehension and the role of deictic shift theory. In J.F. Duchan *et al.* (eds) *Deixis in Narrative: A Cognitive Science Perspective* (pp. 3–17). Hillsdale, NJ: Lawrence Erlbaum.

Slobin, D. I. (1996) Two ways to travel: Verbs of motion in English and Spanish. In M. Shibatani and S. A. Thompson (eds) *Grammatical Constructions: Their Form and Meaning* Oxford: Oxford University Press.

Slobin, D. I. and Bocaz, A. (1988) Learning to talk about movement through time and space: The development of narrative abilities in Spanish and English. *Lenguas Modernas*, 15, 5–24.

Steiner, G. (1977) *After Babel: Aspects of Language and Translation*. Oxford: Oxford University Press.

Tabakowska, E. (1993) *Cognitive Linguistics and the Poetics of Translation*. Tübingen: G. Verlag.

Talmy, L. (1985) Lexicalization patterns: Semantic structure in lexical forms. In T. Shopen (ed.) *Language Typology and Syntactic Description, Vol. III, Grammatical Categories and the Lexicon*. Cambridge: Cambridge University Press.

Temprano, E. (1988) *La selva de los tópicos*. Madrid: Mondadori.

Ubieto, A., Reglá, J., Jover, J.M. and Seco, C. (1977) *Introducción a la Historia de España*. Barcelona: Teide.

Venuti, L. (1996) Unity in diversity: International conference on translation studies, keynote address, Dublin City University, May 1996.

Verschueren, J. (1995) The pragmatic perspective. In J. Verschueren, J.O. Östman and J. Blommaert (eds) *Handbook of Pragmatics Manual*. Amsterdam: John Benjamins.

Vladova, I. (1993) Essential features and specific manifestation of historical distance in original texts and their translations. In P. Zlateva (ed.) *Translation as Social Action: Russian and Bulgarian Perspectives* (pp. 11–17). London: Routledge.

Werth, P. (1995) How to build a world (in less than six days, using only what's in your head). In K. Green (ed.) *New Essays in Deixis: Discourse, Narrative, Literature* (pp. 49–80). Amsterdam: Rodopi.

Zubin, D. A. and Hewitt, L. E. (1995) The deictic center: A theory of deixis in narrative. In J. F. Duchan *et al.* (eds) *Deixis in Narrative: a Cognitive Science Perspective* (pp. 129–55). Hillsdale, NJ: Lawrence Erlbaum.

Chapter 9

Verb Substitution and Predicate Reference

PALMA ZLATEVA

Analyses of translations from English into Bulgarian and Russian (and vice versa) suggest that some of their inadequacies result from insufficient understanding of the mechanism of substitution of whole utterances (or some of their parts in the text), or of referring to non-verbalised elements of the comunicative situation and/or the shared (background) knowledge of its participants. This substitution or reference is achieved by means of a set of pro-forms, to which belong language units, usually — though somewhat arbitrarily — classified into the various traditional parts of speech (or classes of words): pronouns (*this/that, it, which*), numerals (*one*), adverbs (*so, such, thus*), nouns and verbs with a very general meanings (*thing, fact, happening, deed, do, act*), as well as modals and auxiliaries. These linguistic items, mostly deictic in origin, have a peculiar sign character (Bloomfield, 1933; Peirce, 1960; Benveniste, 1966; Lyons, 1977; Paducheva, 1985 etc.). They comprise a system of imitants, of secondary linguistic signs, which reflect the existing system of full-notion words in that their constituents are shaped like them (i.e. like nouns and adjectives, like verbs and adverbs, etc.) and can function like them. These signs of signs, however, are only filled with meaning in a speech situation — they are 'brought to life' in the speech activity of generating an utterance (cf. Benveniste, 1974, quoted in Paducheva, 1985: 42), 'their only content is to serve as a means of identifying the referent [through its relation with the contexts of the speech act or its participants] and, having performed this function, they get off the stage' (Paducheva & Arutyunova, 1985: 15–22). In other words, the deictics, or gesture-words, are somewhat like the dummy symbols, imitative signs, models which reflect [all] the formally relevant features of the word signs, but not their notional meaning. This allows them to fluctuate in their various functions between the poles of the full-notion words and the so-called 'prop-words', or purely functional elements, following Halliday's 'cline of delicacy' (Halliday, 1961).

Deixis is a reflection in language of the physical act of *pointing*, done by people in the process of face-to-face communication. It can safely be assumed that even as far back as the pre-language stages of their development, human beings used pointing in order to include into the field of vision or attention of their interlocutors various objects, as well as certain of their characteristics such as *distance* (close/far), *size* (big/small), *number* (single/non-single), *quantity* (much/ little), etc. They could also express and communicate to others various *actions* (walking, hunting, crying etc.), and the *manner* in which they were performed (quickly/slowly etc.) by simply imitating/mimicking them, and even whole *situations*, by enacting them, thus combining various gestures of pointing with mimicking. All these various gestures, as well as imitating/mimicking in general, are peculiar types of pre-verbal signs which were, and still are, universally understood. With the appearance and the gradual development of verbal signs and human speech in general, the pointing gestures were also verbalised, and different sounds and graphic symbols were assigned to them in the different languages. Thus they lost their universal character in terms of understandability, although they fully preserved their original function of drawing the object of speech into the 'index field' (cf. Bühler, 1934), and even enriched the ways of achieving it, due to the various text functions with which they are loaded. All of these functions, however, have the invariant feature of binding an utterance to the concrete situation in which it is generated, of giving it 'its pragmatic meaning in a referential context of person, place and time' (Mey, 1994: 92).

So the basic function of deictics (also referred to as 'indexicals') or the word combinations of which they are (also referred to as 'indexical expressions') is to enable the speaker/author of a text to point to the object of his speech/text, in order to draw the attention of his/her interlocuter/reader to this object, to help them identify it and then keep it in their field of vision/attention for as long as it is necessary for him/her for the fulfilment of his/her communicative intention, hence for the fulfilment of the communicative function of this speech/text. Normally, the first phase of this process — the introduction of the object — is done by pointing at it by means of a deictical item, and then naming it with a full-notion lexeme (e.g. *this student, [tozi student/etot student]; that sea, [tova more/eto more]* etc.). This non-autonomous way of pointing has the highest degree of definiteness for both the speakers and their interlocuters, and is therefore the most reliable way of non-ambiguous identification of an object. (More on some of the pragmatic problems for the translator when rendering such expressions in an entirely different index field can be found in Richardson: this volume.)

In this chapter I would like to focus, in a somewhat more systematic way, on another textual function of deictics, that of pointing at the object of speech, not as an entity and in combination with its verbal sign in the text, but only at some of its features which are relevant grammatically (e.g., gender and number or tense), and which will prove to be sufficient for its correct identification in the text, thus *substituting* for its [repetitive] verbalisation. By means of this autonomous use of deictics we can refer to an object or situation which has already been mentioned in the text, or to an object or situation which has not been explicitly mentioned, but exists in the framework of the communication act, common to its participants or in their common index field.

There exists a genealogical connection between the deictics which function non-autonomously (i.e. definers, or determiners, accompanying the name), and those which function autonomously, substituting for it (the various pro-forms, or prop-words, or 'pronouns of laziness' etc.) A number of historians of language point to this connection and give convincing evidence in favour of it (cf. Galabov, 1946: 146; Velcheva, 1963: 130–1 etc.) In other words, the linguistic expression of definiteness and the mechanism of substitution are closely connected, and the elements by means of which they are achieved serve as the mortar which binds together the bricks of the 'full-notion' words, thus allowing the speakers to fulfil their communicative intention by building up [systems of] utterances, or texts, that are both cohesive (cf. Halliday & Hasan, 1976: 29–30) and coherent (cf. Tsui, 1991: 111), i.e. meaningful.

Linguists are more or less unanimous in their understanding of substitution as the use of grammatical elements with completely or partially lost/faded semantics in the position of meaningful elements of a sentence or utterance, for the purpose of achieving a complete structure. The structural function of substitution, however, is not the only function of these elements. They have another application, which was first mentioned by L. Bloomfield (1933) and which many contemporary scholars of this mechanism tend to everlook. This is the use of substitutes to refer to an object which has not been verbalised in the text. This function is characteristic not only of analytical languages such as English and Bulgarian but also of synthetic languages such as Russian. I think that we can distinguish at least two cases of such non-structural use of deictic elements:

Case 1

When the speaker, before formulating exactly and unambiguously what he has to say, expresses it as if in a nutshell, e.g.:

Example 1
Tol'ko ya, *eto* . . . Ne kuryu. Vot. Luchshe ne predlagaite.
Chahotka, chto li? — uchastlivo sprosil starshii.
Sportom zanimayus'. *Eto*. Legkaya atletika.
Govoril Artyom skverno i khmuro stesnyalsya. *Emu muchitel'no ne hvatalo slov, i spasitel'noe 'eto' zvuchalo v ego rechah chashche vsego ostal'nogo.*
(B. Vasil'ev)

This use of the Russian demonstrative *eto* [this] resembles cataphoric reference, but its motivation is pragmatic rather than structural, and the author of the text leaves no doubt about it, by stating explicitly the reason for the excessive use of *eto* in his character's speech. The English equivalent of such a pragmatic function would belong to a class of words different from the deictics or gesture-words, but no less ancient and 'pre-speech' in origin — the onomatopaeic *er*. Hence, a possible translation of this excerpt into English would be:[1]

'It's just that I, *er* . . . I don't smoke. So, you'd better not offer me [a cigarette].'
'How come? You haven't got tuberculosis, have you?' the sergeant asked compassionately.
'No, I am going in for sports. *Er* . . . Track and field events.'
Artyom was not a good speaker, and this made him somewhat grim and nervous. *Words kept escaping him, and the blessed 'er' came to his rescue more often than anything else.*

The Bulgarian pragmatic equivalent in similar situations is a deictic too, but an adverbial one: . . . az . . . Ne pusha . . . . . . Sportuvam. *Takova* . . . Leka atletika . . . etc.

Case 2

When the non-structural, pragmatic substitution is a short-cut for a possible lengthy explanation (cf. 'non-syntactic anaphora' in Gensler, 1977: 326), as in the following excerpt from M. Bulgakov's *White Guard*:

Example (2)
[Vasilisa is talking animatedly with the village girl Yavdoha about the price of the milk she is selling, taking his time so as to enjoy her company.]
S kem eto ty? — byistro shnyirnuv glazom vverh, sprosila supruga.

S Yavdohoi, — ravnodushno otvetil Vasilisa, — predstav' sebe, moloko segodnya pyat'desyat.

There is no verbalisation of the wife's jealous suspicions in her question, but the husband's answer comes as a prompt reaction to what was signalled rather than explicitly asked. The Bulgarian equivalent of this function will also be *takova*: Ti s kogo *takova* . . . , but in English we shall have to explicate the 'missing' element by using at least one predicate, e.g.

'Who are you talking with?', asked his wife, shooting a quick glance upwards.
'Oh, it's only Yavdoha,' Vasilisa answered with feigned indifference.
'Can you imagine, the price of milk's gone up to fifty today'.

Similar functions are characteristic of deictics in English too, and, in such cases it is the Bulgarian and Russian translators who sometimes resort to explication. For example:[2]

Example (3)
['Do you suppose Jesse could have been listening?' Maggie asked. . . .
'Jesse? At this hour? He's doing well if he's up before noon.']
Maggie didn't argue with *that*, although she could have. The fact was that Jesse was an early riser and anyhow he worked on Saturdays. (A. Tyler: 8)
(B) . . . Magi reshi da ne osporva *tazi yavna nespravedlivost*, makar che bi mogla. Vsushtnost Djesi ne obichashe da spi do kusno, pri tova v subota raboteshe.
(R) . . . Magi reshila ne sporit' s *nim*, hotya mogla byi, poskol'ko Djesi vsushtnosti lyubil rano vstavat', prichem po subotam rabotal.

As we can see, the Bulgarian translator has rendered *that*, referring to Maggie's husband's words, as *tazi yavna nespravedlivost* [this obvious injustice], thus interpreting and verbalising what Maggie left unsaid, on the basis of her following statement of the fact that her son was actually an early riser, which was quite contrary to what his father had said about him. The Russian translation changes the [antecedent of the] reference in the original from the previous statement (*that* > what her husband *had just said*), to its utterer (ne sporit' s nim > not to argue *with him*, i.e. with *her husband*). Compare also:

Example (4)
Yet another view explained the entire matter by regarding the stranger as a harmless lunatic. *That* had the advantage of accounting for everything straight away. (H. Wells: 143)

(B) Treti smyataha, che nepoznatiyat strada ot nyakakva tiha ludost. *Tova mnenie* imashe predimstvoto, che otvednazh obyasnyavashe vsichko. (p. 34)

(R) Drugie schitali, chto neznakomets stradaet tihim pomeshatel'stvom. *Etot vzglyad* imel to preimushtestvo, chto razom obyasnyal vse. (p. 95)

The English *that* refers to the essence of the view, i.e. to the attitude of *regarding the stranger as a harmless lunatic*, which *had the advantage of accounting for everything*. This attitude is rendered into Bulgarian and Russian by the verb in the main clause *smyataha/schitali* (considered), followed by a subclause stating the attitude — *che nepoznatiyat strada ot nyakakva ludost/chto neznakomets stradaet tihim pomeshatel'stvom* [that the stranger suffers from some kind of lunacy]. The reference in the translations is achieved by a non-autonomous use of the demonstrative, reintroducing the previous predication which has been summed up in a noun: *tova mnenie/etot vzglyad* [this opinion].

This type of pragmatic or situational, rather than structural, reference can also be achieved in Bulgarian by means of the symmetrical autonomous use of the demonstrative *tova* (this) in its various gender forms. For example:

Example (5)
'How many more subs can they throw at us now?'
'Perhaps as many as thirty additional boats, Admiral.'
'THIRTY?' Baker hadn't liked anything he'd been told for a week now. He especially didn't like this.' (T. Clancy: 163)

(B) — Oshte kolko podvodnitsi mogat da hvurlyat sreshtu nas sega?
— Veroyatno ne po-malko ot oshte triiset, Admirale.
— Triiset li?! Veche tsyala sedmitsa nito edna ot *novinite*, koito poluchavashe Beikar, ne mu beshe haresala. No *tazi* beshe osobeno nepriyatna.

The translator could have rendered *anything he'd been told* ... in exactly the same way, i.e. as *nishto, koeto mu byaha kazali*, and then preserved *tova* [this] in the next sentence. But such a use of *tova* would have coincided with the syntactic anaphoric use of tova [this/it] to refer to the immediately preceding predication, and would thus have changed the author's intention by narrowing the scope of his reference. This is the reason why the translator is more explicit and renders *anything he'd been told* as *nito edna ot novinite* [lit. none of the news], referring then by [the structural anaphoric] *tazi*[novina] through *novinite* in the preceding sentence, back to the contents of the last, and particularly nasty, piece of news — that perhaps as many as 30 additional subs may be thrown at Admiral Baker's fleet.

The Bulgarian demonstrative *tova* [this/that] can also function as a translational equivalent of other English substitutes, deictic in origin and performing syntactic prop-up functions, and/or referring to contextual situations or to compound predications from the preceding co-text. For example:

Example (6)
'Were you ever gay?' she asked, she thought now's the time to hit him with some of the big questions.
Mel laughed, he liked *it*. 'Now I'll ask you *one*,' he said. 'What had you rather: that I'm gay or that I'd rather drag your mother out of the supermarket some morning and fuck her.' (L. McMurtry: 154)

(B) — Ti bil li si nyakoga pedal? — popita momicheto, kato misleshe, che momentat e podhodyasht i mozhe da go tsapardosa s nyakoi ot golemite vaprosi.
Mel se razsmya — *tova* mu haresa.
— A sega az shte te popitam *neshto* — kaza toi. — Kakvo bi predpochela: da sam pedal, ili nyakoya sutrin da izmukna maika ti ot supermarketa i da ya nachukam?

By means of the structural element *it* the author refers to both the question itself and to the fact that the girl (whose mind Mel can read only too easily) has decided that the situation puts her in a position to ask such a question. This twofold reference is achieved in Bulgarian by *tova* — which would also have been a perfectly normal use of *that* instead of *it* in both as a structural element, and as a referring one in the English original as well.

Sometimes this twofold function of *it* (cf. Zlateva, 1980; 1981; 1987) both as a structural element (which is a more sophisticated use) and as an anaphoric expression (which is the more common one) can cause misunderstanding, as in:

Example (7)
'Why did you faint?' he said.
'I didn't. Somebody was making an aw'fly boring speech so I went to sleep.
'*It* was you,' he said.
'*What* was?'
'You were making the speech.' (P. Marshal, *The Raging Moon*, 1967)

The misunderstanding is caused by the misinterpretation of the purely syntactic function of the introductory *it* as an anaphoric substitute. This pragmatic effect has to be preserved in the translation. The Bulgarian structural equivalent of *it* is *to*, but it cannot be used for achieving the emphatic word order of the phrase in the original. A possible way of reproducing the pragmatic effect of the English text, though on a different basis, is by using *tova*, i.e. *tozi nyakoi* [this somebody]. Compare:

– Ti zashto pripadna? — popita go toi.
— Ne sam pripadal. Nyakoi iznasyashe uzhasno skuchna rech i me prispa.
— Ama *tova* beshe ti.
— Koe *tova*?
— Rechta iznasyashe ti.

From what we have quoted so far it becomes clear that the non-structural substitution and deictic reference, although a universal mechanism of speech, often calls for various translational transformations in interlanguage communication, where we have a different index field and discourse framework. Translators, however, sometimes resort to such transformations even when a symmetrical structure in the target language is perfectly plausible. It often happens in Bulgarian translations when rendering the relative *which* when it is not used as a simple connector but refers to a previous predication. This function is also characteristic of *koeto*, the Bulgarian structural equivalent of *which*. For example:

Example (8)
'Well, people will always need houses to live in!'— *which* turned out not to be true. Houses were not built, half-built houses stayed half-built, until kids pillaged them or the weather itself beat them down. (J.C. Oats: 18)
(B) "E, horata vinagi shte imat nuzhda ot dom!' A *tova* ne izleze istina. Kashti ne se stroyaha, stroyaha se napolovina, ostavaha si nedostroeni, dokato detsata gi razgrabvaha i dazhdovete gi razrushavaha. (p. 19)

Instead of introducing *tova* [this] in a new sentence, preceded by the conjunction *a* [but], the translator could have preserved the English way of referring to an opinion that proved to be wrong, namely, by *koeto* [which]. Compare: 'E, horata . . . !' — *koeto* ne izleze vyarno. A possible check about the necessity of introducing a change in the translation is to see whether the author herself could have used a different construction. In this particular instance it would have been perfectly possible for her to say '*And this* turned out not to be true', instead of *which* turned out not to be true. She probably made a point of preferring the second construction to the first, and the translator should have respected her choice. Thus she would have achieved the same pragmatic effect by preserving the structure of the original, without interfering with the syntactic norms of the target language.

Here is another example of a linear reference to a preceding predication by means of the relative pronoun *which* in combination with the verb substitute *do*:

Example (9)
And after the stranger had gone to bed, *which* he *did* about half past nine, Mr Hall went aggressively into the parlour . . . (H. G. Wells: 135).
(B) I kogato nepoznatiyat se pribra v stayata si, *koeto stana* kam devet i polovina, Hol vleze napereno v priemnata . . . (25)
(R) I posle togo kak postoyalets ushel v svoyu spal'nyu — *eto bylo* okolo poloviny desyatogo, — mister Holl s ves'ma vyzyvayushchim vidom voshel v gostinuyu . . . (89–90)

The Bulgarian translation preserves the structure of the original, changing only the substituting verb *did* to *stana* [happened], while the Russian translator refrains from using the functionally equivalent *chto sluchilos'/chto bylo/chto on sdelal*, and opts for a somewhat different wording, which is also possible though not required by some structural restrictions in the target language. Compare also:

Example (10)
It occurred to me that if the book were a success, *which* I couldn't doubt, this might smooth my way considerably in the literary world. (I. Murdoch: 64)
(B) Pomislih si, che ako knigata ima uspeh (v *koeto* ne se samnyavah), patyat mi kam literaturniya svyat shteshe da bade znachitelno izgladen. (p. 81)

Sometimes translational transformations when rendering *which* are necessary, and it is usually when the reference achieved by it is intentionally twofold, rather than purely syntactic. For example:

Example (11)
I think they felt that if they hung on to me they'd be in for an entertaining evening, of *which* they were loath to be cheated. (I. Murdoch: 89)
(B) Sigurno predpolagaha, che v moyata kompaniya shte prekarat zabavna vecher i v nikakav sluchai ne iskaha da propusnat *takav sluchai.* (p. 114)

The syntactic reference of the relative *which* is to the preceding noun group, namely *an entertaining evening*, but the pragmatic reference is broader and includes the whole situation, i.e. also the pre-condition of hanging on to the speaker, the fulfilment of which would have guaranteed them having an entertaining evening. The translator has achieved this pragmatic effect by referring to both the pre-condition and to its eventual result by the combination *takav sluchai* [such an event], which is perfectly plausible. If she had preserved the reference by means of the relative pronoun, it would have had to be in the form of the feminine *koyato*, in order to agree with the gender of the headword *vecher* in the preceding noun group. This would have narrowed the scope of the reference, for in Bulgarian we can only refer by *koeto* to whole predications if it is in the neuter form. Thus, the syntactic function would have been fulfilled at the expense of the pragmatic one.

Another deictic, used with a variety of functions, including that of referring to predications (states, situations), is *so*. *So* initially verbalises the speaker's gesture of showing the way something is, or is being done, i.e., is a secondary/shadow adverbial of manner. In its function of referring it is sometimes interchangeable with *this/that*, and its structural equivalent in Bulgarian is the deictic adverb *taka*, but in actual speech this equivalence is only applied very rarely, for example:

Example (12)
'You have put me in danger,' chuckled Socrates. 'Your enemies blame me for making you the way you are.'
'My friends blame you for not making me more *so*.' (J. Heller: 204)

The function of *so* here is to substitute for an unnamed quality or, rather, set of qualities, attributed to Alcibiades and describing him as a person at the moment this dialogue takes place: *the way you are* — in Bulgarian, *takav*, *[kakavto si]*. His enemies do not like him 'the way he is', whereas his friends do, and would like him to have these [unnamed] qualities to a greater extent, to be *'more* the way he is', more *so* — in Bulgarian, *po-takav*. Hence:

—Vragovete ti mi se sardyat, che sam te napravil *takav*.
— A priyatelite mi ti se sardyat, che ne si me napravil *po-takav*.

Of course, other translations are also possible, but they would be more wordy and would say more than the author had intended, so in this particular instance the adjectival deictic *takav* seems to be an adequate functional equivalent of *so*. Compare also:

Example (13)
[But in the absence of law in the state, there is still the law of honor. It is what nations live by, because] honor is nothing but adherence to a code, and those who agree on the code are a nation — they define themselves to be *so*. (W.Holland: 124)

(B) [...] chestta ne e nishto poveche ot pridarzhane kam nyakatak kod, i tezi, koito priemat tozi kod, sa natsiya — te se samoopredelyat kato *takava*.

(R) [...] chest' — eto prosto priderzhivanie k kakomu-to kodu i te lyudi, kotorye prinimayut etot kod, yavlyayutsya natsiei — oni definiruyut sebya kak *takovoi*.

So is often used in such referring functions in combination with verbs of saying, thinking, seeing etc., to substitute for a whole subordinate clause or for a whole presupposition which would specify a certain attitude or opinion. For example:

Example (14)
'Foundry work is heavy work, dirty work.'
'*So* I noticed.' (D. Lodge: 134)

(B) — Rabotata v leyarnata e tezhka i mrasna rabota.
— Zabelyazah *tova*.

(R) — Rabota v liteinoi — gryaznaya i tyazhelaya rabota.
— Ya *etogo* zametila.

Example (15)
'She would never do anything to hurt him.'
'*So* I thought.

(B) — Tya nikoga s nishto ne bi go naranila.
— *Taka* si i misleh.

(R) Ona by nikogda ne obidela ego.
Ya *tak* i dumal.

But:

Example (16)
'Will he be coming tonight?'
'I think so'

(B) — Toi shte doide li dovechera?
— Mislya, *che da*. [lit.: I think yes.]

(R) — On segodnya vecherom priidet?
— Dumayu, *da*.

As can be seen, Bulgarian and Russian vary from English in the units they use for achieving this type of reference. The prevailing equivalent of *so* can be said to be *taka/tak*, and it seems to be a regular correspondence in the rendering of the referring combinations *think so*, *notice so* and the elliptic *if so*. Compare also:

Example (17)
' . . . You never know, something may turn up later in the year. *If so*, perhaps you should go in for it. (D. Lodge: 64)
(B) — . . . Ne se znae, sled nyakoi i drug mesets mozhe neshto da izleze. *Ako stane taka*, tryabva da opitash.
(R) — . . . Mozhet, cherez nekotoroe vremya chto-nibud' i poyavit'sya. *Esli tak*, ty dolzhna poprobovat'.

Example (18)
'What's in *Izvestiya*?' Rollie wondered. 'Anybody getting into Raisa's knickers?'
'*If so*, they haven't reported it.' (W. Holland: 33)
(B) — Kakvo novo v *Izvesiya*? < . . . > Nyakoi da e svalyal gashtichkite na Raisa?
    — I da e *taka*, ne e otrazeno vav vestnika.
(R) — A chto tam novogo v 'Izvestii'? < . . . > Kto-nibud' zabiralsya v Raisinih trusikah?
    — Esli i *tak*, nikto ob etom ne pisal.

When used with referring function that do not imply comparison, *so* embodies the copula *be* as well, and is more or less synonymous with the anaphoric expression *this/that is so*. For example:

Example (19)
Neither would authorize approach to the next higher echelon until the entire proposal had been sifted, costs worked out, market potential mapped, specific recommendations made.
And rightly *so*. Otherwise hundreds of crack-pot schemes would clog the policymaking process. (A. Haily: 316)
(B) Nikoy ne bi otoriziral dostap do sledvashtata instantsiya, dokato ne ogleda vnimatelno predlozhenieto, ne izchisli razhodite, ne pretseni pazarniya mu potentsial i ne napravi neobhodimite preporaki.
    I *tova beshe* savsem razumno. V protiven sluchai protsesat na vzimane na strategicheski resheniya bi bil zadrusten ot stotitsi improvizatsii.
(R) Nikto by [. . .]. I *eto bylo* vpolne rezonno. Esli b ne *tak*, . . .

Both the Bulgarian and the Russian translations explicate the copula and introduce the demonstrative *tova/eto* [this] to refer to the process described in the preceding sentence. *Tak* figures in the Russian translation in the following sentence, as part of the equivalent of *otherwise*, in order to refer both to the process and to its rightness. (*Otherwise* can be paraphrased as *if it were not so*.)

So can also be rendered into Bulgarian and Russian by *sashto/tozhe* [lit. the same].

Example (20)
['Then why did she write you all those letters? She asked us to —
'She didn't. Can't you see that?] They were forgeries and we've been framed.
And *so's* she. (T.Sharpe: 199)
(B) [. . .] Te sa bili falshifitsirani, za da ni zlepostavyat. Neya *sashto*.
(R) [. . .] Ih poddelali, chtoby skomprometirovat' nas. Ee *tozhe*.

Sometimes *so . . . as*, is used in English to refer to a previous predication which denotes a state/quality, attributing the same state/quality to a new object of speech. There is again a cognitive process of comparison involved in this mechanism, and *the sameness* established, but only implied in the original, is explicated in the Bulgarian and Russian translations, as was the case with (18). Compare:

Example (21)
They were shaken by what had happened to their ship. *As* was he.
[Toland's mind kept coming back to the image of the four-inch-thick flight deck steel bent into the sky like cellophane, . . .] (T.Clancy: 285)
(B)   Moryatsite byaha potreseni ot sluchiloto se s tehniya korab.Toland *sashto*. [Umat mu neprekasnato se vrashtashe kam . . .]
(R)   Moryaki byli shokirovany tem, chto sluchilos' korablem. *On tozhe*. [V ego pamyat' to i delo vozvrashchalas' . . .]

So is often used in combination with verbs of saying like *say, tell, warn,* etc., which may at times be the antecedent of a further reference by the auxiliary *do*.

Example (22)
' . . . we'll make out we've lost the way.'
'Bit odd, considering we've got maps and compasses. . . . Still if you *say so*.'

'I *do*,' said Glodstone grimly and heaved himelf to his feet. (T. Sharpe: 94)

(B) — Shte se prestorim, che sme se izgubili.
— Nyama li da e stranno, pri tolkoz karti i kompasi. . . . Ama shtom *taka kazvate* . . .
— Da, *taka kazvam* — zayavi mrachno Glodston i se izpravi na kraka.

(R) — My budem vesti sebya, kak budto poteryali dorogi
— Pazve eto ni stranno, imeya vvidu, cho u nas planshety i compasy . . . Hotya, esli eto vy *tak govorite* . . .
— Da, ya imenno *tak govoryu* — hmuro skazal Glodston i podnyalsya na nogi.

Example (23)
'I assure you I feel her loss very keenly.'
'Probably. But if you will excuse my *saying so*, you don't sound as though you do.' (A. Christie: 121)

(B) — Uveryavam vi, useshtam mnogo silno neinata zaguba.
— Veroyatno. Shte me izvinite, che vi *go kazvam*, no s nishto ne *go* pokazvate.(103)

(R) — Ya vas uveryayu, mne ochen' ne hvataet ee.
— Vozmozhno. Vy uzh ne serdites', chto ya vam *eto govoryu*, no po vashemu golosu *etogo* nikak ne skazhesh'.

So in (22) refers to Glodstone's suggestion that they *make out they've lost the way* and, despite the boy's doubts whether this would be convincing, he emphatically confirms his words by *I do*. The first reference is achieved in Bulgarian and in Russian in exactly the same way — by *taka/tak* whereas the confirmation is rendered by repetition of the verb for *say*, rather than by substituting for it by an emphatic auxiliary, which is only characteristic of English. In (23) we have an instance of cataphoric reference by *so*, and the auxiliary refers not to the immediately preceding verb but to a predication from the words of the previous speaker. Both references in Bulgarian are effected by *go*, which is the accusative form of *to* [it], and in Russian they are done first by *eto*, and then by its case variant *etogo*.

So often performs its referring function in combination with the substituting verb *do*. For example:

Example (24)
'Get your hands on your heads and don't move'.
But the woman had already *done so*. She was off down the drive running as fast as she could. (T. Sharpe: 172)

(B) — Ratsete na glavite i nikakvo dvizhenie!

No zhenata veche se beshe *razdvizhila.*
Tya tichashe s vse sili nadolu po aleyata.
(R) — Ruki vverh i chtob nikto ne dvigalsya!
No zhenshtina uzhe *eto sdelala* — ona begala izo vseh sil vniz po
dorozhke.

Done so in the original refers to the verb *move* in the previous utterence.
The reference, however, becomes more clear after one reads the following
sentence, which specifies that the woman had not only moved — she was
running as fast as she could. The Bulgarian translation renders the order *don't
move* with the elliptic *nikakvo dvizhenie* [lit. no movement], and then
explicates the entecedent of *done so* by using the verb *se beshe razdvizhila* [had
already moved]. In Russian there is a structure parallel to the English one:
dvigalsya is substituted by *eto sdelala* [did this], and what she actually did
comes as an explanation, connected to the substituting phrase with a dash,
rather than separated from it in a following sentence.

Another combination of a deictic and the verb of most general meaning
do, often used in exactly the same way as *do so,* is *do this/that.* For example:

Example (25)
She stared back and he dropped his eyes. *That done,* she decided to have
a little read of her book. (M. Drabble: 20)

(B) Tya vtrenchi pogled v nego i toi navede ochi. *Kato* svarshi i *tova,*
Fransis reshi da prochete neshto ot knizhkata si. (p. 21)

The translator has rendered *that done* in Bulgarian by a symmetrical
substituting combination of the demonstrative *tova* [this] and the verb
svarshi [finished], which has a very general meaning and is sometimes used
as a synomym of *pravya* [do], but still has a very active semantic component
of physical doing. *That done* actually refers to both predications in the
previous sentence, so she probably decided that since the man dropped his
eyes after (and as a result of) Francis's staring, both actions are her own
doing, as the translation *kato svarshi i tova* [having finished that, too]
suggests. I would have preferred a somewhat different way of rendering
this into Bulgarian — either by *sled kato postigna tova* [after she accomplished
that], or by *sled kato tova stana* [after this happened], because the verb *varsha*
has a rather strong semantic component of physical activity, which is out
of place in this situation.

The verbal substitute *do* often performs its referring functions in
combination with *it.* For example:

Example (26)
She had married, she had given birth cheerfully, and produced it seemed cheerful children. Maybe she shouldn't have *done it*? (M. Drabble: 102)
(B) Beshe se omazhila, beshe razhdala bodro i beshe rodila, kakto i se struvashe, vedri detsa. Mozhe bi ne e tryabvalo? (p. 94)

By means of *done it* the author refers to the whole sequence of predications verbalised in the preceding sentence. The Bulgarian translator only renders the modality *ne e tryabvalo* [shouldn't have], without using any prop-expression in the position of the verb. That this position be filled is not required by any syntactic rules of structuring the Bulgarian text.

When *it* comes first in the combination with *do*, it may be the final stage in a longer chain of reference, involving other predicational references as well, for example:

Example (27)
'I'm not interested in what you think. I'm in charge and those are my orders.' And without waiting for an answer, Glodstone went back to the lookout. *That* ought to keep the stupid bastard quiet, he thought. *It did.* (T. Sharpe: 107)

That in the second sentence of the excerpt refers to Glodstone's words to Peregrine, and to some extent also to his following action of leaving the scene abruptly, without giving him a chance to react. *It* in the substituting combination, comprising a separate sentence, refers to *that*, while *did* refers to the predication that follows the deictic subject — *That ought to . . .* If we were to explicate the antecedent of *did*, however, we would have to use the verb in the predicative group in a different form, namely *it did keep* [*the stupid bastard quiet*], where *did* performs not only the grammatical function of marking a different tense for the verb, but also the pragmatic function of emphasising the correctness of Glodstone's assumption, expressed in the preceding sentence. So *did* does not simply fill a slot in the syntactic structure by representing the verb mechanically, it also performs the pragmatic functions of changing the time parameter of the index field and of confirming emphatically the truth value of the speaker's proposition. In Bulgarian and in Russian we do not have structural substitution, so we cannot render equivalently both functions of *it did* as used in (27). The Bulgarian and Russian translators can render either the realisation of the action as foreseen by the speaker and in the new time parameter, e.g. by *Taka i stana / Tak ono i vyshlo* [lit. it became so], or they can explicate the fact that the speaker proved right, e.g. by *i se okaza prav/I vyshel prav* [and he proved right].

The verb *do* can function as a substitute on its own too: in fact, due to its very general meaning of 'performing an action', it is the most widely used verb substitute in English. Even as a purely structural element or as an auxiliary verb, however, it almost always performs some pragmatic function of referring as well. It can be seen clearly in the following example, which illustrates a very interesting blending of the notional meaning of the verb and its structural functions:

Example (28)
'Oh, my God. Someone *do* something!'
Peregrine *did*. [. . .] He found the door and shot into the corridor. (T. Sharpe: 119)

The first *do* here is used in its notional meaning, whereas *did* in the second sentence is used to refer to it, and also in a way to signal the coming in the next sentence of the explicit statement of what it was that Peregrine actually *did*. As in the previous example, if we were to repeat the antecedent of *did*, the full version might be *Peregrine did do something*, i.e. it would contain *did* both as a tense-switching and as an emphatic marker. Again we have to apply transformations in the Bulgarian and Russian translations, opting for either repetition of the equivalents of the first *do* in the second sentence as well, e.g. *Peregrin napravi neshto/Peregrin chto-to sdelal* [Peregrine did something], or for something like *Peregrin reagira nezabavno/Peregrin srazu vypolnil pryzyv* [Peregrine reacted immediately/Peregrine immediately obeyed].

Unlike the grammatical meaning of marking a switch of tense of the antecedent verb, the emphatic pragmatic meaning of *do* when functioning as a substitute, though very common, is not an invariant part of the referring mechanism. Compare:

Example (29)
'Then I'll drink the toast alone,' Osch said. And *did*. (A. Haily: 100)
(B) — Togava sam shte vdigna tost, — kaza Osh. I *go napravi*
(R) — Togda ya sam vypyu, — skazal Osh. I *sdelal eto*.

The Bulgarian and the Russian translations refer back to the predication which renders *I'll drink the toast alone* by means of a combination of a deictic — *go/eto*, and a verb of most general meaning *napravi/sdelal*, semantically equivalent to *do*, which bears the new tense-marker for the switch of the time parameter in the narrative's index field. In other words, the Bulgarian and Russian translations apply the mechanism of reference by *do it/do that* which we discussed in connection with (25) and (26).

Peculiarities of the structural substitution by the auxiliary *do* are that: (a) its antecedent predicate need not immediately precede it; and (b) the auxiliary substitute can serve as a link in a referring sequence and can be referred to in its own right, thus fulfilling the pragmatic function of keeping the notional predicate in the field of the reader's attention, without repeating it. For example:

Example (30)
'Did you know before you came to see me that afternoon?' asks Annie Callendar. 'I can't remember,' says Howard. 'Of course you can remember,' says Annie, 'you *did*.' 'I *may have done*,' says Howard. (M.Bradbury: 229–30)
(B) 'Znaeshe li predi da doidesh da me vidish onzi den?' pita Ani Kalendar. 'Ne pomnya,' otgovarya Hauard. 'Pomnish, razbira se,' kazva Ani, *'znael si!' 'Mozhe i da sum znael,'* suglasyava se Hauard.
(R) — Ty znal [. . .] — Konechno pomnish', *znal!*— *Mozhet, i znal,* — [. . .]

In the Bulgarian and Russian translations the verb for *know* has to be repeated, since knowing something is not really an action, and it cannot be substituted by a verb of even the most general meaning like *pravya* or *vursha/delat'*, since these all have in their semantic structure the component of action or doing. *Znaya*, the Bulgarian equivalent of *know*, in its second use bears a different tense marker, and in its third use is accompanied by the modal *mozhe i da*, whereas the Russian *znal* is in the same form for the past tense — the only possible one in that language — in all its three applications in the Russian text.

Do is used in the structure of English texts to refer to verbs that have not even been uttered, for example:

Example (31)
'Obviously, the police have made a stupid mistake.'
'They ain't made a mistake.'
'My wife would never . . . '
Smokey cut in exasperately. 'Your wife *DID*. Will you get that through your head? And not only *did*, she's signed a confession.' (A. Haily: 396)
(B) — V politsiyata yavno sa napravili glupava greshka.
— Ne sa napravili greshka.
— Zhena mi nikoga ne bi . . .
— Zhena vi *go e napravila*, — prekusna go Smoki, izgubil tarpenie. — Molya vi, nabiite si tova v glavata! I ne samo *go e napravila*, ami e podpisala samopriznanie.

The unuttered verb, to which *did* refers both as a substitute and emphatically, is *steal*. The woman not only stole a bottle of perfume, but signed a confession for the police when caught in the act. Smokey, however, refrains from using this verb, for even in his exasperation he does not want to hurt the husband's feelings more than he can help. So he only emphatically confirms that she *did* what she did, and not only *did* she do it, but even signed a confession to that effect. Since structural substitution is not functional in Bulgarian syntax, as we have already mentioned, the translator has resorted to its pragmatic equivalent, using in place of *did* the verb *napravila* with the general meaning of *doing* in combination with the deictic *go* [it], and then repeating the same combination. The same approach would be acceptable in Russian too — *ona eto sdelala . . . i ne tol'ko sdelala* — for exactly the same reasons.

The next example illustrates an imperative use of the auxiliary *do* in an utterance, aiming to prevent one of the interlocutors from using a specific verb, and not, as is in (31), to substitute for a verb the speaker himself refrains from using. Compare:

Example (32)
['... lay off the feeling part.'
'Yes,' said Glodstone, not too sure if he'd been wise to raise the issue in the first place.] 'All the same ...'
'*Don't,*' said Botwyk menacingly.
['I was going to say ... "I know what you were going to say. And I've answered that one already.'] (T. Sharpe: 126)

The equivalent of this function in Bulgarian, both structural and pragmatic, would be that of the compound lexeme for forming the negative imperative *nedei*, which is fully equivalent to its English counterpart *don't* also in that it contains the same semantic components: the negative particle ne, and the verbal morpheme in the imperative form -*dei*, deriving from the old Bulgarian verb *delati* [do]. Compare also:

Example (33)
['where do you think you're going?'
'Back to Calais,' said Glodstone.
'So why are we on the road to Spain?']
'I just thought ...' said Glodstone, who was too exhausted *to*.
'From now on, *don't*,' said the Countess. 'Leave the brainwork to me.' (T. Sharpe: 182)

This example presents an interesting sequence of references to the predicate *think*, first by the infinitival particle *to*, then by *don't*, which is further in the utterance supplemented by the paraphrase *the brainwork*, synonymous with *the thinking* : *I just thought < too exhausted to [think] < don't [think] < leave the brainwork [thinking] to me*. The closest pragmatic approximation in Bulgarian to this chain of reference, taking into account the structural restrictions for formal syntactic substitution, would be: *Prosto si pomislih < tvarde iztoshten za tova [da misli] < nedei [da mislish] < ostavi umstveniya trud [misleneto] na men*. Or the slightly more explicit: *Prosto si pomislih < tvarde umoren za podobna deinost (too tired for such an activity) < nedei da mislish < ostavi tova na men* [leave that to me].

The verb that *do* refers to may be implied rather than explicitly mentioned in the text. For example:

Example (34)
I've been rotten bad influence. And worst of it, I *did it* on purpose. (E. O'Neil: 165
(B) Uzhasno sum ti povliyal. I nai-uzhasno ot vsichko e, che go *napravih* narochno. (p. 205)

I've been rotten bad influence implies that this influence has been *exerted*, so *do* refers to this implied activity of *exerting bad influence*. The Bulgarian translator has used the active verb *povliyal* to render *I've been [rotten bad] influence*, and then, in order to avoid repetition, refers to it in the next sentence by *napravih go* [I did it], which is a perfectly adequate reference. Compare also:

Example (35)
That gesture of hers with her hand was her habit, he supposed. Yet he had seen somebody else *do it* quite lately. (A. Christie: 237)
(B) Tova dvizhenie s rukata tryabva da i e navik. Savsem neotdavna be vidyal i nyakoi drug da *pravi sashtoto*. (p. 206)

If *the gesture . . . was her habit*, that implies that *she often did it*. So *do it* in the second sentence refers both to the gesture itself and to the act of doing it. *Pravi sashtoto* performs the same twofold reference in Bulgarian, since *sashtoto* [the same], being neuter, agrees with the Bulgarian rendering of gesture as *dvizhenie* [movement] — a noun in the neuter — and can also refer to the whole implied predication of *doing this gesture*. Compare also the function of *koyato* discussed in connection with (11).

The predication, or even a group of predications which can be derived from the context, can be referred to by means of an elliptical *do*-construction, represented by just the negative particle *not* and the *to* which signals the appearance of the *do*-infinitive, although *do* itself may not be verbalised. For example:

Example (36)
'he looked round with angry disappointment at his changed room — the position of everything a little altered and the whole place swept and clean and tidied. He condemned her, 'I told you *not to*'.
'I've only cleaned up, Pinkie.' (G. Green: 213)

Such a structural substitution is not possible in either Bulgarian or Russian, so in rendering *I told you not to* into these languages the translator would most probably have to supply a verb in place of the missing *do* in the referring expression, e.g. *Kazah ti da ne pipash nishto/Ya tebe govoril nichego ne trogat'* [I told you not to touch anything].

Very often the substituting function of *do* is combined with yet another pragmatic function — that of juxtaposition, often accompanied by emphasis as well.

Example (37)
Still, they pay well. Or *did*. (T. Sharpe: 169)
(B) Vse pak, te plashtat dobre. Ili pone *taka beshe* doskoro.
(R) No oni po krainei mere horosho platyat. Tochnee, *platili* do sih por.

Example (38)
The ethic of total possession of the woman you're married to runs very deep. Or *did*. (M. Bradbury: 25)
(B) Razbiraneto za totalna sobstvenost varhu zhenata, koyato e tvoya supruga, e zalegnalo mnogo dalboko. Ili po-tochno *beshe zalegnalo*.
(R) Korni etiki total'nogo pritezhaniya suprugi ee muzhem uhodyat ochen' gluboko. Tochnee, *uhodili*.

Example (39)
'I'll order you a pot of coffee,' I yelled in to him. 'It'll fix you up.'
But it *didn't*. He took it, but it didn't even take time to make itself at home. (R. P. Warren: 93–4)
(B) — Shte ti porucham kafe — izvikah az. — To shte te opravi.
    No *ne go opravi*. [. . .] (109)
(R) — Ya zakazhu tebe kofe, — kriknul ya, — ono tebya vzbodrit.
    No ono *ne vzbodrilo*. [. . .] (p. 107)

Example (40)
'I still don't remember.' Misha shook his head, but Arkadi knew he *did*.
(M. Smith: 264)
(B) — Vse oshte ne moga da si spomnya — poklati glava Misha, no
   Arkadi beshe siguren, che *si e spomnil*.
(R) — I vse zhe nikak ne vspomnyu — pokachal golovoi Misha, no
   Arkadi pochuvstvoval, chto na sammom dele on *vspomnil*.

As can be seen, the opposition of what used to be the case with what it was at the time of the narration in (37), (38), of an expected situation with the actual one at that same time in (39), and of a stated fact with the actual one in (40), are all achieved in Bulgarian and in Russian by repeating the verb from the first predication, marked for the changed time parameter. The difference has at times been enhanced lexically too, by adding the lexemes *po-tochno/tochnee* [more precisely], *pone* [at least] and the phrase *na samom dele* [in actual fact], or by rendering the more neuter verb *knew* by the emotionally stronger *beshe siguren* [was sure].

A reference by means of the substituting *do* can signal a change not only in the time parameter of the predicate, but in its modality, too. For example:

Example (41)
'As we all know,' said the Professor, 'in 1968 she discovered . . . ' and he proceeded , politely, to recap what they all ought to have known but undoubtedly *didn't*. (M. Drabble: 32)
(B) 'Kakto znaem vsichki, prodalzhavashe profesorat, v 1968 g. tya
   otkri . . . ' i prodalzhi uchtivo da rezyumira tova, koeto te bi tryabvalo
   da znayat, no bez samnenie *ne znaeha*.(31)

Example (42)
And yet anyone could tell you it must have some effect. It's obvious that it *does*. (M. Drabble: 99)
(B) A vseki mozhe da vi kazhe, che tova ne mozhe da ne dade
   otrazhenie. Yavno e, che *vliyae*. (p. 91)

As in (37)–(40), the previous examples we discussed, there is juxtaposition in the first of these two examples as well : something *ought to be known*, but *isn't known*. Rather than repeating the whole predication, the author of the English text just signals the change in its time and modal parameters by means of the substitute *did*. The Bulgarian translator has no choice but to repeat the verb, marked in its second use for the new time and modality: *bi tryabvalo da znayat . . . ne znaeha*.

Instead of repeating the verb in the second instance, the same translator uses for the new time and modality parameters a synonymous verb — *ne mozhe da ne dade otrazhenie . . . [yavno e, che] vliyae*. Similar choices will face a Russian translator.

Do can also be used to reject the modal component of the predication.

Example (43)
' . . . Lennie is right, I have to get out of here.'
'No, you *don't*,' he protested.
'Yes, I *do*.' (J. Collins: 176)
(B) — . . . Leni e prav — az tryabva da se mahna ot tuk.
— Ne, *ne tryabva./Ne e vyarno*.
— Da, *tryabva/Vyarno e*.
(R) — Leni prav — ya dolzhna vybrat'sya otsyuda.
— Net, *ne dolzhna*.
— Konechno, *dolzhna*.

Once again, as in almost all cases of structural substitution, Bulgarian and Russian have no syntactic alternative to repetition of the contrasting elements of the predication. Of course, as the Bulgarian translation suggests, it is also possible to reject the truth value of the whole proposition signalled by *do* by using *ne e vyarno* [it's not true]. In fact, this is the only choice of the translator in the next example, where the function of *didn't* is exactly that: to reject the truth value of what the previous speaker has said. Compare:

Example (44)
'How about YOU bein' a proper daughter? Runnin' away from school? Screwin' anything in pants. Goin' from — '
'I *didn't*,' she interrupted, furiously. 'And even if I *did*, so what?' (J. Collins: 62)
(B) — Ami ti shto za dashterya si? Byagash ot uchilishte. Shibash se s vsichko zhivo v pantaloni. Minavash ot —
— *Ne e vyarno!* — prekasna go tya, pobesnyala. — No dazhe *i da beshe*, kakvo ot tova?

As in the previous example, there is a chain of reference here: first the girl rejects the truth of what she has been accused of, then she adds that even if it *were* true, it wouldn't make much difference. The Bulgarian translator explicates the rejection by *ne e vyarno* [it isn't true], but at the next stage of reference drops the full-notion adverb *vyarno*, and represents the whole predication *beshe vyarno* by using just the auxiliary *beshe*.

Finally, I would like to mention one more type of referring substitution by the use of *did*, sometimes classified as idiomatic:

Example (45)
'Mind if I smoke?'
'*I'd rather you didn't,*' said Robyn. 'Could I have Radio Three on?'
'*I'd rather you didn't,*' said Wilcox. The rest of the journey passed in silence.
(D. Lodge: 207)
(B) — Mozhe li da pusha?
    — *Po-dobre nedeite* — kaza Robin. — Mozhe li da poslusham malko radio?
    — *Po-dobre nedeite* — kaza Uilkoks. Ostanalata chast ot patya izmina v malchanie.

Example (46)
'Let me photocopy them, it won't take a minute.'
'*I'd rather you didn't,* if you don't mind.' (Z. Tomin: 8)
(B) — Daite da gi fotokopiram, shte stane za nula vreme.
    — *Predpochitam da ne pravite tova,* ako nyamate nishto protiv.

In the first of the two examples, the translation is more idiomatic and contains the elliptic *nedeite,* standing for the whole compound predicates *nedeite da pushite* and *nedeite da slushate muzika,* so the translation preserves both the pragmatic and the structural peculiarity of the original (compare also (31).) The second translation is less idiomatic and renders more explicitly all the pragmatic presuppositions of the original: *predpochitam da ne pravite tova* [lit.: I prefer you not to do this].

Summary

There are various other ways of effecting predicate reference and verb substitution not just by means of the deictic elements *this/that, it, which, so/as* and by the [auxiliary] verb of most general meaning *do* and their Bulgarian and Russian functional equivalents, but also by means of the [copula] verb *be,* by means of the auxiliaries *have, shall, will,* the modals etc. I have gathered material and I am currently working on a comparative study of these with a view to translation. Here, I have just touched upon some of the problems that the very mechanism of such substitution and reference poses in the interlanguage and intercultural communication, achieved by translation and interpretation. Indeed, some of the more subtle peculiarities of this mechanism, for which there is a common cognitive basis in the various languages, can only be demonstrated and — hopefully — accounted for through interlanguage transformations. The intricacy and the scope of application of this mechanism are closely connected with the level of analyticism that the corresponding language has attained. In this respect, English as a typical analytical language, Bulgarian as a language that has gone the furthest of all of the Slavic languages in its development towards analyticism, and Russian as a typical synthetic language, present a good ground for comparison. As I have tried to show, the system of substitutes and the mechanism of structural substitution are best developed at English, and it is there that we witness the best conditions for economy of linguistic means of expression. This economy of expression, however, often requires much more effort in the process of decoding or understanding, since the scarcity of explicit overt markers often causes ambiguity and can only be compensated for by much background knowledge. For this reason, the translators often have to help their readers and supply for them part of the implied information from the original text. They achieve this by applying various translational transformations, namely:

- repeating the 'economized' items or chunks of the author's message, as in (22), (28), (30), (37), (38), (39), (40), (41);
- introducing synonymous expressions or paraphrases in place of other structural substitutes, as in (23), (33);
- textualising or explicating parts of the non-verbalised linguistic or pragmatic information, as in (2), (3), (4), (24), (36).

The detailed study of the different aspects of reference, which are at the basis of the creation of coherent and cohesive speech products, will also help the development of machine translation and the creation — for good or ill — of artificial intelligence. At this point, however, we who work in the field of translation studies will be happy to have aided, at least to some extent, the natural intelligence of those who are involved in the art of literary translation.

Notes

1.   The translations of all examples after which there are no specific page numbers quoted are mine.
2.   Examples preceded by (B) are in Bulgarian and by (R) are in Russian.

References

Benveniste, E. (1966) *Problèmes de linguistique générale*. Paris: Gallimard.
Bloomfield, L. (1933) *Language*. New York: Holt, Rinehart and Winston.
Bühler, K. (1934) *Sprachtheorie*. Jena: Fischer Verlag.
Galabov, I. (1946) Za chlena v balgarskiya ezik (About the article in Bulgarian). *Izvestiya na narodniya muzei v Burgas. Burgas*, t. 2 (quoted after B. Velcheva).
Gensler, O. (1977) Non-syntactic antecedents and frame semantics. Third Annual Meeting. Berkeley Linguistic Society: Berkeley.

Halliday, M.A.K. (1965) Categories in the theory of grammar. *Word* 17: 241–92.
Halliday, M.A.K. and Hasan. R. (1976) *Cohesion in English*. London: Longman.
Lyons, J. (1977) *Semantics*. Cambridge: Cambridge University Press.
Mey, J. (1994) *Pragmatics: An Introduction*. Oxford: Basil Blackwell.
Paducheva, E.V. (1985) *Vyskazyvanie i ego sootnesennost' s deistvitel'nostyu (The Utterance and Its Relation to Reality)*. Moskva: Nauka.
Paducheva, E.M. and Arutyunova, N. 1985, Istoki, problemy i kategorii pragmatiki (Sources, problems and categories of pragmatics). *Novoe v zarubezhnoi lingvistike XVI* (New Trends in Foreign Linguistics) (pp. 3–40). Moskva Izdatel'stvo inostrannoi literatury.
Peirce, C.S. (1960) *Collected Papers of C.S. Peirce. Vol. 5*. Cambridge, MA.
Tsui, A. (1991) Sequencing rules and coherence in discourse. *Journal of Pragmatics* 15 (2) 111–29.
Velcheva, B. (1963) Kam voprosa za izchezvaneto na trichlennata pokazatelna sistema v bulgarskiya ezik (Towards the problem of the diappearance of the three-member demonstrative system in Bulgarian). *Slavistichen sbornik* (pp. 129–41). Sofia: Izd. BAN.
Zlateva, P. (1980) Funktsii na leksemata TO v savremenniya bulgarski ezik (The functions of the lexeme TO in modern Bulgarian). In *Bulgarski ezik* [Sofia] (3: 3. 230–35).
Zlateva, P. (1981) Funktsionalni ekvivalenti na angliiskoto IT v bulgarskiya ezik 1 (Functional equivalents of the English IT in Bulgarian). In *Contrasive Linguistics,* [Sofia] 2: 39–48.
Zlateva, P. (1987) Leksiko-semanticheskie sredstva osushtestvleniya tsel'nosti teksta (Lexico-semantic means for the realization of textual coherence) — on material from English, Bulgarian and Russian. Dissertation paper. Moscow: Izdatel'stvo MGPIIYaz. im. M. Toreza.
Zlateva, P. (1997) Tekstovye funktsii angliiskoi leksemy *one* i ee bolgarskih i pusskih ekvivalentov *edin i odin* (The textual functions of *one* in English and its Bulgarian and Russian counterparts *edin* and *odin*). In *Contrastive Linguistics* [Sofia] 3–4 (in print).

Sources

M. Bradbury (1975) *The History Man*. London: Arrow Books.
M. Bulgakov: М. Булгаков (1989) *Белая гвардия* — Собрание сочинений в пяти томах т. 1. Москва: Художественная литература.
A. Christie (1969) *Selected Stories*. Moscow: Progress Publishers.
A. Кристи (1979) *Свидетелят на обвинението — Разкази*. София.
T. Clancy (1987) *Red Storm Rising*. New York: Berkley Books.
J. Collins (1986) *Lucky*. New York: Pocket Books.
M. Drabble (1975) *The Realms of Gold*. London: Penguin Books.
М. Драбъл (1983) *Средна възраст*. София: Народна култура.
A. Haily (1990) *Wheels*. New York: Pocket Books.
J. Heller (1988) *Picture This*. New York: Ballantine Books.
W. Holland (1992) *Moscow Twilight*. New York: Pocket Books.
D. Lodge (1991) *Nice Work*. London: Penguin Books
P. Marshall (1980) *The Raging Moon*. London: Penguin Books.

L. Mc Murtry (1988) *The Desert Rose*. New York: Pocket Books.
I. Murdoch (1963) *Under the Net*. London: Penguin Books.
А. Мърдък (1968) *Под мрежата*. София: Народна култура.
J.C. Oates (1986) *Them*. New York: Warner Books.
Дж. К. Оутс (1984) *Тях*. София: Народна култура.
E. O'Neil (1972) *The Long Day's Journey into Night*. In: *Three American Plays*. Moscow: Progress Publishers.
Ю. Нийл (1975) *Дългото пътуване на деня към нощта*. София: Библ. 'Театър'.
T. Sharpe (1983) *Vintage Stuff*. Pan Books.
M. Smith (1983) *Gorki Park*. New York: Ballantine Fiction.
A. Tyler (1989) *Breathing Lessons*. Berkley Books.
B. Vasil'ev: Б. Васильев (1985) *Завтра была война* — Современник, кн. 3. Москва
R.P. Warren (1979) *All the King's Men*. Moscow: Progress Publishers.
Р. П. Уорен (1980) *Вся королевская рать*. Москва: Художесвенная литература.
Р. П. Уорен (1982) *Цялото кралско войнство*. София: Народна култура.
H.G. Wells (1979) *The Invisible Man*. Moscow: Progress Publishers.
Х. Уелс (1979) *Кристалното яйце*. Варна: изд. Г. Бакалов
Г. Уелс (1983) *Избранное*. Москва: Книга.

Chapter 10

Discourse Connectives, Ellipsis and Markedness

IAN MASON

This chapter takes as its starting point the assumption that translating is an act of communication, involving texts as sets of mutually relevant intentions, in which users (including translators) pre-suppose, implicate and infer meaning. From this perspective, we propose to investigate (1) cases of ellipsis of junction (or suppressed connectives) as an interactive feature in French counter-argumentative texts; and (2) translators' responses for particular communicative purposes. Through a qualitative (rather than quantitative) analysis of data drawn from a corpus of examples, the study seeks to show the importance of markedness as a pragmatic variable in relaying meaning in translation and identifies reader-involvement and politeness as contextual effects to be relayed. Thus, the approach has implications which apply, beyond the specific issue of relaying adversative or concessive junction, to the perception and translation of source-text rhetorical purposes.

Explicit and Ellipted Junction

The counter-argumentative text format (or 'straw-man gambit') is a well established textual phenomenon in French, as it is in English. Intertextually, it is so deep-rooted that a *Certes* or an *Of course* serves as a reliable indicator of subsequent development of a text: a concession in argument, followed by an opposing view which is then argued with greater conviction. Text fragments (1) and (2) are characteristic examples.

Example (1)
Il faut *sans doute* tenir compte des traditions locales et des sensibilités nationales. Mais on ne saurait, au nom de ces considérations, revenir sur

une législation communautaire existante . . . (J.-P. Cot, *Eur. Parl.*, 14 February 1996)

Example (2)
Certes, une très forte majorité trouvent normal que les femmes accèdent désormais aux plus hautes fonctions et la plupart se sentent de l'ambition. *Mais* plus des deux-tiers estiment que les femmes peuvent s'épanouir en restant chez elles. (C. Mital, *L'Expansion*, November 1995)

The full text structures of counter-argumentation in French and English are identical and may be stated (following Hatim, 1987; 1991) as consisting of the following obligatory and (optional) elements:

- (Tone-setter)
- Thesis cited
- Opposition
- Substantiation
- (Conclusion)

Given the close resemblance in this respect of French and English (and other Western languages), it might be assumed that there is no particular problem involved in the translation of the counter-argumentative format and that, consequently, it is not an issue of concern to the translator.

While this structure constitutes the norm, however, another recognised phenomenon in French (and, for that matter, other languages) is a *departure from the norm*, in which the same structure occurs but the marker of opposition is ellipted, as in text fragments (3), (4) and (5) below.

Example (3)
C'est de la bonne administration. Gouverner consisterait à . . . (*Le Nouvel Economiste*, 20 October 1989)

Example (4)
Il pourrait donc paraître urgent de . . . transformer ainsi tout le système. Ce serait faire bon marché de l'importance des obstacles et de la faiblesse des ressources. (*Rapport Crozier sur l'évaluation des universités*, June 1990)

Example (5)
Daniel Bell avait prédit l'éclosion rapide d'une société post-industrielle. De là à voir les usines disparaître à l'horizon familier et les entreprises de services fleurir sur le terrain conquis, il n'y avait qu'un pas. Il n'est pas près d'être franchi. (P. Drouin, *Le Monde*, 21 August 1986)

The point about these examples is that, although they do not conform to the norm (cf. (1) and (2)), the occurrence of this ellipsis of junction is sufficiently frequent in French for it to be a recognisable text strategy. The markedness of the structure constitutes no problem for the French reader. In translation into English, on the other hand, straightforward transfer of the ellipsis may create problems of coherence for target-text readers and consequently, as will be shown, there is a tendency for translators to restore explicit junction.

For evidence of the relative incidence of this phenomenon, we may look at what has been said about junction in French and English in studies which view translating from a contrastive linguistic perspective. Is there a regularity of language behaviour involved here? Guillemin-Flescher (1981: 82–3), among others, suggests that there is, referring to a tendency in English towards explicit coordination of clauses and a preference in French for junction-less juxtaposition. Ballard (1995) notes that this general phenomenon is by no means universally accepted and quotes other studies (e.g. Delisle, 1980: 198) which suggest that juxtaposition is more characteristic of English and overt linkage more characteristic of French. He also notes, however, that quantitative empirical studies are few. In this respect, his own detailed distributional study of *and* and its translation into French charts new territory.

Apart from this, the main sources of empirical observation are Guillemin-Flescher (1981) and Chuquet and Paillard (1987; 1992). Their approach is based on Culioli's *théorie de l'énonciation*, applied contrastively to French and English. This approach

> by defining the types of markers and utterance choices at work in both languages, contributes to a contrastive analysis. This analysis in turn serves to throw light on the choices made intuitively in the transition from one language to the other and to guide translators in their work. (Chuquet & Paillard, 1992: 257; my translation)

Guillemin-Flescher (1981: 82) draws evidence from an extensive corpus of translations from English into French and from French into English to show, as mentioned earlier, that propositions which are coordinated in English are often juxtaposed without junction in French. The *explicitation du marqueur de disjonction* [adversative junction] in English is seen as one category within this general phenomenon, as in (6) and (7):

Example (6)
elle aperçut la vase. Elle n'y voulait pas croire.

She saw the mud, *but* would not believe her eyes . . . (Flaubert, *Madame Bovary*, quoted in Guillemin-Flescher, 1981: 189)

Example (7)
Je l'ai attendu pendant deux heures. Il n'est pas venu.
I waited for two hours *but* he didn't come. (Chuquet & Paillard, 1987: 150)

Gallagher (1995) provides ample further evidence of the contrast in French-to-English and English-to-French translations. Tracing the suppression of such connectors in French back to the 17th century, he distinguishes the adversative/temporal function (as in (7)) from the concession-in-argument function, citing as examples of the latter:

Example (8)
Certes tout homme est une totalisation qui se temporalise et rien ne peut lui arriver qui ne l'affecte, d'une façon ou d'une autre, dans toutes ses parties. L'essentiel est que, dans les sociétés intégrées, l'élément psychonévrotique, s'il existe, ne se prend jamais pour le but de l'artiste et moins encore comme la règle de son art. (J.-P. Sartre, cited in Gallagher, 1995: 210)

Example (9)
Un personnage? Oui, certes. La personne se révéla moins brillante. (A. Maurois, cited in Gallagher, 1995: 210)

Gallagher cites published German translations of these examples, reproduced here as (10) and (11), to show the need for explicit junction in that language.

Example (10)
Zwar ist jeder Mensch eine Totalisierung, die sich verzeitlicht, und nichts kann ihm passieren, was ihn nicht so oder so in allen seinen Teilen beeinträchtigt. Wesentlich *jedoch* ist in den integrierten Gesellschaften, daß das psychoneurotische Element, wenn es existiert, sich niemals selbst zum Ziel des Künstlers oder gar zur Regel seiner Kunst macht. (trans. T. König, cited in Gallagher, 1995: 210)

Example (11)
Persönlichkeit? Ja, bestimmt. Als Person *allerdings* zeigte er sich als weniger glänzend. (trans. E. Sander, B. Berger, cited in Gallagher, 1995: 210)

In a similar way, he (1995: 213) claims:

the translator working into English will have to make explicit and to disambiguate relations within and between utterances by the use of adversative and concessive connectors. (My translation)

There can be no doubt that this contrastive regularity is well founded; taken together, the studies cited here provide evidence from a vast corpus of texts and translations, both French-source to English-target and English-source to French-target. They constitute by far the best empirical evidence available to us so far and provide a foundation for further investigation of the phenomenon. There are, however, substantial differences of approach between these works and the present study.

First, although the contrast is between *énoncés* (or utterances), the norms are presented as somehow being properties of the two languages concerned rather than norms of translator behaviour. Thus, Chuquet and Paillard (1992: 257) speak of the 'types of markers and utterance choices at work *in both languages*' (my translation and emphasis) while Guillemin-Flescher (1981: 189), commenting on the example from Flaubert quoted earlier, suggests that 'in English it will be necessary, first of all, to make the relation explicit'. This would appear to imply an unconditional rule of language-to-language transfer. Our concern here, however, is not to contrast the properties and potential of language systems but rather to investigate what text-users (in general) and translators (in particular) seek to do and what choices they make in order to fulfil their goals; in other words, to investigate textual strategies, an exercise in the pragmatics of translation.

Second, the evidence adduced in the studies reviewed so far, valuable though it is, is considered almost without reference to context. Consideration of users' motivations in responding to context and the socio-textual practices they adopt is largely absent. For example, marked use of explicit junction may correspond to particular purposes of a particular user, as in example (12) rather than to universal tendencies of a language.

Example (12)
He swung it once and twice and again. He heard the tiller break and he lunged at the shark . . . (E. Hemingway, *The Old Man and the Sea*, cited in Guillemin-Flescher, 1981: 83)

Over-reliance on instances from a single source may, in this respect, be a pitfall and Gallagher (1995: 218) is constrained to admit that it would be dangerous to formulate generalisations concerning the frequency of ellipsis of junction in French. His corpus shows that while some writers (e.g. A. Maurois), display a strong trend towards the implicit, others, such as J.-P. Sartre, tend towards the opposite.

Third — and perhaps most importantly — it is often hypothesised in translation studies that explicitation is a universal tendency of translating, irrespective of language pair. Blum-Kulka (1986: 19) refers to an 'explicitation hypothesis', which posits that there will often be 'a rise in the level of cohesive explicitness in the target-language text . . . regardless of the increase traceable to differences between the two linguistic and textual systems involved'. Baker (1993: 243) also refers to 'a marked rise in the level of explicitness [in translations] compared to specific source texts and to original texts in general' and further notes a tendency towards simplification and 'conventional grammaticality'. Thus, evidence of the behaviour of (particular) translators may not always be a reliable indicator of non-translational language behaviour. Although, in principle, the contrastivists' consideration of English-to-French, as well as French-to-English, translation examples overcomes this problem, it is revealing that far fewer examples of the former, involving removal of explicit adversative junction, are cited.

Ellipsis of Junction as an Interactive Feature

To account for the phenomenon under discussion in terms of textual strategy, we need to adopt a 'cooperative', rather than a 'conduit', model of communication (Green, 1989: 10). According to the (widespread) conduit view, meaning is transmitted as a definable entity from producer to receiver via the conduit of spoken or written linguistic expression and recovered by listeners/readers exactly as it was sent. From the point of view of a more radical pragmatics, on the other hand, meaning is something which is negotiated between producers and receivers of texts (including translations) according to communicational norms such as those elaborated by Grice (1975).

Now, under standard Gricean analysis, a salient — i.e. marked — omission creates an implicature, through apparent infringement of the maxim of manner (be perspicuous; avoid obscurity of expression; be orderly etc.). That is, the omission (offering less than maximum clarity) creates the need for inferencing on the part of the text receiver. In other words, it creates reader involvement. Thus, ellipsis of the kind we have been considering is an interactive feature. Fowler (1986: 67) comments on the frequency of implicit causative relations in the novels of Raymond Chandler, suggesting that the writer uses this device to involve his readers in constant inferencing 'to retrieve unstated assumptions'.

Sample texts A and B (see Appendix) may now be studied in the light of these considerations. Both exhibit the characteristics of counter-argument. The intertextually established structure of this text type may now be illustrated by application to the French source text of Sample A (see Table 1).

Table 1 The counter-argumentative text structure of sample A

Tone-setter	Sentences 1–3:	France's intervention in Lebanon is a success.
Thesis cited (to be opposed)	Sentences 4–6:	USA is the main actor; nothing has changed.
Opposition	Sentence 7:	USA made no financial commitment.
Substantiation	Sentence 8:	It is Europe which will have to pay.
Conclusion	Sentence 9:	French intervention makes sense.

Among many examples in my corpus, this text is useful in being close to the prototype of counter-argument except for the ellipted *mais* at the beginning of sentence 7. In our earlier cases of ellipted adversative junction, the marker of the thesis cited (normally *certes, sans doute, bien entendu, il est vrai* etc.) was also absent, making the whole structure an implicit one. Here, the thesis cited is explicitly marked by *bien sûr* (sentence 4), creating the strong expectation of an opposing view, to be argued as the text develops.

From a pragmatic perspective, three questions now arise in relation to cases of ellipted junction such as these:

(1) What motivates the ellipsis?
(2) How do receivers retrieve intended meaning?
(3) What are the implications for the translator?

The questions are, of course, interrelated. Indeed, some (e.g. Gutt, 1991, following Sperber & Wilson, 1986) might suggest that the single principle of relevance provides the key to all three problems. Text-users (producers and receivers alike) are motivated by what they perceive to be optimally relevant (providing 'adequate contextual effects at minimal processing cost') to the situation and to each other's communicative needs. In turn, the translator is guided by the same principle within a new situation of communication.

It may, however, be possible to arrive at a more detailed explanatory hypothesis of what is involved. With the assistance of our two sample texts as illustrations, I shall suggest that there are two prime motivations for ellipsis of junction within the counter-argument. They are (1) *informative markedness* and (2) *politeness*.

Informative Markedness

It was suggested earlier (in connection with the ellipsis of causative relations in the style of Raymond Chandler) that implicit causative relations may be preferred to explicit ones to encourage inferencing on the part of the text receiver, who is motivated 'to retrieve unstated assumptions'. The ellipsis of adversative junction, by the same process of creating reader involvement and encouraging inferencing, actually serves to heighten the contrast which the producer intends the reader to perceive. As observed earlier, the ellipsis constitutes a departure from the norm within the conventions of this text type. The markedness of this feature creates a dynamism (Hatim & Mason, 1997: 28), which draws attention to itself and sets up a search for intended effects. This may best be illustrated from text sample B, in which the device is recurrent. The sample is extracted from another *Le Monde* article, this time on the subject of British attitudes towards the policies of the French president, Jacques Chirac. Here, following a tone-setter about Britain's hopes that Mr Chirac might modify his stance, the thesis cited (sentences 2–5) is that Britain was not disappointed by Mr Chirac's policy since it had not entertained any hopes that the policy would change in Britain's favour. The transition is reached in sentence 6: *Voire* ('Indeed'), which casts doubt on the tenability of the thesis cited. The rest of the sequence (sentences 7–13) constitutes the opposition (Britain had indeed entertained hopes) and its substantiation. It is within this unit of text structure that the text producer deploys ellipsis repeatedly to heighten the contrast between hopes and reality. Thus, a series of texts-within-texts is created, piling up evidence and tacitly inviting readers to compare, contrast and draw their own conclusions, as in Table 2.

Table 2 Ellipted junction and heightened contrast in text sample B

Hopes	*Reality*
la Grande Bretagne officielle . . . a sans conteste . . . caressé l'espoir que la politique européenne de la France subirait . . . de sensibles inflexions.	Elle constate, comme tout le monde, que la continuité l'emporte de beaucoup sur le changement.
Pour Londres, les positions franaises sur la monnaie unique ont . . . valeur de test.	Elles suscitent aujourd'hui, outre-Manche, désenchantement et inquiétude.
La Grande Bretagne guettait une défaillance de Jacques Chirac;	elle y croit de moins en moins.
Elle espérait que le marasme de l'économie française et l'ampleur des sacrifices budgétaires . . . obligeraient le président français à demander un report de l'échéance de janvier 1999;	elle observe, à regret, depuis quelques mois, que Jacques Chirac y puise une nouvelle énergie européenne.

This text sample provides the most graphic illustration of the use of ellipsis to encourage inferencing (the unstated assumption of Britain's disappointment) which, we suggest, is at work in many such counter-argumentative texts. This is, however, not the only perceptible contextual effect created by the suppression of connectives.

Politeness

The counter-argumentative text format constitutes in itself a form of positive politeness in that it is a means of 'claiming common ground' (Brown & Levinson, 1987: 102). That is, in order to carry out the face-threatening act (FTA) of countering an opposing point of view, the conventional text strategy is: agree first; then disagree. In the case of the editorial on French policy in Lebanon (Sample A), it is entirely consistent with the discourse of *Le Monde* that a stance of support for French diplomacy will be expressed with subtlety, rebutting the claim of US dominance without being too adversarial about doing so. Recognition of US supremacy has to be ritually made before the FTA of asserting French claims to independent action can be carried out. Further mitigation of the FTA is then achieved by an 'off-record' strategy: understate the opposition by not signalling it explicitly. The opposition still appears, however, and, although the effects of the face-threatening act (challenging US dominance) are mitigated, the text producer still intends receivers to be able to infer the FTA.

At this point, it could be argued that, given what is at stake, the translator's best policy would be always to relay the ellipsis in order to achieve the same purposes. After all, similar ellipsis of junction is an option for text users in English as well. Text fragments (13) — a statement issued by George Bush during the Gulf War — and (14) — from a speech delivered at the European Parliament — provide evidence of this.

Example (13)
As we announced last night, we will not attack unarmed soldiers in retreat. We have no choice but to consider retreating combat units as a threat, and respond accordingly. (. . .). (G. Bush 25 February 1991, cited in Hatim & Mason, 1997: 38)

Example (14)
I acknowledge that the Commission is committed to entrenching the principles of transparency and partnership. It must ensure that there is a real involvement of the social partners, the regional and local authorities and NGOs at all stages. (Cushnahan, *Eur. Parl.* 9 March 1993)

The same strategy of mitigating a FTA is apparent here, together with the same intention that the real threat (13) or implied criticism (14) be nevertheless perceived.

How then do source-text readers retrieve intended meaning? If the adversative nature of the text act is glossed over, how do users ensure that the traces are not covered so well that the text becomes simply disconcerting? The answer is that intentions are indeed signalled but in a more indirect — though more dynamic — way. We would suggest that it is through the interaction of various textural occurrences that the intended text act is perceived. Table 3 lists various devices marking evaluativeness in text sample A, each interacting with the others in the service of a rhetorical purpose.

Table 3 Interactive evaluativeness in text sample A

Tense modality	aura donc valu
Clefts	C'est auprès d'eux que . . .
	ce sont les Européens qui . . .
	Et c'est là que . . .
Intensifiers	se sont *bien* gardés de . . .
	un *quelconque* engagement . . .
Irony	opiniâtreté
	mettre la main au portefeuille

These devices are interdependent and cumulatively relay the pragmatic act of rebutting the case that French intervention was futile. This interactivity will be present whether or not there is ellipsis of junction. Thus, markers of junction in source texts and in translations do not exist in a vacuum and cannot be considered independently of other factors. And what is true of junction is equally so of other cohesive devices. Our study, in fact, constitutes a plea that the issue of junction — and more generally of cohesion — in translating should never be isolated from co-text and context and from the pragmatic factors governing communicative events in their social setting.

In the case of text sample A, the intended act is not easy to retrieve in the published translation since, not only is the marker of junction (however . . .) ellipted; the devices listed in Table 3 are, with one exception, not relayed. Thus, the task of the reader of the translation to retrieve the intended rhetorical purpose is complicated when important interactive clues are removed.

Sample B was also translated almost without explicit junction. So can the same inferencing be encouraged in the target text? Certainly, the safe option will be to uphold coherence in translation by restoring explicit junction. The multitude of examples in the corpora of Gallagher (1995), Guillemin-Flescher (1981) and others bear eloquent witness to this trend. But Chuquet and Paillard (1987) note a certain 'stylistic flattening' in one of the translations in their corpus, in which junction is systematically restored. And, if our hypothesis concerning the motivated use of ellipsis is well founded, then it would follow that some loss is entailed in systematically restoring explicitness in translation. Such loss may, in some contexts, be inevitable. But if explicit junction is to be avoided in translation of the counter-argument, then the opposition has to be made retrievable by the use of other, subtle prompts such as those listed in Table 3 in the case of Sample A. In Sample B, retrievability may depend on the contrastive use of tenses, temporal adverbials, any available intensifiers, the cohesive device of reiteration, word order and so on. For example, key sequences of Sample B might appear in translation as in (15), (16) and (17).

Example (15)
Undeniably, Britain did cherish the hope that, after the election victory, France's European policy would at least be significantly modified, even if there was no U-turn. Now, Britain recognises, like everyone else, that continuity, rather than change, is definitely the order of the day.

Example (16)
Once, Britain was on the look out for . . . ; now, Britain's faith in this is fading fast.

Example (17)
Britain used to hope . . . ; with reluctance, it now admits . . .

In this manner, translators would be seeking to ensure retrievability of a perceived contextual effect without resorting to restoring explicit junction. It is, of course, not being suggested that this consitutes the only appropriate approach; only that it is a possible approach, in fulfilment of particular purposes.

Conclusion

The difference between English and French usage in the frequency of ellipsis of junction within the counter-argumentative text format seems, even in the absence of large-scale quantitative studies, to be an established fact. As a departure from the norm, this ellipsis is an instance of markedness and is thus bound to create contextual effects. These effects, it has been suggested here, lie in the pragmatic dimension of meaning and are motivated by the requirements of informativity and politeness. Preserving the effects in translation is problematic. In many cases, the need to uphold target-text coherence may require that junction be made explicit (as suggested by the contrastivists), thus entailing a loss in translation. Nevertheless, this explicitation is far from being an unconditional rule of translating and the loss should not be assumed to be inevitable. The existence of similarly ellipted structures in English suggests, even if it is less frequent, that similar implicatures can be created by the same means in the target language.

In the translator's attempt to relay contextual effects with as little distortion as possible, it will be vital always to consider the interaction of junction with other text elements and the ways in which inferencing takes place on the basis of the interaction between textual occurrences and the context in which they are uttered. There is, however, an over-riding factor. The communicative, pragmatic and semiotic context of the target text is distinct from that of the source text. Translators' choices have to be made in relation to (i) the task or 'brief' for the particular translation operation; (ii) their audience design (cf. Bell, 1984), these two jointly constituting what Reiss and Vermeer (1984) refer to as *Skopos*. Cohesion and coherence, in other words, are upheld in an entirely new context. Above all, comparisons of source-text and target-text junction can only be made meaningfully in relation to overall rhetorical purposes and the ways in which these find expression in source and target texts.

Appendix
Sample text A

La France dans le jeu libanais	*France's peace role deserves praise*
1. Son opiniâtreté aura donc valu à la France d'être partie prenante à la solution de la crise au Liban.	1. France's persistence has earned her the right to a dominant position in the solution to the Lebanese crisis.
2. Avec Washington, Beyrouth et Damas, Paris fera partie du «groupe de surveillance» chargé de veiller à l'application du cessez-le-feu entré en vigueur samedi 27 avril.	2. With Washington, Beirut and Damascus, France will be part of the 'supervision group' overseeing the ceasefire that took effect on April 27.
3. Il faut s'en féliciter.	3. France must be congratulated.

4. Les sceptiques diront, bien sûr, que les Etats-Unis ont eu le rôle déterminant dans cet «arrangement» et seront le principal garant de son exécution.

4. Of course, the sceptics will say the United States played the main role and is the main guarantor.

5. C'est auprès d'eux que le Liban et Israël s'engagent à respecter les nouvelles règles du jeu militaire, celles que fixe l'accord conclu vendredi.

5. Lebanon and Israel are respecting the rules which the US laid down for this new military game.

6. A peu de choses près, il s'agit d'un retour au statu quo qui prévalait avant la peu glorieuse, mais très meurtrière et destructrice, opération que Tsahal vient de mener au Liban.

6. To some extent, we are dealing with a return to the status quo that prevailed before the not so glorious but extremely murderous and destructive Israeli operation.

7. Les Américains se sont bien gardés de prendre un quelconque engagement financier pour reconstruire les infrastructures civiles détruites par les bombardements israéliens.

7. The Americans have taken care to make no financial engagement for the reconstruction of the civilian infrastructures destroyed by the Israeli bombardments.

8. Une fois de plus, au Proche-Orient, ce sont les Européens qui vont devoir mettre la main au portefeuille.

8. Once again, the Europeans will have to financially support the Middle East.

9. Et c'est là que l'intervention française, forcée et accueillie initialement dans le plus grand scepticisme, prend son sens. (. . .)
(*Le Monde*, 28–29 April 1996)

9. It is here that the French intervention makes sense. (. . .)
(*The Guardian*, 1 May 1996)

Sample text B

Les désenchantements du couple franco-britannique

Can Chirac turn a deaf ear to Britain's pleas?

Comme la Phèdre de Racine, Albion, dans un moment de sincérité, pourrait dire, en songeant à Jacques Chirac: 'Et l'espoir, malgré moi, s'est glissé dans mon coeur'. Mais on s'abandonne rarement à un tel aveu dans les allées du royaume, à la veille de la visite d'Etat du président français. Sur les grands thèmes européens — l'architecture de

As in Racine's Phèdre, Albion might have said in a moment of truth while thinking of Jacques Chirac, 'Despite myself, hope has slipped into my heart'. But such an admission would hardly be made in Britain, especially as the French president begins a state visit.
    When it comes to the important European issues — construction of

l'union, la monnaie unique, les relations franco-allemandes —, on affiche plutôt une sérénité de bon aloi, qu'altèrent à peine de vagues regrets. Pas question de se montrer déçu puisque, vous répète-t-on, Londres n'escomptait de Paris, dans ces domaines, aucun changement spectaculaire en sa faveur.

'Nous ne sommes pas aussi fous que nos vaches, lance un diplomate. Nous n'avons jamais nourri d'illusion excessive!' Voire. Sans prendre ses désirs pour des réalités, la Grande Bretagne officielle, après s'être discrètement réjouie de certains accents eurosceptiques du candidat Jacques Chirac, a sans conteste, au lendemain de sa victoire, caressé l'espoir que la politique européenne de la France subirait, sinon une rupture, du moins de sensibles inflexions. Elle constate, comme tout le monde, que la continuité l'emporte de beaucoup sur le changement.

Pour Londres, les positions françaises sur la monnaie unique ont, à juste titre, valeur de test. Elles suscitent aujourd'hui, outre-Manche, désenchantement et inquiétude. La Grande-Bretagne guettait une défaillance de Jacques Chirac; elle y croit de moins en moins. Elle espérait que le marasme de l'économie française et l'ampleur des sacrifices budgétaires exigés pour satisfaire aux critères de Maastricht obligeraient le président français à demander un report de l'échéance de janvier 1999; elle observe à regret, depuis quelques mois, que Jacques Chirac y puise une nouvelle énergie européenne. (. . .) (*Le Monde*, 14 May 1996)

the union, a single currency, Franco-German relations — the British would rather not show their feelings — tinged as they are with slight regret. There is no question of them showing their disappointment because London no longer expects from Paris any dramatic changes in its favour.

'We are not as mad as your [*sic*] cows', a French diplomat says. 'We have never fed anyone excessive illusions'.

Without substituting hope for reality, Britain, the day after Mr Chirac's victory (after discreetly rejoicing about some hints of Euro-scepticism), hoped that France's European policies would suffer some kind of break, or at least be susceptible to flexibility.

Understandably, London sees France's position on the single currency as a test. It creates worry and disenchantment across the Channel. Britain had suspected a weakening on Mr Chirac's part, but is increasingly no longer so sure. Britain hoped that French economic stagnation and increased budgetary sacrifices required to satisfy the Maastricht criteria , would have forced the French president to ask for a report [*sic*] on the elections of January 1999. Recently they have noticed with regret that Jacques Chirac has found a new European energy. (. . .) (*The Guardian*, 15 May 1996)

References

Baker, M. (1993) Corpus linguistics and translation studies: Implications and applications. In M. Baker, G. Francis and E. Tognini-Bonelli (eds) *Text and Technology: In Honour of John Sinclair*. Amsterdam: John Benjamins.

Ballard, M. (1995) La traduction de la conjonction *and* en français. In M. Ballard (ed.) *Relations discursives et traduction* (pp. 221–93). Lille: Presses Universitaires de Lille.

Bell, A. (1984) Language style as audience design. *Language in Society* 13, 145–204.

Blum-Kulka, S. (1986) Shifts of cohesion and coherence in translation. In J. House and S. Blum-Kulka (eds) *Interlingual and Intercultural Communication: Discourse and Cognition in Translation and Second Language Acquisition Studies*. Tübingen: Narr.

Brown, P. and Levinson, S. (1987) *Politeness. Some Universals in Language Usage*. Cambridge: Cambridge University Press.

Chuquet, H. and Paillard, M. (1987) *Approche linguistique des problèmes de traduction*. Paris: Ophrys.

Chuquet, H. and Paillard, M. (1992) Enonciation et traduction chez les linguistes francophones. *Journal of French Language Studies* 2, 237–59.

Delisle, J. (1980) *L'Analyse du discours comme méthode de traduction*. Ottawa: University of Ottawa Press.

Fowler, R. (1986) *Linguistic Criticism*. Oxford: Oxford University Press.

Gallagher, J. (1995) L'Effacement des connecteurs adversatifs et concessifs en français moderne. In M. Ballard (ed.) *Relations discursive et traduction* (pp. 201–20). Lille: Presses Universitaire de Lille.

Green, G. (1989) *Pragmatics and Natural Language Understanding*. Hillsdale, NJ: Laurence Erlbaum.

Grice, H.P. (1975) Logic and conversation. In P.Cole and J.Morgan (eds) *Syntax and Semantics 3: Speech Acts*. New York: Academic Press.

Guillemin-Flescher, J. (1981) *Syntaxe comparée du français et de l'anglais. Problèmes de traduction*. Paris: Ophrys.

Gutt, E.-A. (1991) *Translation and Relevance. Cognition and Context*. Oxford: Blackwell.

Hatim, B. (1987) A text-linguistic model for the analysis of discourse errors: Contributions from Arabic linguistics. In J. Monaghan (ed.) *Grammar in the Construction of Texts*. London: Frances Pinter.

Hatim, B. (1991) The pragmatics of argumentation in Arabic: The rise and fall of a text type. *Text* 11, 189–99.

Hatim, B. and Mason, I. (1997) *The Translator as Communicator*. London: Routledge.

Reiss, K. and Vermeer, H. (1984) *Grundlegung einer allgemeiner Translationstheorie*. Tübingen: Niemeyer.

Sperber, D. and Wilson, D. (1986) *Relevance: Communication and Cognition*. Oxford: Blackwell.

Chapter 11

Hedges in Political Texts: A Translational Perspective

CHRISTINA SCHÄFFNER

In a recent editorial, the *European Voice* referred to Great Britain as 'a unitary state *par excellence* which treats any notion of federalism as anathema' (*European Voice*, 13 February 1997).

'Par excellence' can be classified as a hedge. Hedges are defined by Lakoff (1973: 471) as 'words whose meaning implicitly involves fuzziness', as 'words whose job it is to make things fuzzier or less fuzzy'. Fuzziness can be related to vagueness, indeterminateness, variation of sense, which are constitutive characteristics of natural languages.

In linguistic research, such phenomena have been described both from a semantic and a pragmatic perspective. The interest of linguistic semanticists has been aroused by the problems which vagueness poses for semantic models of meaning. Lakoff, for example, criticised truth-conditional semantics for dividing sentences into true, false and lacking a truth value, and he argued for studying fuzzy boundaries (cf. Channell 1994: 10). Pragmatic research has contributed particularly by introducing the distinction between the propositional content and the illocutionary role, i.e. speech acts and, based on Grice, by differentiating between conventional and conversational parts of the utterance meaning.

In this chapter, I want to take the case of hedges and find out what happens to them in the process of translation, using the language pair English and German. For the empirical research, I have chosen political texts, mainly speeches by politicians, based on the assumption that hedges are a typical feature of these texts. However, the frequency of hedges depends on the text types (genres) and the context of situation. They are more frequent in, for example, challenging interviews in contrast to, for example, speeches at party congresses, where the speaker is 'preaching to the converted'. More specifically I want to ask: What kinds of hedges might

185

pose problems for translation? Why? What can a translational perspective contribute to our understanding of hedges and their functioning in (political) communication?

The choice of text type(s) is determined by the question of whether they actually get translated. Challenging interviews, for example, are usually intended for the home audience and are hardly ever translated. Texts that do get translated are texts whose content is of relevance beyond national boundaries, either because a new government outlines its future policy (e.g. de Maizière's government declaration, cf. appendix), or because of some diplomatic act (e.g. Kinkel's speech). In the majority of these cases, there will be a change in the function of the target text (TT) compared to the source text (ST). The STs often aim at the general public (de Maizière's speech was simultaneously transmitted by radio and TV). The addressees of the TTs, however, are mainly politicians. In this case, we have a change from external political communication (politicians speak to the public) to internal political communication (politicians speak to politicians). Kinkel's address-ees are the TT audience who were invited to a specific event (the opening of the Centre for the Advanced Study of European and Comparative Law in Oxford). For diplomatic reasons, the ST has to be produced in the source language but from the outset with the intention of having it translated for use in the target culture. There are hardly any 'proper' addressees of the ST (apart from German-speaking members of the immediate audience). One possible use of the ST in the source culture could be as a reference point for subsequent media reports (the text was indeed distributed as a press release by the German embassy in London). In this case, then, we have a change from internal political communication to external political communication. Speeches by the leader of a political party, too, may be translated for distribution to news agencies. However, Tony Blair's speech to the 1995 Labour Party Conference was simultaneously interpreted and then written up. But the written German version of the interpreted speech still has all the characteristic features of spoken language.

Politicians are (almost) always speaking as representatives of a political party or of a government, and as such they are engaging in policy-making ('doing politics'), outlining or defending their own political decisions, directly or indirectly criticising or commenting on ideas or actions of their political opponents. This is why, in addition to the immediate audience, other political parties or groups, friends or foes alike, at home or abroad, are also among the addressees of a political speech. There is an intricate network of audience constellation and the functions of a political speech, which is reflected in its linguistic structure, of which hedging devices are assumed to be a decisive part. These will now be discussed on the basis of examples from authentic texts and their authentic translations.

Evidentiality-Hedges

There are numerous words and phrases that can be classed as hedges or hedge-like. 'By qualifying of modifying a word or statement, hedges measure the word or idea against what is expected' (Tannen, 1993: 17/18). Hedging devices are, for example, verbs with a modal meaning (e.g. think, suggest), adverbs (e.g. just, obviously), downtoners (e.g. some, there is some evidence to suggest . . .), qualifiers (e.g. kind of, in this respect), approximating expressions (e.g. this is about right)[1] and also metalinguistic comments (e.g. I must say).

Hedges can be used to introduce fuzziness with respect to the speakers' degree of commitment to the truth of the proposition being conveyed. Sweetser (1981) calls them evidentiality-hedges because they 'indicate the evidential status of the statement being made' (Sweetser, 1981: 32). Examples are 'I think, it seemed that, to the best of my knowledge, for all I know'. Such a strategy of reducing or avoiding commitment can be found in political interviews (cf. Simon-Vandenbergen, 1996) and also in speeches by politicians.

As Simon-Vandenbergen (1996: 406) argues, such verbs as 'think', 'believe', only have a modal meaning and can thus be classified as hedging devices when the clause expresses a verifiable fact and not an opinion. Therefore, (1) and (2) would contain hedged statements, but (3) would not (hedging is indicated by italics).

Example (1)
His name was George Orwell. But actually it wasn't. That was his pen name. His real name — was Eric. His surname? You've guessed it. It was Blair. Eric Blair. He changed his name. I can't say the same thing about my opposite number. He's changed everything else. His politics. His principles. His philosophy. But — *to the best of my belief* — he hasn't changed his name. (Major, 1995)

Example (2)
And *I honestly believe* that if we had not changed, . . . we could not change the country. (Blair, 1995)
[Und *ich glaube wirklich daß*, wenn wir uns nicht geändert hätten . . . könnten wir das Land nicht ändern.]

Example (3)
Diese Werte zeigen die Richtung auf, die ich — *und ich denke, wir alle* — einschlagen wollen. (De Maizière)
[These values indicate the direction which — *and I think we all* — intend to pursue.]

In (1) to (3), it is not so much the truth of the facts which is at stake but the function of the hedges — which calls for a pragmatic explanation. Although (3) expresses a personal opinion, this has to be seen in its context, i.e. the government declaration of the first freely elected Parliament in the German Democratic Republic (GDR) in 1990, shortly before German unification. De Maizière, the leader of the East German Christian Democratic Union (CDU, which had got the majority of the votes) was the head of a coalition government which represented various political parties and groups, all committed to a democratic renewal. Speaking as an equal among equals, de Maizière indirectly invites confirmation and agreement from the other members of the coalition government. (1) and (2) are quotations from the speech of the leader of a political party at its annual conference. In (1), the hedge functions as an (ironical) reinforcement — by analogy — of the statement that a political opponent changed his convictions for the sole purpose of winning future elections. The function of the hedge in (2) is to solicit credibility for the statement, to reinforce the speaker's position, (this reading of 'I honestly believe' as a hedge requires, of course, the acceptance of the presupposition 'we have changed' as expressing a true fact).

In political discourse, hedging devices which function to relieve authors of some of the responsibility for their statements (and thus to avoid criticism), may be found in televised debates between the main candidates before an election. In the texts I have looked at, however, evidentiality-hedges mainly contribute to presenting a positive image of the leader as a knowledgeable, honest, trustworthy, decisive and witty politician (cf. Chilton & Schäffner 1997), confirming Simon-Vandenbergen's finding that 'politicians not only use the 'negative' strategy of avoidance of commitment, they also employ the 'positive' strategy of inspiring confidence by sounding fully committed to the truth of their claims' (Simon-Vandenbergen, 1996: 390). Evidentiality-hedges do not seem to pose a major problem for translation.

However, there is one area of political discourse where we could argue that the speaker wishes to reduce the risk of being criticised for his or her statements — diplomacy. For example, (4) is taken from a speech by the German foreign minister Kinkel which he made in England. He comments at length on European integration, presenting the German government's view in a straightforward way, but uses a lot of hedging to avoid open criticism of the British government's attitude, cf.

Example (4)

Aus britischer Sicht — so mein Eindruck — könnte alles so harmonisch sein, *wenn da nicht* diese unbegreifliche 'deutsche Vision' von Europa *wäre*. Verfolgt *man* die Europa-Debatte in Ihrem Lande, *dann könnte man fast glauben*, daß einige 'Europa-Phantasten' auf dem Kontinent, vor allem in Bonn und Paris, einen europäischen Superstaat errichten wollten, in dem Brüsseler Enarchen und deutsche Zentralbanker das Sagen haben. Speziell uns Deutschen *wird unterstellt*, unter dem Deckmantel der europäischen Integration eine 'hidden agenda' für ein deutsches Europa zu verfolgen. Für Großbritannien *scheint* mehr Gemeinsamkeit in Europa heute automatisch den Weg in den Föderalismus zu bedeuten.

I have the impression that *the British believe* that everything *would* be so harmonious *if it were not for* the incomprehensible 'German vision' of Europe. Following the debate on Europe in your country, *one could almost think* that some starry-eyed idealists on the continent, particularly in Bonn and Paris, wanted to establish a European superstate in which top Brussels bureaucrats and German central bankers have the say. We Germans in particular *are accused* of pursuing a hidden agenda on a German Europe under the guise of European integration. *It seems* that for Britain today more common ground in Europe automatically implies a move towards federalism.

The German text is full of hedging devices (use of modal auxiliaries: 'könnte', 'wäre', 'scheint'; impersonal constructions: 'man'; agentless passives: 'wird unterstellt'; restrictions: 'könnte man fast glauben'). In addition, the word order in the first sentence contributes to the vagueness ('so mein Eindruck' in second position restricts the commitment to the truth of the proposition). In the TT, however, the change of the word order and the transposition from a more passive form to an agentive structure ('the British believe'), makes the statement more factual, because some of the vagueness gets lost (a reproduction of the vagueness could have been achieved by a more literal rendering, e.g. as 'In the British view/from a British perspective — so, at least is my impression — everything could be so harmonious if . . .). Particularly in diplomacy, such a factual statement could more readily lend itself to a critical reaction by the audience than one which is very vague due to hedging devices — a point which needs to be taken into account for translation.

In political speeches, policy is often presented by simple statements and claims, often claims to the truth. Many of these assertive speech acts appear to be felicitous on no other basis than the authority of the speaker in his role defined by the particular speech situation. But something else has to be added: some of the assertions only have relevance in relation to background propositions which the speaker is rejecting or contradicting. Hedges may play a role here, as in (5).

Example (5)

Wir gehen davon aus, daß wir wohl *auf absehbare Zeit* nicht auf die Nutzung von Kernenergie verzichten können. (de Maizière)
[In our view it will not be possible to do without nuclear energy *within the foreseeable future.*]

'Auf absehbare Zeit' modifies the validity of the proposition by adding a condition. Demands (although it is not said by whom) to stop the use of nuclear energy immediately are implicity rejected as not being on the government's agenda, but the statement is hedged, which at least could be interpreted as a signal to opponents to discuss the matter.

Hedges which are used to relativise or apologise can be interpreted as signals of communicative insecurity. In politics, however, hedging also functions for strategic manipulation and to enhance the image of the speaker. In other words, hedges may function interpersonally in that the hearers' acceptance of the speaker's claim is the goal (cf. Powell, 1985). Such phrases which operate as evidentiality-hedges or have a definite interpersonal function do not pose problems for translation.

I now want to look at semantic hedges, i.e. expressions whose meanings can be described with reference to the notion of category membership, i.e. in terms of prototype structures.

Hedges and Category Membership

Lakoff's study of hedges started out as a semantic analysis. It has subsequently been pointed out that his hedges should be subdivided into different types, and that they are related both to semantic and to pragmatic indeterminacy (e.g. Kay, 1979; Lakoff ,1982; Channell, 1994). Both Kay and Lakoff link hedges to cognitive schemata or to 'idealized cognitive models (ICM)' (Lakoff, 1982). 'Par excellence' from the introductory quotation functions semantically to form categories consisting of representative members.

By using hedges, the speaker explicitly adds or modifies contextual information, which makes it possible to operate relatively freely the scope of precision of an utterance. Pinkal (1985: 48) classifies hedges according to the way in which they influence the status of precision of the modified expression. He speaks of 'präzisierende Hecken' [defining or specifying hedges], 'depräzisierende Hecken' [despecifying hedges], 'modifizierende Hecken' [modifying hedges] and 'quantifizierende Hecken' [quantifying hedges]. I will give examples from the texts I have analysed for each of these four types, discussing the question whether their characterisation as semantic hedges is sufficient and describing how they were dealt with in the process of translation. At the end of the chapter, some of these translation strategies will be summarised and evaluated.

Not all of these four types (which are not always easy to keep apart) occur with the same frequency. The most frequent, and most interesting, type from a translational perspective, is the specifying hedge, which will be discussed last.

Modifying and quantifying hedges

Modifying hedges (e.g. 'fairly', 'too', 'typical') shift the scope of indeterminateness of the utterance, as we have already seen in (5). Such hedges often modify relative expressions which are based on a scale of degree (e.g. something can be done with more or less hesitation).

Example (6)
Mit der Einführung der Länder wird die Polizeihoheit *im wesentlichen* bei den Ländern liegen. (de Maizière)
[With the introduction of the *Länder* as administrative units, police powers will *essentially* rest with these.]

Example (7)
Die bisher *zu* zaghafte Entrümpelung europäischer Regelungen muß politisch weiter vorangetrieben werden. (Kinkel)
[The hitherto *over*-hesitant clear-out of European regulations must be further advanced politically.]

These hedges can be characterised as semantic in that they modify 'bei den Ländern liegen' and 'zaghaft', respectively. However, as already stated earlier, in political speeches the speaker usually (also) engages in an often implicit debate with the political opponent(s), who, for example, may have demanded police powers to be given exclusively to the Länder. In this sense, these hedges function pragmatically.

Quantifying hedges (e.g. 'in every respect', 'in some respect') relate to characteristics of the whole scope of precision, e.g.:

Example (8)
Dazu brauchen wir Schutzmaßnahman *jedweder Art* für eine mehrjährige
Übergangsperiode. (de Maizière)
[For this purpose we need protective measures *of every kind* for a
transitional period extending over several years.]

Example (9)
The Tories set up the Nolan Committee on Standards in Public Life . . .
We will implement it. *In full.* (Blair, 1995)
[Die Tories haben das Nolankomitee über den Standard im öffentlichen
Leben eingesetzt . . . Labour wird das *voll* durchführen.]

Here too, we have both a semantic and a pragmatic function of the
hedges. The pragmatic reading is due to the implicit speech acts: a request
in (8), where the context is making East German agriculture fit for the
requirements of the European Union, and a promise in (9).

Despecifying and specifying hedges

Despecifying hedges (e.g. 'kind of', 'roughly') extend the scope of
indeterminateness, particularly of expressions which are indeterminate as
to the periphery. Despecifying hedges are surprisingly rare in my corpus.
But we find one very telling example at the beginning of John Major's
speech at the 1995 Conservative Party Conference:

Example (10)
As you know, in June I resigned as Leader of our party and called a
leadership election. I did so because speculation was drowning out
everything we were trying to do. How could you argue our case on the
doorstep with that *sort of thing* going on? Well, of course, you couldn't.
It had to end — whatever the risk. (Major, 1995)

This hedge, too, calls for a pragmatic explanation which presupposes
knowledge of the previous event, i.e. the leadership challenge by John
Redwood (whose name is not mentioned, though). Since the topic of
disunity within a party and disloyalty to its leader is not a pleasant one, it
is treated in this very vague way, avoiding a more precise label such as
'fight'. However, a few sentences later in the speech, 'fight' suddenly is
used, though in combination with a specifying hedge:

Example (11)
But, that was yesterday. Today, we meet united, healed, renewed — and
thirsting for the *real* fight: with Labour. (Major, 1995)

The concept 'fight' can be explained by recourse to prototype theory (cf. Rosch, 1977) and to Lakoff's ICMs. The prototypical fight seems to involve opponents, whereas clashes within a — supposedly — homogenous party or group would not be classified as 'fights'.

Are defining, or specifying hedges (e.g. 'real', 'genuine', 'true', 'exactly'), then 'proper' semantic hedges? These hedges are related to vagueness in terms of category membership in that they narrow down the scope of indeterminateness of a concept or a proposition, thus making it more precise. This type is most common in my corpus and most interesting, both from the point of view of analysis and of translation.

Example (12)
Nicht die Staatssicherheit war die *eigentliche* Krankheit der DDR, sie war nur eine ihrer Auswüchse. Die *eigentliche* Erbkrankheit der sozialistischen Gesellschaft war der diktatorische Zentralismus . . . (de Maizière)
[The State Security Service was not the disease that afflicted the GDR, but only one of its symptoms. The hereditary disease that plagued socialist society was a dictatorial centralism . . .]

Example (13)
Die *eigentlichen* Probleme in unserer Welt — wir wissen es alle — sind nicht die deutsch-deutschen oder die Ost–West-Probleme. Die *eigentlichen* Probleme bestehen in der strukturellen Ungerechtigkeit zwischen Nord und Süd. (de Maizère)
[We all know that the *real* problems confronting our world are not the German-German or the East-West problems, but rather the structural injustice between North and South.]

In contrast to John Major, Lothar de Maizière does not leave information implicit but explicitly opposes two different specifications of 'eigentliche Krankheit' and 'eigentliche Probleme'. The syntactic structure in (12) and (13) is identical: a negating sentence followed by a specification (not $x = y$, [but] $z = y$). It is due to this syntactic structure that 'eigentlich' functions as a semantic hedge. But when we ask for the function of the hedge, it becomes obvious that it is used to put the statement in a historical perspective, thus relativising the role of East Germany's State Security Service in (12) and of the problems of the upcoming German unification in (13). In both cases this can be interpreted as indirectly engaging in a debate with political groups who held a different view. In both TTs we notice a deletion of the hedge (I will come back to this translation procedure later). In (12), both occurrences of 'eigentlich' (real, intrinsic) are deleted, with the effect that the relativising function has been lost. In (13), only the second occurrence has been deleted, but this is not a loss because it has been compensated for by a different syntactic structure ('but rather').

The following examples reveal another aspect of specifying hedges which can again be explained both from a semantic and a pragmatic perspective.

Example (14)
Bürgerinitiative, Länderverantwortung und gesetzgeberisches, hoheitsrechtliches Handeln des Staates sollen sich nach dem Willen der Regierung in einer *wahrhaft demokratischen Baukultur* . . . (de Maizière)
[The government suggests that the initiative of the people, the responsibility of the *Länder* and the legislation and sovereign jurisdiction of the state shall be combined to devise *a truly democratic culture of building* . . .]

Here, the hedge 'wahrhaft' functions as a signal to the hearers to give a specific meaning to the concept 'demokratische Baukultur'. This interpretation, however, is related to a presupposition, namely that what existed before in the GDR and which was also officially called 'demokratisch' did not really deserve this label. De Maizière engages in a critical dialogue with the previous political authorities, rejecting their language use and establishing a new meaning. This new meaning, however, is not explicitly spelled out, but indicated by the specifying hedge. The audience will have to activate knowledge about the meaning of 'democratic' in the official public discourse of the GDR in order to fully understand the pragmatic function of the hedge. The hedge, so to speak, functions pragmatically as a signal for a presupposition (or an implicature). In political discourse, presuppositions may have prominent ideological functions in that they introduce ideological positions whose truth, however, is often not at all uncontroversial.

We can see the same strategy in Tony Blair's speech to the 1995 Labour Party Conference. His preferred hedge is 'proper', or 'properly', which is used to specify (future) Labour policy in contrast to the current policy of the Tory government.

Example (15)
Proper assessment for all five year olds. (Blair, 1995)
[*Richtige* Beurteilung der Fähigkeiten aller Fünfjährigen.]

Example (16)
Teachers would be *properly* rewarded. (Blair, 1995)
[Lehrer werden *gut* bezahlt werden.]

Example (17)
Ballots, peaceful picketing, *proper* conduct of disputes, these laws are staying. (Blair, 1995)
[Abstimmung, friedliche Streikposten, *aufrechtes* Vorgehen bei Strei- tigkeiten, diese Gesetze werden bleiben.]

Example (18)
This nation needs a *proper* national integrated transport system ... (Blair, 1995)
[Dieses Land braucht ein *neues*, integriertes, nationales Transportsys- tem ...]

Example (19)
The privatised utilities will be *properly* regulated. (Blair, 1995)
[Wir wollen Betriebe der öffentlichen Versorgung *vernünftig* regulieren.]

In all these examples, Blair implicity accuses the Tories. An interpreta- tion of the statements builds on the knowledge that the Tory policy with respect to the actions and institutions referred to is not appropriate and that a Labour government would conduct a better policy. It is interesting to see that in the German simultaneous interpreting of the speech, different equivalents for 'proper' and 'properly' were used.[2] When we look at them closely, we see that they are all adjectives or adverbs which refer to something desirable and which implicitly reject their semantic opposites: 'richtig' ['proper', 'correct'], 'gut' ['good', 'well'], 'aufrecht' ['honourable'], 'neu' ['new'], 'vernünftig' ['reasonably']. One might argue whether the one or the other of these German equivalents is perhaps too specific (or an 'over-translation'), but they are all evidence of the interpreter's awareness of the pragmatic function of the hedges.

Hedges, like 'proper', 'real', are linked to concepts or categories. As Lakoff (1991: 54) states, 'the human category system is based on basic-level and prototype-centred categories of various kinds — graded, metonymic, and radial'. What is typical of political discourse is abstract concepts, but it is difficult to explain 'democracy' or 'rewarding' in terms of basic-level concepts or prototypes. Meaning is based on the understanding of experience. In contrast to natural categories or artefacts, the meanings of abstract concepts are exclusively acquired through their use in discourse. In the field of politics, some key concepts are used with different meanings, depending on the ideology of the users (cf. van Dijk, 1995). Combinations of such concepts with 'genuine' or 'real' have the function of differentiation, i.e. one representative of the category is given a specific status (cf. Schäffner, 1990). However, this is not a status in the sense of a prototype as the most representative exemplar of the category, but as a particular concept which serves a specific discursive purpose, i.e. to set the meaning which a particular political party hosts apart from meanings used by opponents with each party often presenting its meaning as the only true one.

Thus, specifying hedges can also be explained pragmatically. From the point of view of translation, it boils down to the question: will the TT audience be able to interpret this pragmatic function of the hedge? Will they be able to see the presupposition that an interpretation of the political opponents is being criticised or rejected? In the characterisation of my sample texts, I have said that, in the process of translation, their textual function changes: the TTs are used for internal political communication, i.e. by politicians or other knowledgeable readers in the target community. It can reasonably be assumed that the TT users are acquainted both with the political background situation of the ST (e.g. a new East German government outlines a totally new policy) and with the characteristic features of the text type political speech. Therefore, it can also be assumed that the pragmatic function of the specifying hedges will be correctly interpreted.

Translation Strategies

In the majority of the examples here, the hedges in the ST were rendered by hedges in the TT. In the last part of this chapter I want to discuss some examples where hedges were either deleted, or added, or where changes occurred, and I want to examine the effects.

A first strategy was the deletion of hedges. In example (12), the deletion had the effect that the relativising function of the ST statement got lost. Deletions occurred with all four types of hedges, illustrated below with modifying hedges ('mere' in (20)) and quantifying hedges ('as widely as possible' in (21)).

Example (20)
Europa darf sich aber nicht zu einer *bloßen* Zweckgemeinschaft für Freihandel und Prosperität zurückbilden. (Kinkel)
[However, Europe must not regress into a community of convenience in pursuit of free trade and prosperity.]

Example (21)
Den Kommunen muß das Recht zukommen, das Bauen in ihren Territorien *weitestgehend* selbst zu bestimmen. (de Maizière)
[The communities must have the right to decide on building activities in their area of responsibility.]

In (20), the speaker refers to a specific view of the European Union which is widely held among British politicians and which he implicity criticises. 'Eine bloße Zweckgemeinschaft' ('a community merely for the purpose of') is a negatively evaluated idea of a European Union in a very limited sense of purpose. The criticism is obvious to the TT audience, and the deleted hedge is compensated for by the addition of 'community of convenience'. In (21), we have both a semantic and a pragmatic effect. In semantic terms, the communities' scope of action is restricted in the ST, but not in the TT. This restriction in the ST goes hand in hand with the pragmatic function of making a promise (or an implicit warning — depending on how the communities interpret this statement against the background of their previous rights).

Another translation strategy was the addition of hedges. This occurred rarely and was related to evidentiality-hedges:

Example (22)
It sounds harsh but it is actually fair. (Blair, 1995)
[*Ich weiß*, einiges davon klingt *vielleicht* hart, es ist *aber nur* fair und gerecht.]

Example (23)
Aber wer den positiven Besitzstand der deutschen Geschichte für sich reklamiert, der muß auch zu ihren Schulden stehen, unabhängig davon, wann er geboren und selbst aktiv handelnd in diese Geschichte eingetreten ist. (de Maizière)
[*But we think* that one cannot claim to be solely the heir of the positive aspects of German history and let others bear responsibility for the negative sides — regardless of when they were born and when they themselves became actively involved in this history.]

In (22), it may well be that Tony Blair had actually added 'I know'. The TT is the transcribed version of the simultaneous interpreting of his speech and it is quite common for politicians not to read the prepared (and then published) speech word for word but slightly divert from the written text whenever the situation invites such a diversion. Adding 'vielleicht' and 'aber nur', however, adds vagueness to the TT which is absent in the ST. In (23), the addition of the evidentiality-hedge results in a change of perspective. The ST is vague in that it calls for a conversational implicature (cf. Grice, 1989; Liedtke, 1995); the audience will have to activate background knowledge in order to identify the referent of 'wer' ('those who claim'), which in this specific case is the former communist party of East Germany, the Socialist Unity Party (SED). But for this implicature to operate, background knowledge about the political system in the GDR is necessary. At the time of the speech, the GDR was still in existence, and although unification was declared as the aim of the coalition government, no concrete date had been given. For pragmatic reasons, therefore, a too open criticism was not considered politically wise. In the TT, the added hedge transforms the sentence into a programmatic statement. It is more difficult for the TT audience to recognise the intended implicature and, in addition, the 'they' is ambiguous.

A third phenomenon with the translation of hedges was a change in the perspective. I hesitate to speak of a translation strategy here, because I doubt that the observed changes were made deliberately. In (24), a quantifying hedge in the ST ('sufficiently') was changed to a modifying hedge in the TT:

Example (24)
Der Krisenzustand in unserem Gesundheitswesen ist *hinlänglich* bekannt. (de Maizière)
[The crisis in our health care system is *well* known.]

The quantification here actually implies the quality (i.e. if something is sufficiently known it is well known), so that the change is an expression of an implied proposition.

Example (25)
Die Beziehungen Deutschlands zu Großbritannien sind eine Freund-schaft *besonderer Art*. (Kinkel)
[Germany and Britain have developed a *particular friendship*.]

Kinkel characterises the relationship between Germany and Great Britain as a 'friendship of a specific kind' and goes on to explain it:

Unspektakulär und nüchtern, aber von großer Dichte und Intensität. Ich möchte das deutsch-britische Verhältnis eine 'Allianz der Über-zeugungen' nennen: . . .
[Unspectacular and down-to-earth, but very close and intense. I would like to call the Anglo-German relationship an 'alliance of convictions': . . .]

This 'Allianz der Überzeugungen' is then further specified by listing some examples of common opinions and political actions. In the ST, the speaker starts with a general, but very neutral, characterisation. The pragmatic function of 'besonderer Art' is to signal to the audience that a more specific definition is about to follow. For the TT audience, however, 'a particular friendship' is not a neutral characterisation but rather a modification which can easily be interpreted as an accusation — depending on the activation of ideologically relevant background knowledge.

In (26), Kinkel argues for a common European currency:

Example (26)
Mit seiner stabilitätspolitischen Performance wäre *gerade Großbritannien* ein Gewinn für die Endstufe. (Kinkel)
[Britain would be a *particular gain* for the final stage due to its performance in terms of stability.]

We have to bear in mind that Kinkel is speaking in Great Britain and his purpose here is to stress the positive role Great Britain would play as a member of the European Monetary Union. In the ST, 'gerade' ('particularly') specifies 'Great Britain', but in the TT the specification is moved to 'gain'. This change is accompanied by a change in the focus, in the evaluation and also in the topic-focus structure of the sentence.

When we ask for effects of such deletions, additions and changes for the TT, we must not forget that the texts were relatively long. Apart from the fact that hedges are not very frequent in these political speeches anyway, I have discussed only individual sentences, more or less taken out of their contexts. The effects at the micro-level will rarely have a far-reaching effect at the macro-level of the speech or for politics in general. It can be argued that sometimes even the effect for the micro-level will go unnoticed by the speakers due to the specific communicative situation, e.g. when the speech is simultaneously interpreted. There may, however, be unwanted perlocutionary effects on the addressees when changes of hedges occur too often in the TT, as in the speech by Kinkel (cf. also Example (4)), but this would need a separate study.

Conclusion

In the context of political speeches, no clear dividing line between semantic and pragmatic aspects of hedges can be drawn. From a semantic point of view, hedges like 'genuine' or 'real' give specific, ideologically determined, prominence to one exemplar of the category. From the pragmatic point of view, particularly specifying hedges, but also modifying hedges, are often used in implicit argumentation with the political opponent(s). In this sense, hedges are linked to presuppositions and implicatures. In order to fully comprehend the message, the hearers will have to activate background knowledge, which will often be culture-specific.

From the point of view of translation, there may be comprehension problems whenever the TT audience does not have the relevant background knowledge. However, in the case of political speeches, the TT usually functions for internal political communication, in other words, compared to the ST, there is a narrower audience in the target community. Since this audience consists normally of knowledgeable politicians, it can be assumed that they will have the background knowledge which is needed to comprehend the intended message.

Some hedging devices are used to make a statement more vague. This occurs whenever politicians want to reduce their commitment to the truth of a proposition being conveyed or when they want to mitigate possible negative perlocutionary effects on their audience, i.e. hedges function interpersonally. As Channell (1994: 198) argues, understanding vague expressions 'requires hearers to bring to bear not just knowledge of the lexis and grammar of English, but also pragmatic knowledge about how language is used, and how it relates to its settings'.

It is particularly this aspect of understanding the function of hedges which is of high relevance for translation as cross-cultural communication. Translation difficulties can arise because of inadequate attention to hedged utterances and to the presuppositions that these hedges invite. Thus, the most important factors for the translator are the purpose of the target text and its addressees. Whenever there are differences in the background knowledge of ST and TT addressees which might affect the comprehension of the message, the translator would have to take decisions as to the textual format of the TT, for example making implicit information explicit.

As we have seen, in their respective context of political speeches, all hedges call for a pragmatic explanation. In most cases discussed, the hedges did not pose major difficulties for translation. This statement, however, cannot be generalised because it is based on just some preliminary observations of a specific text type. Wilss (1996) calls for a detailed description of hedging configurations. He argues that '[t]heir properties are adequately describable only in the context of their own functional system as a powerful softening strategy' (Wilss 1996: 121). Such a detailed description will also allow for further conclusions as to translation strategies. This chapter is meant as a step in this direction.

Notes

1. Channell (1994) excludes from hedges those expressions which introduce fuzziness *within* the proposition that the speaker is expressing e.g. 'He has a somewhat low interior larynx'. "Here, each speaker makes an unhedged (unshielded) statement about a phenomenon of which their knowledge is vague" (Channell, 1994: 17). Such expressions are called 'approximators'.

2. This is not to imply that in a written translation 'proper' and 'properly' would always have been rendered by one and the same German equivalent. The specific requirements of simultaneous interpreting call, of course, for an immediate solution, not allowing much time for reflection on consistency or variation.

Appendix: Analysed texts

I. Regierungserklärung des Ministerpräsidenten der DDR, Lothar de Maizière, Neues Deutschland, 20 April 1990.
   Policy statement by the Prime Minister of the GDR, Lothar de Maizière, at the third session of the GDR People's Chamber on 19 April 1990 (Foreign Affairs Bulletin, No. 9–10/1990, translated by Intertext).

II. Rt Hon. Tony Blair MP, Leader of the Labour Party, Speech to 1995 Labour Party Conference, 3 October 1995 (Issued by the Labour Party Conference Media Office).
   German simultaneous interpretation of the speech.

III. Speech by the Rt Hon. John Major MP, Prime Minister and Leader of the Conservative Party, to the 112th Conservative Party Conference, Blackpool, 13 October 1995.

IV. Die Europäische Union im 21. Jahrhundert, Rede von Bundesminister Dr. Klaus Kinkel in Oxford anläßlich der Eröffnung des Centre for Advanced Study of European and Comparative Law, 17 January 1996.
   'The European Union in the 21st century — more of the same?'. Speech by Dr. Klaus Kinkel, Federal Minister of Foreign Affairs, at the opening of the Centre for the Advanced Study of European and Comparative Law, Oxford, 17 January 1996.

References

Channell, J. (1994) *Vague Language*. Oxford: Oxford University Press.
Chilton, P. and Schäffner, C. (1997) Discourse and politics. In T.A. Van Dijk (ed.) *Discourse Studies. A Multidisciplinary Introduction* Vol. 2. *Discourse as Social Interaction* (pp. 206–30). London: Sage.
Grice, H.P. (1989) *Studies in the Way of Words*. Cambridge, MA: Harvard University Press.
Kay, P. (1979) The role of cognitive schemata in word meaning: Hedges revisited. Unpublished manuscript.
Lakoff, G. (1973) Hedges: A study in meaning criteria and the logic of fuzzy concepts. *Journal of Philosophical Logic* 2, 458–508.
Lakoff, G. (1982) Categories and cognitive models. Cognitive Science Report, University of California at Berkeley (mimeo).
Lakoff, G. (1991) Cognitive versus generative linguistics: How commitments influence results. *Language & Communication* II, 53–62.
Liedtke, F. (ed.) (1995) *Implikaturen. Grammatische und pragmatische Analysen*. Tübingen: Niemeyer.

Pinkal, M. (1985) Kontextabhängigkeit, Vagheit, Mehrdeutigkeit. In C. Schwarze and D. Wunderlich (eds) *Handbuch der Lexikologie* (pp. 27–63). Königstein/Ts: Athenäum.

Powell, M.J. (1985) Purposive vagueness: An evaluative dimension of vague quantifying expressions. *Journal of Linguistics* 21, 31–50.

Rosch, E. (1977), Human categorization. In E. Warren (ed.) *Advances in Cross-Cultural Psychology Vol. I* (pp. 1–49). New York: Academic Press.

Schäffner, C. (1990) Sind Abstrakta im politischen Bereich prototypisch beschreibbar? Überlegungen anhand des *Economist*. In C. Schäffner (ed.) *Gibt es eine prototypische Wortschatzbeschreibung? Eine Problemdiskussion (Linguistische Studien A 202)* (pp. 46–64). Berlin: Zentralinstitut für Sprachwissenschaft der Akademie der Wissenschaften der DDR.

Simon-Vandenbergen, A.-M. (1996) Image-building through modality: The case of political interviews. *Discourse & Society* 7, 389–415.

Sweetser, E. (1981) The definition of 'lie': An examination of the folk theories underlying a semantic prototype. Unpublished manuscript.

Tannen, D. (1993) What's in a frame? Surface evidence for underlying expectations. In D. Tannen (ed.) *Framing in Discourse* (pp. 14–56). New York/Oxford: Oxford University Press.

Van Dijk, T.A. (1995) Discourse, opinions and ideologies. *Current Issues in Language and Society* 2, 115–45.

Wilss, W. (1996) *Knowledge and Skills in Translator Behavior*. Amsterdam/Philadelphia: Benjamins.

Chapter 12

Translating the Pragmatics of Verse in 'Andromaque'

IAN HIGGINS

Using verse to solemnise a speech act, or to get people or gods to respond, is an ancient practice, the conventional rhythmic and phonic patterns of verse being held to give extra force to vows, prayers, hymns and incantations. Where such utterances are public or collective, the verse has a second function — typically, to strengthen the faith or banish the doubts of the audience or participants, or to prompt them to action. In literature, verse has been used from the start for similar purposes — as well as for its mnemonic value — in drama, love poetry, satire and so on. While the pragmatics of verse is relatively easy to appreciate in a dialogue, it can seem more problematic in a poem. Did Marvell really say or send those lines to his coy mistress? And if he did, did they do the trick? Countless love poems seem at least as much to be inviting a third party to admire, or to empathise with, the expression of the feelings of the other two, as to be actually addressing the beloved.

It is in verse theatre, particularly tragedy, that these various pragmatic functions of verse occur together most clearly and most conveniently for brief analysis. In so far as we empathise with these exemplary and (in tragedy) sacrificial characters, we are being persuaded both to accept the value of the theatrical ritual and to take part in it. In this essay, I am going to look at some implications of these observations in a speech from Act II, scene 1 of Racine's *Andromaque* (1667) and in three translations. In concentrating on the pragmatics of verse translation, I shall naturally leave undiscussed important aspects of both ST and TTs. I shall also take three things as given. First, that we react to the speech both as addressed by Hermione to Cléone (and to herself) and as addressed to us by Racine. Second, that if verse is preferred to prose for the TT, this is in order to exploit the expressive potential of TL verse conventions in a manner analogous to

that of the ST. Third, that the very fact that a text is in verse creates in the
reader or listener certain *a priori* expectations regarding genre, tone,
subject-matter, theme and the organisation of discourse. In respect of this
last, the conventions of verse lend themselves particularly well to the
expressive exploitation of, and departure from, more or less complex
patterns. I am going to look specifically at translation challenges posed by
the pragmatics of four features that Racine particularly exploits in this
manipulation of patterns: word order, the mute e (when heard as a schwa),
the caesura and rhyme. My analysis will principally show that each of these
features, especially the first three, has implications for thematisation and
emphasis. It will also show that this emphasis is affective, especially when
generated or reinforced by phonic and prosodic features: every line wrings
emotional reactions from Hermione, from her confidante and from the
spectator. The analysis is far from exhaustive, because there is only space
for discussion of a few samples of each feature. I shall examine Racine's text
first, and then the translations by Ambrose Philips (1712), John Cairncross
(1967) and Douglas Dunn (1990). Racine's lines will be referred to by the
number they have in the play, preceded by 'ST'; the lines in each of the TTs
are numbered from 1, and in references will be preceded by the translator's
initials. In notating English speech, a main stress will be shown as bold
italics, a secondary stress as italics alone. Here is Racine's text:

[*Contextual information*. The Greek princess Hermione is betrothed to
Pyrrhus, king of Epirus and destroyer of Troy. Pyrrhus, however, is in
love with his captive, Hector's widow, Andromaque. Andromaque
rejects him, ceaselessly mourning Hector and fearful for Astyanax, her
son: the Greeks have sent an embassy to secure his death. Pyrrhus is so
besotted with Andromaque that he has offered to protect the boy if she
will relent. Hermione has been told by her father to return to Greece if
Pyrrhus refuses to hand Astyanax over to the Greeks. Her confidante
Cléone tells her that her reluctance to turn her back on Pyrrhus shows
that, despite professing now to hate him, she does still love him.]

> HERMIONE
> Pourquoi veux-tu, cruelle, irriter mes ennuis?
> Je crains de me connaître en l'état où je suis.
> De tout ce que tu vois, tâche de ne rien croire;
> 430   Crois que je n'aime plus, vante-moi ma victoire;
> Crois que dans son dépit mon cœur est endurci;
> Hélas! et, s'il se peut, fais-le-moi croire aussi.
> Tu veux que je le fuie? Hé bien! rien ne m'arrête:
> Allons, n'envions plus son indigne conquête;

435 Que sur lui sa captive étende son pouvoir;
   Fuyons . . . Mais si l'ingrat rentrait dans son devoir!
   Si la foi dans son cœur retrouvait quelque place!
   S'il venait à mes pieds me demander sa grâce!
   Si sous mes lois, Amour, tu pouvais l'engager!
440 S'il voulait . . . Mais l'ingrat ne veut que m'outrager.
   Demeurons toutefois pour troubler leur fortune;
   Prenons quelque plaisir à leur être importune;
   Ou, le forçant de rompre un nœud si solennel,
   Aux yeux de tous les Grecs rendons-le criminel.
445 J'ai déjà sur le fils attiré leur colère;
   Je veux qu'on vienne encor leur demander la mère.
   Rendons-lui les tourments qu'elle me fait souffrir;
   Qu'elle le perde, ou bien qu'il la fasse périr. (Racine, 1965: 54–5)

In discussing word order, I shall concentrate on inversion and its consequences for thematisation. Let us take first ST 431. A prose alternative is 'Crois que mon cœur est endurci dans son dépit'. This has 12 syllables, but no median caesura. It also has a different focus, 'endurci' acquiring theme status as the sentence progresses to the climactic announcement of 'dépit'. Racine's order gives 'dans son dépit' a causal nuance; looked at purely grammatically, 'dépit' is thus reduced to a mere stage on the way to the climactic 'endurci'. As we shall see later, however, if one also looks at 'dépit' phonically and prosodically, it acquires quasi-rhematic force, which gives the line greater complexity and intensity; in effect it says: 'Crois (1) que j'ai sombré dans le dépit, et (2) que mon cœur s'est endurci'.

In ST 435, too, the word-order differs from the obvious prose alternative: 'Que sa captive étende son pouvoir sur lui'. In Racine's line, the listener is briefly held in suspense, so that special weight falls on 'captive'. Two other factors increase the emphasis still more; the three unvoiced plosives alliteratively tighten the link with 'conquête', and 'captive' falls in the privileged end-of-hemistich position. The irony and sarcasm are therefore greatly reinforced: while 'conquête' and 'captive' stand out primarily for reasons of versification, phonic factors throw them into further relief. The important conqueror/captive paradox is then finally highlighted by the line-terminal position of 'pouvoir'.

ST 437 is moving testimony to Hermione's distraught wishful thinking. The first hemistich has to be spoken with a slight hesitation after 'foi', to prevent possible misconstrual, viz 'la foi qui est dans son cœur'. There will also be a slight pause after 'cœur', because of the caesura. The pause naturally emphasises the vital word 'cœur', but it also briefly introduces the possibility that 'dans son cœur' does qualify 'foi' and not the coming verb. The bathos of the second hemistich then imitates Hermione's cruel disillusion by taking away that reading: there is no faith in Pyrrhus's heart after all. The rhematisation of the vague, pathetic 'quelque place' is far more desolate, and desolating, than if the more obvious 'cœur' had come at the 12th syllable.

One other example of inversion is especially worth discussing. ST 445 departs from unmarked word order, which would have 'le fils' after 'colère': 'J'ai déjà attiré leur colère sur le fils'. This would have rhematised 'fils', setting up the obvious end-of-line contrast with 'mère'. Unfortunately, it would have 13 syllables and a masculine rhyme. A 12-syllable possibility might be 'J'ai déjà attiré sur le fils leur colère'; but this thematises 'attiré sur le fils' and implies that what she wants to do now is get the Greeks to adopt an even more violent attitude than anger. Putting 'fils' at the caesura confirms it as rheme, and gives it particular stress because of its syntactic oddness.

In some cases, the effect of the inversion depends in part on another feature specific to verse, the systematic sounding of the mute e when it occurs between pronounced consonants within the line. For instance, in ST 435, 'étende' might be glossed over if the line were read as prose, the verb being treated more or less as a synonym of 'exerce', simply a means of arriving at the focus of interest, 'pouvoir'. As it is, the mute e is sounded, and the tonic syllable receives significant emphasis. The effect is to bring out the point that Andromaque already has power over Pyrrhus: 'He's pathetic,' it is implied, 'let him grovel still more'.

The mute e is fully exploited in other lines, where an inversion is not present. The effect is usually to introduce emphasis, as above. ST 430 is a good example, where 'aime' receives its full due. Taking ST 429–431 together, it is notable that on four occasions the first syllable of the hemistich is accented ('crois' twice, 'tâche', 'vante') . This is in itself unusual, and the use of the mute e heightens the effect in 'tâche' and 'vante', the tonic syllable receiving extra stress. The overall effect is one of rhythmic disruption: the lines do not slip smoothly off the tongue, but take an effort to speak. Our own breathing is disturbed as we listen to Hermione's distress.

ST 448 is an interesting case, in that the subject pronoun is rarely stressed in prose or in verse, even where, as here, the mute e in 'elle' has to be sounded. There is, however, a case for stressing 'elle' here, to compensate for the lack of a contrastive 'lui' in the second hemistich: 'que lui (,il) la fasse périr', which would have given one or two syllables too many (and is in any case, in either variant, an unlikely form in classical tragic verse). In the same line, the sounded mute e in 'fasse' attracts emphasis both to 'périr' and to Pyrrhus's agency as instigator of a Greek persecution of Andromaque. The line is slightly slowed, and attention is drawn to Hermione's manipulative vindictiveness.

There is virtually always a median caesura in the classical alexandrine, marked by a natural grammatical division and by some degree of pause and emphasis. As we have seen, inversion is often doubly expressive because it brings key words to either side of the caesura (or to both), as in ST 429, 435, 445. The same effect is often produced even where there is no inversion. In ST 428, the natural focus on 'connaître' helps to keep our attention focused on one of the play's key themes, self-knowledge and ignorance of self. The two occurrences of 'ingrat' at mid-line (ST 436, 440) emphasise Hermione's swings between clear-sightedness and wilful blindness: Pyrrhus *has* turned from her, but she sees him first as a penitent 'ingrat' and then as an insulting one.

The fourth significant feature is rhyme. Rhyme, too, can enhance the effect of inversion. In ST 429–430, for example, the inversion in the first line brings the vain hope of self-delusion to the fore, and the rhyme in 'croire/victoire' underlines the vanity of this victory. In ST 445–446, where the inversion avoids the obvious end-of-line contrast of 'fils/mère', it also permits the rhyme of 'colère/mère'. This emphasises Hermione's vindictiveness, Andromaque being earmarked for particular suffering almost as punishment for being the breeding female ('la mère', not 'sa mère').

Internal rhyme is also exploited by Racine, usually at the caesura, sometimes away from it. Seeing is believing, but Hermione is wishing it were not so. The intrusive hammer-blows of [wa] in ST 429–431 ('vois/crois/moi/crois'), one at the caesura, two in the marked first-syllable position, suggest her agitation and despair, an impression reinforced by the assonance with 'croire/victoire'. The dominant [wa] is abruptly replaced by the return (after ST 427–428) of [i], at the end of each hemistich in ST 431, at the end of ST 432, and at the sixth syllable in ST 433. This combination of internal and terminal rhyme on the high-pitched [i] is insistent and unrelaxed. It stresses the intellectual and emotional bathos of the second half of ST 432, and suggests that flight ('Tu veux que je le fuie?'), rather than persuasion, really is the only way of resolving her position. Then, after 'fuie', the end-of-hemistich sound changes in 'rien ne m'arrête': this is a real relief to the ear, suggesting that perhaps she herself is relieved finally to have decided to cut the Gordian knot and leave.

This resolve lasts for less than three lines, however. Her acceptance of the inevitable is confirmed by the echoes in 'ingrat' (ST 436, 440) and 'foi' (ST 437), each heightened by a slight pause. This makes her final switch back to self-delusion, in ST 441, all the more brittle, especially as the momentary slowing-down engineered in part by the sounded mute e in 'toutefois' throws into relief the near-rhymes (at the caesura) of 'ingrat' and 'toutefois': she knows very well that he is an 'ingrat', so her 'toutefois' is all the more laden with pathos.

All the effects I have been discussing derive especial power from the text's being in verse. Racine uses the basic prosodic and phonic characteristics of classical verse both to charge Hermione's agitation, anguish and vindictiveness with greater intellectual and emotional complexity and to give them specific illocutionary force and greater expressive power. The translator's job is to ensure that Hermione's and Racine's illocutionary projects function in the TT in a manner as closely analogous as possible to that of the ST.

In *The Distrest Mother*, Ambrose Philips does sometimes use major compensation to exploit his blank verse almost as successfully as Racine did his alexandrine:

HERMIONE

Why dost thou heighten my distress? I fear
To search out my own thoughts, and sound my heart.
Be blind to what thou seest: believe me cur'd;
Flatter my weakness; tell me I have conquer'd;
5   Think that my injured soul is set against him;
And do thy best to make me think so too.

CLEONE

Why would you loiter here, then?

HERMIONE

Let us begone! I leave him to his captive:
Let him go kneel, and supplicate his slave,
10   Let us begone! — But what if he repent?
What if the perjur'd prince again submit,
And sue for pardon: what if he renew
His former vows? — But, Oh, the faithless man!
He slights me! drives me to extremities! — However,
15   I'll stay, Cleone, to perplex their loves;
I'll stay, till, by an open breach of contract,
I make him hateful to the Greeks. Already

> Their vengeance have I drawn upon the son,
> Their second embassy shall claim the mother:
> 20   I will redouble all my griefs upon her! (Racine, 1776: 21)

ST 428 is given more than one line in the TT. In the ST, the crucial 'connaître' is in an emphatic position. This ensures that we do not miss the double meaning it has here: 'explore' and 'know'. It implies both emotional acquaintance and rational assessment and knowledge. The first hemistich of ST 428 implies the former, the second implies an affective state; the movement from one to the other reflects Hermione's vacillations. This typical use of metrical symmetry for expressive purposes cannot pass into a pentameter other than through compensation. Philips's longer formulation successfully covers both mind and heart as objects of discovery, though the 'knowledge' that would be acquired is only connoted, in 'search out' and 'own thoughts'. This is compensated for through the alliteration and assonance in 'search out' and 'sound', and through the accents on 'search' and 'sound', more marked than they would be in prose because they coincide with metrical stress.

AP 3–4 go beyond the ST, perhaps partly for metrical reasons. They do have several advantages, however. 'Flatter my weakness' is an implicit admission that she is failing: it restores the emphasis on *her* behaviour that is present in 'Crois que *je n'aime plus*' and absent from 'Believe *me cur'd*', and it compensates for the loss of the pitiable 'tâche de'. 'Tell me I have conquer'd' is a skilful rendering of 'vante-moi ma victoire', in that the loss of the boastfulness of 'vante' is counterbalanced by the metrical stress on 'tell' and 'I'. Further, as we have seen, ST 429–431 do not only denote Hermione's agitation, they also imitate it. Philips produces analogous effects. For instance, the jumps from verb to verb reflect Hermione's instability. The colons and semicolons, too, break the lines so much that the actress's delivery is awkward and agitated, as in the ST. And the compensatory power of 'Flatter my weakness' is all the greater as the fluttery rhythm interrupts the otherwise regular iambic beat of AP 3–4. In these two lines, Philips's manipulation of metre and rhythm offsets to some extent the loss of the phonic effects that Racine achieves through internal and terminal rhyme, alliteration and assonance in ST 429–433.

AP 7 is one of many instances where Philips gives speech to an interlocutor who is silent in the ST. In some cases, this breaks up speeches which are longer than English convention generally allowed. In others, as here, it picks up on one of the 'hidden' stage-directions that Racine builds into his texts: 'Tu veux que je le fuie?' is in part a response to a gesture from Cléone. Philips marks Hermione's momentary decisiveness through repetition ('Let us fly! Let us begone!'), where in the ST it is marked phonically, through the change from dominant [i] to the rhyme of 'arrête' and the highlighted 'conquête'.

AP 9 is another example of the exploitation of metre as compensation for a translation loss. Lexically, the line is a modulation of the ST, Pyrrhus being the agent instead of the patient. The sarcastic emphases wrought in ST 435 on 'lui', 'captive' and 'étende' by word order and the mute e are therefore lost. Philips compensates for this by having Pyrrhus 'kneel' and 'supplicate', his double act of submission corresponding to the stresses on 'lui' and especially on 'étende'. Phonically, the alliteration on stressed syllables in 'supplicate' and 'slave' marks the contradiction which, in the ST, was marked by inversion, with 'captive' and 'pouvoir' being brought to the end of successive hemistichs.

AP 10–14 correspond to ST 436–440, but — for whatever reason — are structurally very different. Philips does not match the pragmatic potential of English metrics to Racine's as fully as he did in the opening lines. He compensates for this lexically and phonically. Lexically, the imagery of 'repent', 'perju'd prince', 'submit' and 'sue for pardon' is a powerful development of the imagery in AP 9, and it is reinforced phonically, in the alliteration on [p] and [s].

The climactic murderous intensity of ST 447–448 is lost, as is the typical Racinian balanced antithesis of the last line. 'Redouble' has the two senses of 'double' and 'rebound', but the speech does end far less strongly than in the ST. However, AP 20 offers a good example of how breaking with conventional metrical pattern can change the illocutionary force. The actress can indeed compensate for some of the losses by disrupting the regular iambic flow ('I will redouble all my griefs upon her'), in three ways. First, she can ensure that we respond to both senses of 'redouble' by speaking it slowly and very emphatically, lengthening the first syllable enough to give it secondary-stress status. Second, she can give the line an anapestic ending ('upon her' versus 'upon her'). The unexpected anapest rhematises 'her', and Hermione's vindictiveness would come over more powerfully than in a simple iambic delivery. Third, this effect could be heightened still further by putting the mid-line stress on 'my' rather than 'all'. This would also help to compensate for the loss of Hermione's self-centred sense of persecution in AP 14 ('He slights me! drives me to extremities!' versus 'Mais l'ingrat *ne veut que* m'outrager') — an important quality, which she shares with Oreste. This climactic line of the speech would therefore be spoken like this: 'I will redouble all my grief upon her'. The departure from metrical convention would to a great extent restore by compensation the illocutionary force and the expressive power which Racine derives from metrical constraint and which would otherwise be lost.

This would be an entirely appropriate exploitation of the fact that the text is in verse.

Cairncross also uses blank verse, but with a close line-to-line correspondence between ST and TT:

HERMIONE

Why must you, cruel one, inflame my wounds?
I fear to look into a heart distraught.
Each thing you witness try to disbelieve.
Believe I love no more. Cry Victory.
5   Believe my heart is steeled against him, and,
If that may be, make me believe it too.
You tell me flee. Well, nothing holds me back.
Envy no more his paltry conquest. Let
His captive over him extend her sway.
10   Let's flee. But if the ingrate felt the call
Of duty and some twinge of faithfulness,
If he came back, sought pardon at my feet;
If you could bind him, love, to my command,
If . . . But he seeks only to outrage me.
15   Let us stay on to spoil their happiness,
And find some joy in being in their way;
Or, forcing him to break so strong a tie,
Make him a criminal to all the Greeks.
I have already drawn their anger on
20   The son. They must demand the mother too.
I'll pay her back for all she's made me bear.
Let her be *his* downfall or he be hers. (Racine, 1967: 62–3)

In this TT, the effects of some of Racine's inversions are successfully rendered through inversion, a similar degree of stylisation ensuring a certain dignity which is far from always being as unconvincing as the lexically dilute JC 2, in which, too, the inversion of noun and adjective suggests metrical constraint and nothing more. The slightly archaic order in JC 8, however, works well, 'his paltry conquest' being given rheme status, to match the ST emphasis thrown on to 'conquête' by the mute e in 'indigne'. But the clear self-address of 'envions' is lost. In JC 9, on the other hand, the inversion coincides perfectly with the iambic metre to invite a sneering emphasis on 'over *him*', although this does imply a weakening of the sense of 'extend' to something like 'exert' — precisely the effect Racine avoids through the mute e in 'étende'.

JC 19–20 ingeniously convey something of the effect wrought by the inversion in ST 445, an inversion which would have been far-fetched in the only slightly archaising English that Cairncross uses. There is real menace in the curt 'They must demand the mother too', which compensates to some extent for the loss of the effect produced by the rhyme of 'colère/mère'.

Cairncross felicitously renders some pragmatic effects that, in the ST, are worked by other means than simple inversion. In JC 5, 'steeled against him' combines 'endurci' and, by modulation, 'dépit' (which implies hostility towards the cause of the 'dépit'). It does, however, lose the vehemence that word order and the rhyme in [i] give to the ST. This could perhaps be compensated for if the noun 'steel' were substituted for 'steeled': for the line to be clear, the actress would have to give aggressive emphasis to 'steel', and pause slightly after it; and it would have a stronger connotation of 'weapon' than of 'steeled'.

The 'twinge of faithfulness' in JC 11 is a clever rendering of ST 437 in a short space, when the material of JC 10–11 was threatening to overspill and spoil the overall line-for-line correspondence of ST and TT. The physicality of 'twinge' skilfully connotes 'cœur' and 'quelque place'; and, through its collocative meanings of 'regret' and 'remorse', it gives back to Hermione the combination of yearning and sarcasm which is generated in the ST by the position of 'dans son cœur'.

In JC 14, the effect of the repetition of end-of-hemistich 'ingrat' is lost. However, there is some metrical compensation for this loss. A natural stressing of the line is something like this: 'If . . . But he seeks only to outrage me'. After the second foot, the line becomes trochaic, which forces a slight hiatus after 'seeks' and therefore throws emphasis on Hermione's warped self-centredness, just as Racine's line does. If further compensation is felt necessary, the actress could again call the metre to the rescue. She would stress the 'If' and, after a distraught silence, speak the rest of the line like this: 'But he seeks only to outrage me'. For this to work, she needs, not to gloss over 'seeks', which is vital, but to linger, in quivering (almost tearful) anger, over 'he'. This way of stressing 'he' compensates for the loss of 'ingrat'. And, given the assonance in 'he seeks', the syntagm could have an almost uniform intonation: while 'he' is granted full metrical stress status, 'seeks' is also lengthened, and followed by a (slight) indignant pause, so that it retains its importance in pointing to 'outrage me'. The effect is completed by giving 'to' greater prominence than in the 'natural' reading suggested above, lengthening it and perhaps pausing fractionally after it.

Overall, Cairncross's TT is less intellectually complex and emotionally intense than Philips's; this is mainly because Cairncross is less willing to compensate for the loss of ST textual effects, whether by creating corresponding effects at different *places* in the TT or by using different *types* of textual effect in the TT.

Douglas Dunn's translation is longer and much freer than the other two. Few of the effects specific to Racine's versification are rendered through TL versification. He has chosen the iambic pentameter, rhyming it in couplets, although the rhymes are often approximate:

HERMIONE

You torturess! You touch my wounds with salt.
I fear for what I feel, and what I've felt.
Though you discredit everything you see,
Trust in this — *I don't love.* That's victory!
5   And here's another truth — my angry mind
Confronts its obstacles and I'm determined.
Please, if it can be done, teach me to trust
My heart and what it says, because I must.
You think it's best to leave? Nothing stops it.
10   Come on, then. Envy's inappropriate
To what he's done. We'll let her mistress him;
He'll be a prisoner to his prisoner's whim.
We'll go . . .
        But what if Pyrrhus should relearn
His duty, and replace his unconcern
15   With all the love he used to feel for me,
And beg forgiveness on his bended knee?
If, if, O Love, if only you obeyed
The laws of love that you claim to have made!
Insulting me's the only thing he wants.
20   Oh, no, we'll stay; we'll be their irritants —
We'll laugh at them by worsening their luck,
And, by obliging Pyrrhus to unpluck
His solemn ties, present to every Greek
The renegade and outcast that they seek.
25   I've drawn their hatred to the Trojan child;
His mother, too, I want dead and defiled.
For what she's made me suffer she must pay
In suffering; and this Andromache
Shall cause Pyrrhus to fall, and Pyrrhus err
30   In such a way he'll cause the death of *her.* (Racine, 1990: 19)

Occasionally, the rhyme creates a highlight effect analogous to an ST highlight achieved by other means. For example, in DD 15–16, the rhyme 'me/knee' emphasises the dream of dominance conveyed in ST 438 by the position of '(à mes) pieds' at the caesura and 'grâce' at the end of the line. The effect is felicitously reinforced by the alliteration and assonance of 'beg [. . .] bended'. However, the heavy stress on 'me' that is needed if the rhyme is to work creates an unwanted illocutionary force. The intended contrast in the sentence is between 'unconcern' and 'love', not 'Andromache' and 'me'; so the natural focus of the line is 'love', or possibly 'used to'. Consequently, a weak, virtually dactylic ending to the line is required, 'me' being spoken more as [mɪ] than as [miː].

In DD 11, on the other hand, it is essential that 'him' be heavily stressed, for three reasons. In the first place, it ensures that the splendid oxymoron of DD 12 is announced in DD 11. Second, it enables the rhyme with DD 12 to cement the oxymoron, *she* dictating to *him*. Finally, it prevents the iambic DD 11 petering out as 'we'll let her mistress him': this dactylic ending is the most tempting 'natural' reading, but it would allow the sexual connotations of 'mistress' to smother the use of 'to mistress' as a substitute for 'to master'.

Apart from these examples, the intended function of the rhyming is unclear. The need for rhyme seems sometimes actually to have led to additions or contortions which do not altogether harmonise with the emotional and intellectual complexity of either ST or TT (e.g. DD 7–8, 17–18, 21–22, 23–24, 25–26, 29–30). The TT is indeed eight lines longer than the ST. This is doubtless also because, in respect of verse pragmatics, Dunn has apparently tried to compensate, in three main ways, for the sorts of loss we have seen it is easy to incur in translating into verse: he introduces concrete imagery, spinning out ST images or particularising ST terms (e.g. DD 1, 5–6, 7–8, 9, 11, 20, 22–23, 24, 26); he introduces repetition (e.g. DD 12, 17–18, 27–28, 29); and he makes extensive use of alliteration and assonance (e.g., in addition to the repetitions, DD 1, 2, 15–18, 21–22, 26).

The result of this approach is a series of vivid images, conceits and phonetic agglomerations which do not cohere into a whole, sometimes even contradicting each other or simply not making sense. They seem only approximately to correspond to the tone, complexity and intensity of the ST, and hardly at all to the illocutionary power of Racine's versification. DD 2, for example, not only loses the mind/heart complexity and the crucial tension between knowledge and illusion, but it is so distant from the ST as to be virtually meaningless: it surely paraphrases as 'I'm afraid harm will come to what I feel and what I've felt'. In DD 3, the sense of ST 429 is totally lost: few people will construe 'Though you discredit' as 'Even if you discredit'; and 'discredit' is bound to be understood as 'bring discredit on'.

DD 7–8 are also baffling. In DD 5, it is her *mind* that is determined. Now she wants to trust her *heart*. Any spectator will register this as an instance of the old opposition of mind and heart. Yet it is surely her heart that tells her she still loves Pyrrhus? Are heart and mind opposed here, or are they as one? If, next, in DD 10–16, we do momentarily catch her drift, the conceit in DD 17–18 ensures that we lose sight of it again. The audience will inevitably take 'Love' to be addressed to the absent Pyrrhus, because (unlike Racine's Hermione) she has explicitly introduced 'all the love he used to feel for me' in DD 15; ST 439 is lost without trace. By the time we have worked these lines out (or given up trying), we will return to what she is saying just in time to assume (in some puzzlement) that the 'renegade and outcast that they seek' is Astyanax: here, too, the crystal-clear ST 443–444 disappear almost completely.

Not surprisingly, the very condensed ST 447–448 are expanded into four lines in the TT. The repetitions are skilful attempts at compensation for losing the expressive force of the various occurrences of pronounced mute e, but the awful rhyme in 'err/*her*' and the bathos of DD 30 (trying *not* to sound like Frankie Howerd) ruin the effect.

It is clear from the foregoing that the defining features of verse have illocutionary potential. Nowadays, this potential is indeed one of their major *raisons d'être*. Further, regardless of the local effects produced as the text develops, the very fact of writing in verse triggers certain expectations in readers, listeners and spectators. It is not enough, however, simply to decide to write a TT in verse. Once the decision has been taken to render verse with verse, as much attention has to be paid to the big differences between SL and TL versification systems as to the characteristic differences in the ways in which the two languages create emphasis. With care, skill and good luck, the translator into English will sometimes be able to use the defining features of, say, blank verse to achieve illocutionary effects similar to those created by, say, Racine's use of versification. Philips, Cairncross and Dunn have done this, Philips more consistently than Cairncross, and Cairncross than Dunn.

All three, however, depend on the actress's sensitivity to verse for these effects to be realised in performance — good examples of this are AP 20; JC 5, 14–15; and DD 11–12. In such cases, a crucial consideration in the pragmatics of translating verse is the need to supply stage directions, italics or punctuation marks that are not necessarily present in the ST. Cairncross does use italics in JC 22, but he could usefully have italicised 'her' as well. Dunn's italics in DD 4 are a sensitive way of compensating for the loss of 'vante-moi [. . .]': the lady doth protest too much for us to take this as anything but wishful thinking. As they stand, however, all three TTs would have done themselves and Racine a favour if they had added some stage directions, to help the English-speaking actress do what it is, after all, completely natural to do in prose as well as verse — to use vocal stress and intonation for emphasis where, so often, French uses grammatical devices. It is perhaps significant in this respect that Racine has so few stage directions: 17th-century convention apart, the characteristics of classical French versification quite simply indicate thematisation and emphasis more clearly than do those of English versification. But as long as one accepts that translation loss is inevitable at every turn, and that there is an inexhaustible repertoire of ways in which those losses can be more or less compensated for, there is no reason for holding Racine's plays to be more 'untranslatable' than other texts. Philips showed the way, in his blend of literality and adaptivity. In our own time, Cairncross has favoured the literal way, Dunn the adaptive. Step forward an Ambrose Philips for the year 2000.[1]

Notes

1. Craig Raine calls his '1953' a 'version' of *Andromaque*. (It takes place in Rome, the Axis powers having won in the West and razed London. Annette, the widowed mother of Angus LeSkye, claimant to the British throne, is in captivity. Turning his back on his German fiancée, Ira, Mussolini's son lusts after Annette, but she spurns him.) Raine takes the adaptive strategy to its limits. He does not translate the ST, but, keeping its plot structure and often matching speech to speech, he uses vivid imagery and alternating, loosely iambic, pentameters and tetrameters (the latter rhyming with one another) to produce a thematic and affective cogency which is often — as in this speech — comparable to that which Racine creates by other means. It worked well at the Citizens' Theatre, Glasgow, in 1992, and was staged at the Almeida Theatre, London, in 1996, in a production I did not see. It is well worth study but, by its very nature, it would have taken this discussion beyond the parameters set for it.

References

Racine, J. (1965) *Andromaque*. Paris: Larousse (Classiques Larousse).
Racine, J. (1967) *Andromache* (translation J. Cairncross). London: Penguin.
Racine, J. (1990) *Andromache* (translation D. Dunn). London: Faber & Faber.
Racine, J. (1776) *The Distrest Mother* (translation A. Philips [1712]). London: John Bell.
Raine, C. (1990) '1953'. London: Faber & Faber.

Chapter 13

Perlocutionary Equivalence: Marking, Exegesis and Recontextualisation

LEO HICKEY

Perlocution

In distinguishing locutionary, illocutionary and perlocutionary acts, Austin (1962) was referring to what a person says, does and brings about, or is likely to bring about, in or on somebody, respectively. In uttering a certain sentence, then, a speaker says something (thus performing a locutionary act, as in 'Get lost!'), does something (performing an illocutionary act, such as insulting or giving a command) and brings or may bring about some effect on somebody (performing a perlocutionary act, perhaps causing the hearer to feel upset and to go away). These three 'acts' are so inextricably interrelated as to be regarded by some as no more than different perspectives of one and the same transaction (see Davis, 1980: 37; Leech, 1983: 201–3).

On perlocution Austin (1962: 101) wrote:

> Saying something will often, or even normally, produce certain consequential effects upon the feelings, thoughts, or actions of the audience, or of the speaker, or of other persons: and it may be done with the design, intention, or purpose of producing them; and we may then say, thinking of this, that the speaker has performed an act . . . We shall call . . . the act performed, where suitable . . . a 'perlocution'.

He went on to describe a perlocutionary act as 'what we bring about or achieve *by* saying something, such as convincing, persuading, deterring, or even, say, surprising or misleading' (p. 109).

Davis (1980: 39) distinguishes the perlocutionary act (the speaker's causing the hearer to do something or something to be done to the hearer), the perlocutionary cause (the speaker's saying something) and the perlocutionary effect (the hearer's doing something or what happens in, on or to the hearer). Thus, for our purposes, an original or source text (ST) may perform a perlocutionary act and constitute a perlocutionary cause of certain perlocutionary effects.

Imagine that Paul has received a bill for a large sum which he cannot pay. It will probably worry him, send him scurrying to his bank manager and eventually get him to pay up. His wife happens to read the bill, she also gets worried and shows it to her friend to explain why she is worried; the friend feels and expresses sympathy for Paul's wife. One and the same text may thus bring about different reactions in different readers. Now imagine a similar bill comes to Ann, written in a language she does not understand, from an overseas supplier. She has it translated and the translation or target text (TT) worries her, gets her to scurry to her bank manager and eventually pay up. In this second case, clearly the ST and the TT produce different perlocutionary effects on Ann, and the ST does not directly cause any of the effects intended by the writer. Nevertheless the ST is capable of stimulating effects analogous to those that derive from Paul's bill and the TT must likewise be capable of stimulating all these effects: otherwise the translation is defective.

In studying perlocution in translation, let us keep in mind that a translator is not concerned with real effects (if any) produced on real readers (if any) of the TT, but only with the potential effects. Let us also be aware that the writer's subjective intentions are irrelevant and can be ignored, except in so far as they are objectively maifested in the ST (see Austin, 1962: 106)

Following Austin's admission (1962: 110) that *'any*, or almost any, perlocutionary act is liable to be brought off, in sufficiently special circumstances, by the issuing, with or without calculation, of any utterance whatsoever', Gu (1993: 408) explains that 'the utterance exerts *no binding force* on the effects produced', it may produce 'an infinite and indefinite number' of effects and consequently it is impossible to infer, from what a speaker says, what consequences may ensue. Gu, therefore, rejects any strict line of causation between an utterance and its perlocutionary effects, stressing instead the hearer's 'legitimate claim to agency' (p. 420). He argues that it is in fact the hearer who produces the reaction and that perlocutionary effects, psychological or mental events, are 'response-acts' of which the hearer is the agent. A perlocutionary act then 'is a joint endeavour between S(peaker) and H(earer). It involves S's performance of speech acts and H's performance of response-acts' (p. 422). In other words, the speaker's saying something plays (merely) a triggering role in the whole transaction and different individuals in different contexts may respond differently to one and the same trigger.

In accepting the broad thrust, though not the extreme details in all cases, of Gu's arguments, I will regard the speaker's locution and illocution as a trigger and I will deal here, not with perlocutionary acts or even causes, but with perlocutionary effects potentially brought about in or on the hearer. To be practical, a translator must treat all such responses, however 'infinite and indefinite', as being analogous to one another on the ground that they have at least their trigger or cause in common, even if the readers and their contexts may be different. Although such perlocutionary effects may fall outside the study of pragmatics and linguistic communication, as some argue (see Gu, 1993: 428; Leech, 1983: 203), in dealing as she thinks best with the locution (what the ST says) and the illocution (what the ST does), a translator (see Gutt, note 1: this volume) must examine all potential perlocutions (the effects and responses reasonably predictable — on the basis of the common trigger or cause — in or on the mind, imagination, feelings or actions of a reader of the TT) as a check to ensure that perlocutionary equivalence — 'perlocutionary analogy' might be a more accurate term — has been achieved.

My contention then is that, just as the ST is capable of producing or likely to produce or stimulate one or more analogically related perlocutionary effects on its original readers, so also any TT must, in turn, be capable of producing 'analogous' perlocutionary effects on its readers. The use of the adjective 'analogous' rather than 'similar', allows for the fact that, just as not all ST readers or their contexts are the same, so also the TT readers may be quite different, and situated in different contexts, from any of the ST readers.

Perhaps I should recall here that philosophers have interpreted the concept of perlocution in varying ways. Grice (1957), for example, seems to believe that to say something and mean it is a matter of intending to perform a perlocutionary act, whereas Searle claims that saying something and meaning it is precisely a matter of intending to perform an illocutionary act; he argues that (simply to produce) understanding of what is said is not a perlocution (Searle, 1969: 46–7). With this divergence in mind, I wish to suggest that understanding or knowledge of what has been said — if such a reaction or effect is ever possible on its own in real life or if, to parody Austin, there is such an animal — comes under my (broadened) category of perlocution, on the grounds that it is something that takes place within the domain of the hearer's response allowing him to react further as he thinks best after the speaker has performed her part in the event.

Therefore by perlocutionary effect I mean, for the purposes of this study, any effect, result or response, which may range from (mere) understanding to being alarmed or frightened and even to shooting someone (Austin's example), produced in or on the hearer by a locution/illocution either alone or in combination with some relevant features of the context and the reader. It therefore extends to any change in the hearer's state of mind, emotion, actions etc.

Perhaps I have arrived, by a circuitous route, at a position quite close to Nida's 'dynamic' or 'functional' equivalence (see de Waard and Nida, 1986: 36–40), or to Newmark's 'equivalent effect' (see Newmark, 1988: 48), which the latter sees as a desirable result rather than as the aim of any translation. Yet my contention is that the concept of perlocution outlined here means that the translator must aim to provide a text capable of offering its readers the opportunity of experiencing an analogous effect to that which the ST offered its own readers, that it must do this always and not just in certain cases, as Newmark seems to suggest, nor just allowing them to 'comprehend the translated text to such an extent that they can understand how the original receptors must have understood the original text', as Nida requires (see de Waard and Nida, 1986: 36).

Let us take a fairly realistic example. Suppose a commercial letter ends as follows: 'Thanking you for the prompt settlement of your account', any translation of this phrase, however locutionarily (or literally) accurate or illocutionarily similar to the ST with regard to the linguistic level or the act of thanking the addressee, which gives the latter either a feeling of satisfaction at having paid the bill (if he has not) or convinces him that he must pay it (if he has already done so) will be inadequate from the perlocutionary point of view; the translator must produce a version that will be as perlocutionarily ambiguous as the original, which is locutionarily and illocutionarily clear (unless we wish to distinguish the speech act of 'thanking in advance' from that of 'thanking in arrears') but leaves the 'prompt settlement of your account' perlocutionarily unclear as to whether the reader should feel satisfaction at having already paid or be convinced that he must now pay the bill.

I now wish to look at three factors that are closely involved with perlocution.

Marking

Whatever emerges from the pen of the translator, it seems certain that it will be, or have some connection with, reported speech. After all, a translator is *de facto* a mediator, a third person, intervening between the writer of the ST and the reader of the TT. Whether this mediation is quite 'visible' (as in a word-processed document headed 'Translation' and signed by the translator) or virtually 'invisible' (as when a brief text on mathematics, consisting mainly of formulae, is translated from one language to another on an otherwise blank sheet of paper), the translator has accomplished a task that yields an output, the TT, which is one step away — in some real or metaphorical sense — from the original. The TT reader, consequently, will read something which is necessarily different from what the ST author wrote.

I suggest, therefore, that a TT is somehow 'marked' in the sense that it may carry a kind of notice or signal, however notional, along the lines: 'Read the following text as a translation', 'The original text refers not to Britain but to Spain' or 'An original text says, does and may cause you to . . .'. The result is that, at some level, the reader should or is bound to read the TT in a way that differs from the way in which the original text is read: for example, by imagining that he is in a 'world' or society which he would not immediately imagine, by mentally adapting references, allusions or terms that he does not automatically recognise, or by simply making adjustments of the type 'When the text says "I" or "my", it doesn't mean the writer of what I am reading but rather some third person'.

I am not referring necessarily to such overt marks as the translator's name on the title page of a work of literature, blatantly foreign names and addresses on word-processed sheets or even explicit references to foreign terms, currency, place-names or customs. I am referring, rather, to the reality interposed between the ST and the final reader, a textual operator which ensures that the reader is told what the original text says, does and may stimulate, rather than being obliged or permitted to experience the original for himself at first hand.

This is not to say that some translated texts may not themselves function as original texts: for example, multilingual public notices, Acts of Parliament passed in all relevant languages or other texts which are signed or validated by whatever person or process is competent to validate them, such as the President of the Republic, the Company Secretary or the author of a bilingual text in a multilingual or diglossic situation.

Exegesis

The view that translations are *ipso facto* mediated and marked to that effect leads easily to the question of exegesis or explanation of the ST. The difficulties readers may experience in understanding a TT may be due to the fact that it is not 'about', does not 'refer to' or 'use' the culture, including the language or other realities, that would be accessible or known to them. A legal text is likely to be 'about' certain concepts and realities (constituting, amending or discussing them), a literary text may 'refer to' certain realities in order to stimulate a particular type of (aesthetic) experience, and humorous texts at most 'make use of' certain realities which may be quite peripheral to what is being aimed at (usually to amuse the reader).

For example, if a Spanish text states that the 'juez' visited the scene of a crime as part of his investigation, a translator will have to decide whether simply to translate 'juez' as 'judge' or perhaps 'investigating judge' or to explain that some Spanish 'judges' are more similar to English police officers than to English judges.

Since the TT will be marked as referring to Spain, the perlocutionary effect which it is capable of producing will be a function of the level of any exegesis provided. Perlocution derives from locutionary/illocutionary acts + context + reader, and TT context = ST context + exegesis + marking; therefore the perlocution will depend — among other factors — on the levels of marking and exegesis which operate to adjust the TT reader's context and his 'suitability' as a reader, in order to make him a more 'suitable' reader and situate him in a more 'suitably fitted' context to the TT. The more strongly or visibly the text is marked as a translation of a text from a given source culture, the less exegesis will be appropriate: this is clear in the case of legal texts; the more weakly, invisibly or notionally the marking, the more exegesis may be required to make the text suitable to be read by a TT reader.

Recontextualisation

In discussing marking and exegesis I have posited a situation in which a translator may strongly mark a TT as deriving from an ST of a certain culture, leaving the cultural, linguistic and other references more or less intact or, alternatively, may give a strong exegesis or explanation of the ST background, thus requiring weaker marking. I now posit the possibility that an original context (including features of the language) may play such an essential part in the perlocution that no degree of exegesis or marking combined will achieve the desired effects. For example, humour frequently depends for its effect on some characteristic of the original language, which it may not share with the target language.

By recontexualistation I refer to a radical approach to the translation of a particular text, which consists of totally or partially abandoning the literal, propositional or locutionary level, while maintaining the illocutionary act (usually 'telling') as far as possible and focusing strongly on the perlocutionary effect, directly or accurately reproducing it.

For example, a teacher is explaining proverbs to the class and asks one little boy: 'Now Johnny, cleanliness is next to what?', 'Impossible, Miss', replies Johnny. The humour here is caused by a one-word deviation from the well known proverb, which nevertheless makes perfect sense to any reader and makes more sense to a child than the expected 'godliness'. If a translator were to explain this (approximately as I have just done) he might achieve an exegesis but the perlocutionary effect (amusement) would be destroyed. Recontextualisation will involve finding a proverb in the target language and distorting it in the same way as the original: 'En boca cerrada no entran caramelos', 'De noche todos los gatos son ruidosos', 'A quien madruga Dios le da sueño' etc. Here there is no marking or exegesis and the perlocutionary effect is virtually identical to that of the ST.

Perlocution in Practice

I now propose to exemplify how in some texts (legal) very strong marking and very weak exegesis may contribute to perlocutionary equivalence, in others (literary) weak marking and weak exegesis may achieve the same objective, while in yet others (humorous) very weak or no marking or exegesis together with recontextualisation may be effective. In Table 1 what I hope to show is as follows:

Table 1

Type	Perlocution	Marking	Exegesis	Recontextualisation
Legal	inform etc.	very strong	very weak	—
Literary	evoke etc.	weak	weak	—
Humorous	amuse etc.	weak/none	—	very strong

The concept of marking, strictly speaking, conflicts with that of perlocution because, if we interpret marking literally, we reduce all TTs to the function of informing. If a text begins with a mark signalling: 'The text of which the following is a translation says that . . . ', then it can literally or directly perform no speech act other than that of informing its readers of what the ST says, does and is capable of bringing about, just as a person who reports that a third party is performing, or has performed, a certain act is not, by doing so, herself performing any act other than reporting. Yet, of course, we are accustomed to being affected — and very deeply — by indirect speech, not to mention indirect speech acts. It still remains, however, that all the effects produced on the TT reader will be *de facto* at one remove from the ST. Just as an intended addressee's wife or casual visitor may react differently to a bill addressed to the intended addressee, so also — but no more so — a reader of a TT may react differently to the TT from the way in which the original ST readers reacted. This, it seems to me, is an intrinsic feature of translation and is itself neither positive nor negative.

Legal Translation

Legal translation covers a wide range of texts, from a country's Constitution or Acts of Parliament, to a single-sentence fax from a client to a legal adviser, with all sorts of public and private documents, forms and paperwork in between, having in common only some link with the Law. However, we may generalise and say that legal texts usually make or amend the law or regulate relationships between persons, being informative, explicative and factual, rather than literary or humorous, often referring in specialised terminology and complex style to realities, concepts and distinctions that are not material, concrete or physical.

Any translation must, as I have said, be capable of potentially (that is, given an appropriate reader and context) affecting its readers in whatever way the ST was capable of doing to its readers: for example, moving them to take or refrain from taking some action, including feelings produced by illocutionary acts (such as thanking or promising) that some authorities explicitly argue are not perlocutionary and which, as it happens, frequently occur in legal documents (see Davis, 1980: 47).

Indexical or deictic expressions, which acquire their meaning directly from some features of the situation in which they are uttered (such as 'I' or the first person singular of verbs), will usually appear in some very similar form in the TT, since this will normally produce analogous effects to those produced by the ST. However, some referring expressions (like 'the Law', 'the Constitution', 'our Criminal Justice system' or 'the Sale of Goods Act') may require 'marking' to show that they refer to realities in the ST culture and not in the TT culture: 'the Spanish Law', 'the French Constitution', 'the Senegalese Criminal Justice system', 'the English Sale of Goods Act' etc. This is one form of marking and an alternative to labelling the whole text at or near the beginning (see Richardson: this volume).

We may assume that a translation of a translation, whether into a third language or back into the source language (in which case it will presumably be done either in ignorance of its TT status or as an attempt to recover the original, and in no case can it be attributed to the author of the ST, since it is highly unlikely to reproduce her words), is doubly marked. This would mean something like: 'Another text says that an original text says that . . .'. Interestingly, this indirectness reflects quite accurately the intuition that each translation takes the reader one step away from the original text, which is, in a way, the point I am treating under the heading of marking.

I come now to exemplify exegesis. Let us imagine that an English lawyer drafts a memo to his trainee saying: 'Re SoGA, see 1 All ER 135 1987 and advise'. The intended reader understands that this concerns the Sale of Goods Act 1979 and he is to look up Volume I of the *All England Law Reports* 1987 and let his boss know whether the decision in the case reported on page 135 (Aswan Engineering Establishment Co. versus Lupdine Ltd.) is relevant to a case on which they are engaged at present. The TT must produce analogous effects in a Spanish lawyer and this will be achieved by spelling out 'Sale of Goods Act 1979' and 'Volume I *All England Law Reports* 1987' and by translating 'advise' as meaning 'inform me of your findings'. However, an English lawyer will be familiar with the Sale of Goods Act and will know whether, for example, if the thing to be sold is a crop of wheat growing in a field at the time the contract is made, this will be counted as 'goods' for the purposes of the Act, whereas a Spanish lawyer might not know this or even see its relevance. Nevertheless, it is no part of the translator's task to provide an exegesis of this or any other substantive point of law. The translator must ask herself how the original text reader would have been affected and ensure that an analogical TT reader will be affected similarly by his reading of the text (hence his marking and spelling out) but not by any other means. She will thus be expected to explicate anything that is explicated in the text surface and nothing else.

Take another example: an English text about a Coroner's Court is to be translated into Spanish, Spain being a country which has nothing exactly like a coroner. Since it is no part of the translator's task to teach her TT reader about the English system relating to coroners, she will have fulfilled her function if she drafts a TT which can produce on a (notional) reader who knows what a coroner is an analogous effect to that which the ST was likely to have on the ST reader, using any term for 'coroner' (including 'coroner', 'forense', 'juez', 'juez correspondiente' . . . but perhaps not 'médico forense', as this might lead to misunderstandings because of its similarities and differences from the coroner), which will trigger in the TT reader recognition without adding information not explicit in the ST: any information on the coroner's functions, methods of working, relationships with other officials or the legal system (and perhaps especially how he differs from the Spanish 'médico forense') would constitute exegesis in my sense.

In particular, I suggest that a translator should not over-assimilate concepts or realities in the source and target cultures. This becomes relevant, for example, in cases of synecdoche or metonymy, where one system may use the name of part of something to refer to the whole and vice versa, or may simply name something closely associated with something else. In English to say that a car 'passed its MOT' means that it passed its annual roadworthiness test, even though the Ministry of Transport (MOT) fulfils countless functions other than overseeing this test: so a phrase meaning 'annual test' would provide a reasonable translation and it would be *ultra vires* if the translator were to give further information. Similarly, in Spanish 'Hacienda' (referring to the Ministry of Finance, though containing no overt mention of any ministry, and much less of any particular branch of the ministry) is the normal word corresponding to 'Income Tax' or the 'Inland Revenue', and these would provide reasonable translations without further explanation. In cases like these also, marking without exegesis might be the most appropriate translation procedure.

To sum up, then, legal texts being very culture-based or culture-specific, many of the concepts, realities and terms which condition them will not be readily accessible to readers of their translations. A TT should show therefore, by clear marking, that it is a translation, and this exonerates, indeed precludes, it from explaining the realities, concepts or terms; rather, it leaves them as they are, translated but unexplained, within the framework of the marked text so that the reader may seek legal advice or explanations exactly as he would if confronted by a technical text in his own language.

Literary Translation

Here I have in mind mainly novels and short stories which, according to Pratt (1977: 143, referring to Grice and Searle), 'fall into the class whose primary point is thought-producing, representative or world-describing', rather than action-stimulating. The pragmatic status of such texts may be unsettled (see Pratt, 1977: 90; Searle, 1979: 58–75 for claims that fiction seems to pretend to perform speech acts), but in any case their perlocutionary effects must be safeguarded in translation.

Indeed, although Austin included under perlocution both overt, objective, actions on the hearer's part (like shooting someone) and covert, subjective reactions (such as being convinced of something), and although clearly some literary works may stimulate readers to take action, it is more normal and perhaps more essential that they induce or evoke in the reader some purely internal reaction: aesthetic experiences of pleasure, feelings of appreciation, enjoyment or admiration, images and mental activities such as relating singular characters or events to general or universal levels of meaning.

Although some aspects of literary texts, such as the story, characters, descriptions of places etc., usually 'carry over' fairly easily from a ST to a TT, yet even these 'transferable' realities will elicit somewhat different reactions in the TT reader: at some psychological or aesthetic level, any reader of a translation will react differently from a reader of the original. Nevertheless, the aspects of the ST which are more directly related to the language, including the stylistic choices, figures of speech and other language-specific features, tend to give translators more difficulty.

What kind of perlocution should the literary translator aim at? Should she try to adapt the whole work to the target culture, for example, situating a novel originally set in Barcelona in Manchester and changing the Ramblas into Market Street or Deansgate? Should she replace original proper names with English ones? Should she, in short, present the TT as an original text, as if it had been written in English in the first place? The most realistic answer to these questions is that, in practice, this is not done: translators do not present translated literary works as originals (see Newmark, 1981: 70–83). It is partly by marking the TT as such, signalling in effect, 'The following is a translation of a Spanish novel', that the translator can offer the TT reader the opportunity of experiencing the aesthetic effects offered by the original. In fact, part of the marking may take the form of leaving names of characters and places, of institutions and other sociocultural realities, in the original language.

This differs from an original English work set in a foreign place in that the presuppositions, psychologies and values of such a work will be English and even the descriptions will be those selected by an English writer for English readers.

Within these constraints, a translator may make a list or inventory, however mental or approximate, of the strategies and features of the ST which seem to be directly transferable and then ask herself whether she can evoke in her TT readers effects analogous to all of those evoked in the ST by 'reproducing' these features in the target language or whether some other steps are required.

The markings situate the reader in a context or situation foreign to him, thus compensating for any interstices that remain after the translator has done his best to provide — usually in the form of presupposition (see Hickey *et al.*, 1993a; b) or other style-preserving means — any relevant background information that a ST reader would be likely to possess but a TT reader might not. In other words, the fact that the intended readership is, and is marked as being, different from the original readership will tacitly justify the fact that certain features are 'spelled out'. For example, Hickey *et al.* (1993b) suggest that 'Coronation Street' in an English novel might be translated into Spanish as 'el culebrón "Coronation Street" ' [lit., 'the soap opera "Coronation Street" ']; 'suburban gardens' might become 'jardines típicos de aquellas zonas residenciales' [lit. 'gardens typical of those residential areas', since 'suburban' suggests to Spanish readers inner-city slums]; and intertextual references to a 'brave new world' might be elucidated as 'Huxley reconocería su mundo feliz' [lit. 'Huxley would recognise his brave new world'].

The perlocution in these cases is effected by conveying to the TT reader just sufficient information about the 'content' and using a style that will evoke in him approximately the same reaction as would have been evoked in a ST reader, who would know that 'Coronation Street' was a soap opera, that suburban gardens are usually well kept and, perhaps, that *Brave New World* is the title of a book. When I say 'style', I refer basically to the fact that no translator's note, additional sentence of explanation calling attention to itself need be used, but rather that the clarifications appear as brief presupposition-bearing adjectival or adverbial phrases.

In literary translation, as I have already suggested, the marking may be weak since the text is not essentially set in the ST world but is usually universal in its import. The exegesis may also be fairly weak because it will normally refer to realities that are 'accidentally' culture-based but might have coincided with those of the target or any other culture. Unlike legal translation, where exegesis might well involve technical or professional explanations of concepts, institutions and terminology, where such exegesis would be for denotational purposes only and would lie outside the competence of a translator who was not also a qualified lawyer, whose mistakes might have horrendous consequences, and where the text would make sense without exegesis, in literary translation, exegesis will involve only general world knowledge of realities and cultural concepts, it will be for detonational and, more crucially, connotational purposes, a normal translator will be qualified to provide it, if she gets it wrong, the consequences will be 'purely' literary, not extraliterary, and the text will make little sense without it.

One aspect of literary exegesis that merits special mention is the question of time deixis (see Levinson, 1983: 73–9; Richardson, this volume). I refer to the fact that literary works remain for ever as they were originally drafted, whereas a translation may be done at any time after that date; consequently the language and all linguistic features may be chosen for the TT in relation to the moment either of the original composition, of the translation itself or of some moment in between. This is relevant to perlocution in that the effects caused on a reader of the ST will differ depending, among other factors, on when he is reading it, since as time elapses the context will become more and more distant from that of the original. A literary translation, therefore, being a weakly marked text, may attempt to replace a corresponding ST context with a later (for example, contemporary) TT context, arguing that a reader of the original ST would equally have been in a contemporary ST context. Since a translation can carry marks — such as diachronically significant language features — situating it in virtually any time relationship to the ST, a translator will have to consider the perlocutionary effect potentially accessible to her TT readers.

My suggestion, then, is that literary translators consider the possibility of balancing some marking (situating the text openly in its original context, leaving proper names etc.) with some exegesis (conveying a degree of background information in a non-intrusive manner), thus offering the TT reader an aesthetic experience similar to that of the original readers' and evoking a perlocutionary effect or effects analogous to theirs.

Translation of Humour

The perlocutionary effect usually associated with humorous texts is the recognition and appreciation of some kind of innocuous incongruity or non-threatening inappropriateness (see Chapman & Foot, 1976; McGhee, 1979; McGhee & Goldstein, 1983) either in the linguistic level of a text or in the propositional content, with the reader's consequent amusement often manifested in a (more or less overtly articulated) laugh, smile or cringe, depending on the context, personality, mood and social manners of the reader. Three considerations of particular relevance to this type of translation deserve mention or reiteration.

First, if a translation of the ST is to arouse in a TT reader an effect analogous to that aroused or potentially aroused in a ST reader, it will not be sufficient to inform the TT reader of the locution or illocution performed in the ST or to 'explain the joke', for example, by presenting an analysis of the basis on which it is founded, such as an ambiguity or pun in the source language. In other words, no amount of exegesis is likely to bring about perlocutionary equivalence in this type of translation; on the contrary, attempts to explain a humorous text usually end up boring the reader and killing the humour.

Second, the strength of the perlocutionary effect should be roughly similar in both texts; for example, the translation of a text which is likely to provoke only a cringe of embarrassment does not need — indeed, strictly speaking, should not, (though this will seldom be criticised) — provoke a hearty guffaw. Third, although a perlocution should be caused by a text that bears the closest possible similarity to the locution and illocution of the ST, in the case of humorous texts this is usually of secondary importance and is frequently impossible or irrelevant to the production of the desired perlocution (see Hickey, forthcoming). Of course, if the locution and illocution are, in the translator's opinion, capable of evoking a reaction in the TT reader analogous to that of the ST reader, then she can translate as she would a literary text, and in fact humorous texts share with literature many features: 'tellability' (see Pratt, 1977: 136–47), narration and description of events and situations, dialogue etc.

If, however, the perlocution depends on a specifically linguistic or intertextual feature, then she should extricate the underlying formula on which the potential effect is based and thereupon generate another, new, text or joke in the target language, keeping as close as possible, or relevant, to the propositional content of the original. Whether the new text will in itself provide sufficient similarity with the original text will depend on the overall desired perlocutionary effect: if the text was essentially about some topic that was central to the discourse, this topic will have to survive reformulation even at the cost of some other aspect of the perlocution, whereas if the text is relatively 'free-standing' and independent of the discourse, then, so long as the formula is respected and maintained, the TT will count as a translation.

For example, in Sharpe (1982: 18) much of the reader's amusement derives from the protagonist's inability to distinguish the metaphorical from the literal meaning of language; when a teacher in anger tells him to 'get lost' the boy hides in a barn ten miles away and the police with alsatians have to search for him. Here the 'formula' consists of acting on the literal sense of an idiom which is normally understood only metaphorically; the perlocutionary effect derives from the double meaning and an inappropriate choice. In a TT, any similarly metaphorical idiom may be used: for example, in Spanish a companion of the boy may suggest to him 'que dé un sablazo al profesor de inglés, y al día siguiente le encuentran con un dedo de menos'. An attempt to generate another joke in English on the basis of the 'recycled' formula which has given rise to this Spanish version would be: a companion suggests to the protagonist that he should 'touch the English teacher for a few quid', but he is unable to claim the money he thinks he has been promised for groping the master, because the punishment meted out to him for such indecent intimacy has left him in the infirmary for three days.

Let us take an example of humour which is directly dependent on a lexical ambiguity. In San-Antonio (1991: 19) the narrator says of his driver 'Il a reçu des instructions (à défaut d'instruction)', a mild pun on the word 'instruction', meaning both instructions and education. A translator might decide to translate this as 'He has received his far from holy orders', where the perlocutionary effect — mild amusement — is not transferred or conveyed but rather recreated on the basis of the same formula as the ST. On the same basis, and remembering that the potential perlocutionary effect (mild amusement) is the aim, other perlocutionary causes might have been set up: 'He had not been well trained, or bussed either for that matter', 'He was never properly taught, indeed he was quite lax', 'The office floor was carpeted and so was he' etc.

Exegesis, therefore, is normally neither required nor appropriate in translating humour, at least in the sense of 'explaining the joke', since the perlocution depends on 'seeing' the fun or incongruity and enjoying it as a result of grasping both levels: the incongruity and an alternative congruity at the same time. Decontextualisation withdraws the text from its original setting in so far as may be necessary to reformulate it, or recycle the formula, either in a new context — more or less relevant to the discourse of the TT — or in a neutral context. This process or device also removes the need for marking: since the reader does not have to situate himself in a new context or culture, no very visible marking will serve any purpose.

It will be obvious that I have applied only to three types of translation the suggestion that a TT's effectiveness in bringing about perlocutionary effects analogous to those of the ST may depend directly on its strength of marking, degree of exegesis and use of decontextualisation. The validity or usefulness of the suggestion itself, not to mention its applicability to other types of translation, remains to be tested.

References

Austin, J.L. (1962) *How To Do Things With Words*. Oxford: Clarendon Press. Page references are to the 1986 OUP edition.

Chapman, A.J. and Foot, H.C. (1976) *Humour and Laughter: Theory, Research and Application*. London: John Wiley & Sons.

Davis, S. (1980) Perlocutions. In J.R. Searle, F. Keifer and M. Bierwisch (eds) *Speech Act Theory and Pragmatics* (pp. 37–55). Dordrecht: D. Reidel.

De Waard, J and Nida, E.A. (1986) *From One Language to Another: Functional Equivalence in Bible Translating*. Nashville: Thomas Nelson.

Grice, P.H. (1957) Meaning. *Philosophical Review* 66, 377–88.

Gu, Y. (1993) The impasse of perlocution. *Journal of Pragmatics* 20, 405–32.

Hickey, L., Lorés, R., Loyo Gómez, H. and Gil de Carrasco, A. (1993a) A pragmastylistic aspect of literary translation. *Babel* 39 (2), 77–88.

Hickey, L., Lorés, R., Loyo Gómez, H. and Gil de Carrasco, A. (1993b) Información 'conocida' y 'nueva' en la traducción literaria. *Sendebar* 4, 199–207.

Hickey, L. (forthcoming) Aproximación pragmalingüística a la traducción del humor. *Actas del Simposio Internacional sobre traducción*. Alcalá de Henares: Instituto Cervantes.

Leech, G. N. (1983) *Principles of Pragmatics*. London: Longman.

Levinson, S.C. (1983) *Pragmatics*. Cambridge: Cambridge University Press.

McGhee, P.E. (1979) *Humor: Its Origin and Development*. San Francisco: W.H. Freeman.

McGhee, P.E. and Goldstein, J.H. (eds) (1983) *Handbook of Humor Research* Vol. I. New York/Berlin: Springer.

Newmark, P. (1981) *Approaches to Translation*. Oxford: Pergamon.

Newmark, P. (1988) *A Textbook of Translation*. New York: Prentice Hall.

Pratt, M-L. (1977) *Towards a Speech Act Theory of Literary Discourse*. Bloomington: Indiana University Press.

San-Antonio. (1991) *Le Hareng perd ses plumes*. Paris: FleuveNoir

Searle, J.R. (1969) *Speech Acts: An Essay in the Philosophy of Language*. Cambridge: Cambridge University Press.

Searle, J.R. (1979) *Expression and Meaning: Studies in the Theory of Speech Acts*. Cambridge: Cambrdige University Press.

Sharpe, T. (1982) *Vintage Stuff*. London: Martin Secker and Warburg. Page references are to the 1983 Pan Books edition.

Index

Authors

Subjects